ENGAGING VIOLENCE

Cultural Memory
in
the
Present

Hent de Vries, Editor

ENGAGING VIOLENCE

Civility and the Reach of Literature

David Simpson

STANFORD UNIVERSITY PRESS

STANFORD, CALIFORNIA

Stanford University Press
Stanford, California

Printed in the United States of America on acid-free, archival-quality paper

Library of Congress Cataloging-in-Publication Data

Names: Simpson, David, 1951– author.
Title: Engaging violence : civility and the reach of literature / David Simpson.
Other titles: Cultural memory in the present.
Description: Stanford, California : Stanford University Press, 2022. | Series: Cultural memory in the present | Includes bibliographical references and index.
Identifiers: LCCN 2021055751 (print) | LCCN 2021055752 (ebook) | ISBN 9781503632745 (cloth) | ISBN 9781503633087 (paperback) | ISBN 9781503633094 (ebook)
Subjects: LCSH: Literature and morals. | Literature and society. | Violence in literature. | Courtesy in literature.
Classification: LCC PN49 .S5545 2022 (print) | LCC PN49 (ebook) | DDC 823.009/353—dc23/eng/20220316
LC record available at https://lccn.loc.gov/2021055751
LC ebook record available at https://lccn.loc.gov/2021055752

Cover design: Angela Moody
Cover photo: The book, *The House of Leaves*, being burned. Learning Lark, via Flickr. CC 2.0

Do literary and linguistic studies or discussions of education have any effects commensurate with the needs of the world? Are we fiddling in the burning city? Could our fiddling really make any future city less inflammable?

—I. A. Richards, 1940

Contents

Acknowledgments

Taken seriously, acknowledgment is the hardest of genres. Who has not helped us think what we think? Who has most provoked, most inspired, most encouraged? This book is the result of thirty years of on and off meditation, first about civil society in its 1990s manifestations in relation to rhetorics of civility (not quite the same thing) and then more and more about violence and literature (and literary pedagogy) in relation to both. It may be easiest to start with my most recent gratitude to the anonymous readers of this manuscript who have devoted generous and detailed attention, well beyond the norm, to its arguments and made suggestions that I have almost always gladly accepted; and to Erica Wetter, my editor, and her colleague Caroline McKusick, whose support and professionalism have been exemplary. Way back when, Georges van den Abbeele and Ron Saufley, who ran the Davis Humanities Center, encouraged me to help set up a conference on civility and incivility, which was a crucial early opportunity to focus some of the questions here pursued. I thank them both. More recently, residencies in South Africa (at the Stellenbosch Institute for Advanced Studies) and Australia (at the Humanities Research Center in Canberra) proved critically stimulating. So too a visiting fellowship at King's College, Cambridge, in the fall of 2019. I thank the provost and fellows for their warm welcome and for providing the stringent intellectual and social environment that makes lives like ours most rewarding. Many friends and colleagues over the years have taught me things that have, whether they know it or not, gone into this book: among them are Jonathan Arac and Paul Bové and the *boundary2* collective, David Atwell, John Barrell, David Clark, Stefan Collini, Peter de Bolla, Susanna Ferguson, Bishnu Ghosh, Kevis Goodman, Ryan Heuser, John Higgins, David Lloyd, Roger Malbert, Tobias Menely, Liz Miller,

Tom Mitchell, Tim Morton, Pablo Ortiz, Michael Oruch, Bruce Robbins, Cliff Siskin, Matthew Stratton and Penny Wilson.

Sarah Maza gave my draft introduction a very helpful critique. Margaret Ferguson read and talked through everything here, often more than once, with a focus, intelligence and generosity I have not, after many years, yet learned to take for granted.

ENGAGING VIOLENCE

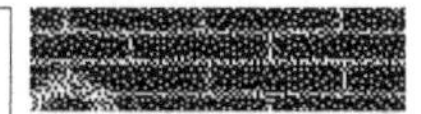

Introduction

Violence, civility and literature are all difficult words, or words of complicated conceptual scope: setting the terms involves upsetting the terms. Despite various absolutist determinations of what is and is not literature, it is a noun that commonly requires a limiting adjective of some sort: high or low, bad or good, harmful or improving. Civility can describe a near-moral virtue, a hypocritical pretense, a habit of good manners or a disciplinary regime, and everything in between; and violence covers a spectrum stretching from the atomic bomb to deep psychological formations that may not even be visible to a third party. While it is a truth widely (though not universally) acknowledged that civility works against violence and that literature generates or accompanies civility and engenders tolerance, civility has been understood as violence in disguise, and literature, which has only rarely sought to claim the power of violence, has often been accused of inciting or approving it. This book sets out to describe the ways in which these English words and the concepts they evoke are mutually entangled and the uses to which these entanglements have been put.

Each word and concept invokes the others in ways that are both implicit and explicit but are not subject to definitive specification. The claim to assure a secure and peaceable life has become a major component of the political rhetoric of statehood through the Euro-American modern period, one that has been accompanied by a projection of violence as the attribute of others and civility as the birthright of the West. But civility has also been conceived as a disciplinary agent for disorderly domestic populations. It is thus under strain both for what it is in itself—a potentially coercive practice that never quite comes naturally—and for what it conjures up as other to itself, a violence consigned exclusively to those outside the group that deems itself to be behaving properly. Ambivalence is constitutive of our ideas of civility. It evolves historically from being a courtly-aristocratic protocol exercised by elite men to a behavioral model for an emergent middle class and thence for many more; as such it seems almost bound to generate confusion and paradox about who possesses it and who does not. Literature has also functioned variably, both as a means of nation-state confirmation and interpellation ('the English novel,' 'the national poet') and as a critique or testing out of habitual practices and assumptions. It moves in and out of acknowledging the violences of history and of the individual psyche and across a range of options explaining, justifying or opposing them. The spilling of brains and intestines has never been better described than in the *Iliad*. But between then and now more and more forms of violence have been specified as demanding attention, both descriptively and conceptually: global war, mass destruction, ecological crisis, slavery, colonization and its aftermaths, violence against women, racialized violence, violence in the name of religion, psychological violence and so forth. Western nations have needed violence even as they purport to diminish it, whether to discipline their own populations or to impose their rule over others. Meanwhile, civility continues to be invoked by both scholars and ordinary citizens as a necessary restraint, and literature continues to be written and disseminated, both as a market event and as a component of the educational apparatus. This study builds upon the work of historians, political scientists, literary scholars and philosophers but ventures a new argument about the complex and often mystified entanglements between literature, civility and violence in the anglophone Atlantic sphere. It does not lay claim to being a comprehensive historical philology, and for literature and violence it attempts no philological analysis at all. Civility is treated in more detail because its senses are limited enough to be describable and because it is, I argue, a key connector between the other two terms, in ways that have yet to be understood. The details I explore are mostly but not entirely anglophone, and they suggest that literature, civility and violence have been in play in mutually constitutive ways that delineate the ambitions and the limits of the project of culture in its broadest sense: the furtherance of social behavior that has the support and models the behavior of a critical mass of a population, though not necessarily (indeed probably not) of a majority. There are of course far more coercive forces at play in the management of populations: Marx describes some of them in *Capital*. Work regimes, wage policies, antistrike legislation and outright violence in policing were and are all deployed in maintaining the peace that allows the few to continue to profit from the life and labor of the many. But other kinds of persuasion also matter, those embodied in notions of good manners, attention to others and responsiveness to art and literature. These are less definitive and less obvious in their operations and incur certain ambiguities and perhaps uncontainable effects. They can work against habits of obedience in approved behavior, but also encourage it by distracting us or, in their pedagogical forms, enacting the performance of a freedom and independence, including freedom and independence from violence, that cannot surely be known categorically as either real or illusory.

Circulating literature and performing civility developed together as ways of calling out violence and displacing its threats. They originated in small-group, elite subcultures and came to be imagined as key to the well-being of many more, while being never quite open to all. At first privileged young men and a few women mastered good manners along with a proficiency in reading and writing and in acquiring foreign languages (Greek, Latin, French, Italian) and the literatures produced in them. This became the attribute of a professional and bureaucratic class able to administer a nation and then an empire. Competence in classical languages remained relatively restricted, leading to the construction of a national literary tradition built upon Shakespeare and later upon novels that could be made to embody and publicize the values and benefits of civil exchange. But what would happen if we were to suggest a canon founded on *Oroonoko* rather than *Robinson Crusoe*, *Clarissa* rather than *Pamela*, *Evelina* rather than *Pride and Prejudice*? The radical and often incorrigible violences against black people and women that are frontal in these novels could never have sustained the model of interiority and proper conduct that has allowed the (predominantly English) novel to flourish as the centerpiece of a British national literary education. They offer a benchmark of recognition for what the favored narratives often seem to ignore or push to the margins. But even the more acceptably canonized novels can be read against the grain to reveal an encounter with forms of violence that cannot easily be assimilated by representations of an established peace upon earth. The American novel, meanwhile, is almost always too cognizant of the power of an intransigent violence to offer itself as the bearer of any patriotic idealism about manifest destiny. Both literature and civility project their own inadequacies in this respect. But they also generate utopian aspirations that are not completely undercut by their own limitations. In relation to violence and nonviolence, they inhabit the world of both/and. The ethical complexities of literary reading are like those associated with civility: each can be seen either as a creative virtual experience fostering the exercise of sympathetic instincts or as an evasive indulgence substituting for consequential decisions about real-life events.

We live at a time in which the value of a humanities education is regularly called into question, not least by the very institutions of higher learning that have sustained it for more than two centuries. They vote with their wallets: funding for arts and literature has been under great pressure and in some places has entirely disappeared. These same institutions, like other sectors of society, publish civility codes designed, sometimes quite coercively, to foster the values of community and respect. It mostly goes unrecognized that arts-based pedagogies themselves developed as both agents and apostles of this same civility, seeking to rehearse conflict in the classroom by way of imagined rather than immediate situations and thereby teaching people how to disagree without calling forth actual violence. The study of literature in particular has also been committed to cherishing the aesthetic pleasure deriving from imaginary forms while hanging on to a mediated reference to a real world in which moral judgment and witnessing historical events remain urgent imperatives. That means engaging with the violence that literature's own formal protocols, devised as representations rather than enactments, discourage. There is a risk involved: that the representation of violence will be taken as its endorsement. The long-standing debates about the messages of Joseph Conrad's *Heart of Darkness* reflect the persistence of the problem and the difficulty of resolving it. So too the perplexities that arise from the apparent ignoring or finessing of violence, which inform (for example) discussions of Jane Austen's *Mansfield Park*. For all that has been written about them, these books (and others like them) continue to provide provocations rather than definite answers.

The disposition toward *engaging* violence is common to both literature and civility and invites at least two readings. First, literature and civility face up to violence, address and contest it, in ways that are both direct and indirect: engaging *with* violence. Second, they can make violence itself seem engaging and even entertaining, whether as an imagined life in a book or as polite manners performed to rebuke those who do not share them. Friend-enemy narratives often function by subjecting the other to some sort of violence, often enthusiastically. Here it can be hard to hold on to the representational identity of literature as not the thing itself. But hold on we must. Political philosopher Étienne Balibar, whose *Violence and Civility* has been pivotal in my thinking, not least in its honest admission of a besetting confusion and obscurity around the whole concept of civility, has invoked the idea of "inconvertible violence." By this he signals a component of contemporary life that cannot be avoided or sublimated as conducive to some greater good: a violence that must be avowed and engaged (for example, as cruelty and racism) in its very intransigence, and one that requires a more stringent and perhaps as yet unthinkable civility to contest it. By insisting on the inevitability of a recurrent violence, he interferes with the narrative that makes its subsumption a feature of 'civilization,' a civilization that has indeed arguably regressed toward more pervasive violences even as it has developed greater technological accomplishments. No incarnation of civility devised to engage with this situation is going to subsist as intact and unmixed. The difficulty of imagining a kind of civility that subsists despite its own incompletion presents challenges for the practices of both civility and literature. Civility already bears within it an exclusionary and punitive legacy, the result of its limiting itself to some and denying it to others. It has figured in this way as a tool for separating so-called civilization from so-called barbarism, as well as in the more local social distinctions between classes and occupations, all this while also claiming to bring about a peaceful world. Literature, insofar as it relies upon a subsidiary notion of the nonliterary, can also be made to appear exclusionary, and familiarity with fine writing has certainly been employed as a mechanism for social distinction. Matthew

Arnold's contempt for those he called philistines is a famous case in point, and those who can quote *Hamlet* often do sense themselves as a cut above those who cannot. But when it comes to discussing the play, outcomes are less predictable and conclusions often indecisive, as some find the Danish prince himself to be. Literature in its modern sense declares its identity as a virtual medium, existing by a commitment to representation, which preempts its own capacity for direct violence. Its role in the educational system has often been one of encouraging the suspension of belief and the habit of conducting inquiry without a guarantee of clear outcomes. In this it invites and models civility and a mode of argument that tolerates uncertainty and diversity of opinion. At the same time, while still remaining within the parameters of representation, an always-mediated rhetoric, literature can claim the power of historical witnessing, including the witnessing of violence. This can have the effect of inviting or inciting others to act in a way that literature alone and in itself never does. Pedagogy can thereby also incorporate an activist incentive along with its inclination to detachment: we tend not to teach *Uncle Tom's Cabin* as a tribute to the virtues of irony and disinterest. Some readers may find themselves resisting its deployment of sentiment, but few if any doubt its call for judgment and response.

Both literature and civility work toward holding violence in abeyance, but only to some degree and never to the point of its disappearance. Invoking civility may perform minor violence as it discredits or represses those deemed to be ignoring its protocols, while literature can never be fully settled beneath the protective shell promised by the claim to be always and only mere representation or fiction. Each articulation of literature or civility, or of the relation between them, thus always renegotiates anew, and renders always to be decided, an attitude to or implication in kinds and degrees of violence. Nothing is given in advance or in principle. Some have said that literature can save the world, but there is nothing in the record to suggest that it will or that it can guarantee an immunity to enacting or suffering significant violence. Only a universal and hegemonic community of enlightened readers—readers in the literary mode—could even begin to lay the ground for posing the question of how much good literature can do: this we have never had and are far from having now. And yet intelligent thinkers like Matthew Arnold and I. A. Richards have come close to suggesting just this, because literature may indeed be among our best resources for diminishing the acceptability or inevitability of violence. Meditative solitary reading, or face-to-face discussion of complex language proceeding as an un-co-opted event, habits that do not give up on incentivizing us toward real-world agency while still insisting on a procedural commitment to the sphere of representation alone, are capacious mediums for exploring a wide range of attitudes and projections. They require an extended commitment of time devoted to noninstrumental outcomes and are thus physiologically nonviolent at the same time as they tend to produce 'meanings' that go in more than one direction and take yet more time to evaluate. The importance of these activities does not depend on a conviction that violence is not innate, or indeed that it is. The evidence of extreme violence enacted by humans upon one another goes all the way back; the historical record is pretty clear about this, whether one prefers to attribute it to hardwired biological or psychological traits, to socially contingent circumstances or to some measure of each. It seems unlikely, to say the least, that we can promise a world where violence is a thing of the past. But every instance of violence is in itself open to investigation and to the projection of alternatives. And violence is not the only human trait that goes all the way back. So too does sociability, the habit of association in groups that raises so many of the issues that a concept of civility is designed to address. The play between the two means that the expression of violence has always raised the question of violence: Is it justified, beneficial to some, avoidable? Is there an available recourse to sociability that might offset the onset of violence?

And then there is a third human activity that seems never to be absent from the archaeological and historical record: the apparent compulsion to make things, to alter in some way the world as it is given. This making of things has commonly gone well beyond the point at which something is merely rendered useful for survival; a flint ax, for example, can take on a sculptural form that elicits judgments that it is a thing of beauty, and who is to say that its makers were not of the same mind? What the Greeks called *poesis* included both utilitarian and 'artistic' activities. And objects that we consider purely decorative are there from the start, or very close to the start, of human evolution. Aesthetic culture is up there with violence and sociability as a primary human imperative. To some, like Shelley, it is the first among all human drives, the one without which no social or historical development of any kind can be imagined as possible. And it has one trait that the others do not share: it takes on fixed form and endures through time in more or less the form in which it was invented. Passing through historical time, it can be celebrated, analyzed, imitated or simply ignored; it can be rediscovered or reimagined in contexts and for purposes that could not have existed in the world in which it first took form. This is obviously true of the neolithic ax that ends up in a museum, but it is true also of the biblical or Homeric text that can never be thought of as finished or seen as whole because it comes to us in too many bits and pieces. In all such cases, attention in the aesthetic mode takes up time that is not being directed at irreversible outcomes. Thus it is that the *Iliad*, so full of descriptions of violence, is a story that holds violence to account. And yet it can never offer a guarantee against the arrival of readers for whom it will stand as an endorsement or glorification of that same violence. Those are the readers who decide not to abide by the conventions of the aesthetic mode, which must depend upon some form of continual enactment (like teaching) to stake its claim.

My argument follows a broadly historical trajectory through the long modern period to the present day, but it is not exhaustive or seamlessly continuous. It does not aspire to a comprehensive historical account; it is an inquiry into some exemplary formations. Most obviously it hardly touches on the long war period of 1914–45, when violence was inescapable and at the front of so many people's minds. I may be wrong in thinking that civility was not then much of an issue, or at least an interesting issue, though it would be surprising if no examples could be found of civility protocols being disputed or defended in discussions of, for example, appeasement, pacifism or the allocation of rations, let alone whether or not to obliterate German and Japanese cities in firestorms or atomic explosions. My hunch is that that these instances and others like them are somewhat straightforward to articulate, although not of course to resolve. My focus here is on the less widely recognized articulations that govern the long modern formations of violence, literature and civility. I do take it as an operational assumption that literary aesthetics and civility are to be taken seriously, not simply dismissed as liberal ideology or bad faith, and thus my argument does take the risk of being deemed by some to be already co-opted. I accept the risk, and I have attempted not to underplay the need for critique. Decisions about inescapable violence cannot be made in advance and anyway cannot expect to hold good for all persons at all times. Even when they seem to attract a working consensus, there is always another side to be heard. All violence generates a holding to account, and to that end the coarticulation of literature and civility offers an enduring resource.

Chapter 1 introduces the varieties of literature's relation to violence and the questions it generates, with some famous examples from Auden, Yeats and Austen. What happens when a literary work seems to endorse or excuse violence? Is violence perhaps always in the picture, if we look hard enough, but always open to the productive uncertainties of aesthetic representation? Like civility, literature seems constitutively ambiguous or paradoxical. I go on to ask why the historically persistent commitment to civility seems not to have produced any settled decision about exactly what it is. Civility falls short of philosophical or legal specificity (for instance, as a moral law) but is habitually imagined as something more than just being nice to others. Its apparent well-disposedness has been interpreted as a crucial social bond or as nothing more than a front for hypocrisy. It has moved well beyond its original Latin sense denoting mere membership of the body politic (*civilis*), itself never a neutral qualifier as long as citizenship remains restrictive. While apparently pitched against violence—as in Norbert Elias's thesis about civility's work in controlling aristocratic (male) aggression—it has been accused of imposing its own violent norms and exclusions. Insofar as it makes men's treatment of women a yardstick for civil behavior, it both elevates and degrades the figure of the female. Under the heading of *courtesy*, it was embroiled not only in domestically violent social relations but also in the project of early modern colonization, as is vividly represented in Spenser's *The Faerie Queene*. It shares with literature a constitutive ambiguity or obscurity (what 'is' literature?), as well as a commitment to what Elias called reflective detachment. Literature stages its own relations to violence: even representation itself and alone has, ever since Plato, been accused of dangerous incitements. As teaching literature is absorbed into institutions of education, and eventually mass education, these questions become of more concern to more people.

So too does the nature and extent of violence, with some (like Steven Pinker) suggesting that it is decreasing in our own time, while others are convinced of its increasing incidence and new penetration of every facet of life, from the global to the interpersonal, a case made in Frantz Fanon's analysis of the decolonization process. Meanwhile, the conditions set by Kant and Schiller for the identification of the aesthetic—nonutilitarian, disinterested, strictly representational—continue to dominate the modern discussion, even as they have come under critical inspection for being dependent upon racialized categories that perpetuate the very violence they purport to displace.

Chapter 2 addresses the constitutive and foundational relations between literature and civility in the eighteenth century. It opens with a bizarre moment of spectacular politeness in Daniel Defoe's depiction of Crusoe's island, where the performance of civility and the power of violence are staged together by a lapsed gentleman who seems not to have forgotten his manners even after decades of solitude followed by more years of companionate authority over another man. Crusoe missed much of the violence of the English Civil War period, a violence the Earl of Clarendon (Edward Hyde) attributed in considerable part to a failure of civility. Following an extended investigation of public manners by the early eighteenth-century essayists, the publication of Richardson's *Pamela* provoked a vigorous debate about the place of ordinary people in polite culture and about the potential of small, private reading groups for displacing violence, notably male sexual violence. Another major controversy over civility came in the 1770s with the posthumous appearance of Chesterfield's *Letters*, an informal conduct manual that reenacts the sixteenth-century debates about courtesy and civility for a later generation. Here a cosmopolitan, aristocratic affect (antithetical to *Pamela*'s national-patriotic localism) aligns with a visibly middle-class language register in what was widely received as a cynical exposure of the hypocrisies implicit in the performance of deference to others and of a purely apparitional displacement of violence.

Chapter 3 explores the literary basis of eighteenth-century British philosophical writing, which indeed projects civility and literature as each the natural expression of the other. Philosophy, novels and journals are all pursuing the same ends in the same ways. Shaftesbury, Hume, Smith,

Ferguson and Kames all theorize a role for civility and civil society, one whose goal is the diminishing of violence. At the same time they signal the limits of small-group formations as suitable models for managing larger social aggressions. The project of political economy takes on the task of balancing the necessary instability and conflict that drives an entrepreneurial culture with the needs of a manageably peaceful state: civility keeping violence to a minimum. Meanwhile, philosophy, fiction, history writing, criticism and belles lettres evolve together to constitute a general mode of communication that is visibly literary: self-reflective, unassertive and dialogic. Adam Smith's *The Theory of Moral Sentiments* is an important example of the synthesis. But after Chesterfield, and in the light of concerns about an imminent mass reading public, civility is under stress as a viable solution to social conflict, and literature begins to look elsewhere for alliances against the threat of violence that becomes more identified with urgently apparent class divisions and with the experiences of global war and militant empire building. Mary Wollstonecraft's feminist critique further calls into question the long-standing convention imaging the treatment of women as the measure of courtesy, civility and the progress of civil society.

Chapter 4 traces the near extinction, in Britain and America in the nineteenth and early twentieth centuries, of any deep investment in the concept of civility (though it is partly subsumed into anthropological ideas of civilization). Manners, often still an attribute of women, remain an important topic of debate, but it is above all an invocation of personal culture (in the spirit of the German *Bildung*) that is dramatized in literature and literary criticism and given the task of managing violence and keeping it below the level that requires physical policing. Matthew Arnold adapts Schiller toward a literature-based education that makes an explicit place for criticism as central to a culture that depends upon disinterestedness and a free play of the mind, while the novelists move away from civility as a sufficient or trustworthy term for managing conflict. The turn to culture fits better with the inward-looking habits of British literature, which keeps the violence of empire at a distance while trying to manage that of class relations, than with those of American literature, which is much more direct in representing the conditions of slavery and of the destruction of Native America. Perhaps because of this frankness about the omnipresence of violence, literature in the United States is mostly not presented as a medium for civilizing the new nation. Tocqueville deflects attention away from both literature and civility as essential ingredients of public life, but the natural democracy he finds viable in America is premised on excluding black slaves, Native Americans and women from the possibility of citizenship. Assertions of masculine power and violence also reappear as antidotes to a perceived feminization and degeneration of the national culture. In Britain, the synthesis of literature and culture leads up to an influential twentieth-century pedagogy, devised in the wake of World War I, by I. A. Richards, F. R. Leavis and others, which incorporates civility protocols into the classroom and once again seeks to combine the small-group experience with a widely distributable public paradigm.

Chapter 5 addresses the explosion of civility and civil society theory in the wake of the fall of the Soviet Empire, as civility becomes the go-to concept in social and political science, most notably in the United States and in Tony Blair's Britain. The celebration of round tables, the British 'Third Way' and the renovated American fascination with town meetings all affirm the potential of nonstate mechanisms for the creation of a healthy public life that can avoid the recourse to any critical violence. When a political scientist like Geoff Mulgan announces that "the defining questions are all about relationships," we can sense the degree to which the model of literary engagement (dialogical, conversational, nonhierarchical) has become the prototype for theorizing political conduct. The expansion of the European Union inspires another dramatic rethinking of whether civility and civil society theory are adequate to the task of adjusting to an increasingly diversifying transnational entity, one bringing with it seemingly unnegotiable forms and degrees of violence: the breakup of Yugoslavia, increasing immigration, new inequalities of wealth and health. Europe has always been a shifting and contested idea, one imagined as a concept to include some and exclude others. Literary theory in the 1990s plays a role in the projection of an ideal of Europe as an alternative to the Washington consensus: Jacques Derrida, Jürgen Habermas and Étienne Balibar, among others, propose the estrangement of Europe from itself in another version of civility-as-literature transforming violence. Anglophone philosophers like Richard Rorty and Martha Nussbaum also project the literary mode as exemplary for the cultivation of a nondestructive citizenry. The novel of migration is attuned to representing the besetting violences of neoliberal culture, undercutting its pretensions to civility, but it also stages a commitment to the imagining of a better world.

Chapter 6 brings us to the current moment when aesthetic theory and literature itself respond to what Balibar calls the inconvertible presence of violence, no longer imaginable as an alternative to civility but as part of its immanent fabric. Among those who pay attention to the humanities at all, conservatives, liberals and leftists alike continue to share some kind of faith in the value of the literary imagination, and the literary mode (art, theory, pedagogy) continues to work for deployment against violence, even as no language, creative or quotidian, is immune to a possible capture by violent interests. One notable response to this predicament is, following Roland Barthes, a reinvention of John Keats's idea of negative capability: a recourse to the neutral, to gestures of minimalist intervention that seek to keep potential violence at arm's length. Literature also remains implicated in a project of witnessing, of registering conditions that an author may feel unable to change but can prevent being forgotten. And witnessing, taken up by others, can become incentivizing, a passage to the kinds of doing that Schiller's aesthetic mode conventionally disavows: putting right what is wrong with the world. Meanwhile, the model of imaginative disinterest and free play devised by Kant and Schiller remains central to the discussion of why aesthetic and literary response matters, even though it has been identified, most coherently by David Lloyd, as proffering a fake universality. At the present time the task of assessing the balance of civility and violence in and through literature falls principally to the novel, and increasingly to what we recognize as the global novel. For this genre (hardly any longer a subgenre) Lloyd's articulation of the category of subalternity, evolving as theorizing both the colonial encounter and the mechanics of decolonization (and thus the icon of a violence that so often targets both gender and race), functions as an important figuration of both the brute conditions of history as it happens and the imaginary realm of the uncanny that marks it as memorable and thinkable in new ways, for example, in Mohsin Hamid's echoing (in *The Reluctant Fundamentalist*) of Robinson Crusoe playing the gentleman (as discussed in Chapter 2). In representing the predicaments of subalternity, from Conrad and Forster to Hamid and Kamila Shamsie, civility's residual indeterminacy is well suited to the articulation of an always unstable subjectivity that does damage only by claiming to have fully consolidated itself as an identity. Civility can here acknowledge its affiliation with and function within an aesthetics of radical discomfort, unable to keep a clear distance from the violence that it must still hold up to an ongoing critique, while committed also to keeping open an incentive to social bonding, like the romance plot to which the novel can still resort as the bearer of some measure of hope for the future.

1

Civility and Literature and Their Discontents

Necessary Murders?

In 1970, Richard Hofstadter projected that "the rediscovery of our violence will undoubtedly be one of the important intellectual legacies of the 1960s."[1] His anthology on the history of American violence, published by a major commercial house, seemed to be bidding for a place on the college and school syllabi that, if he were right, should be populating our classrooms. Today, the book, with its nearly five hundred pages of material, is almost impossible to find outside major libraries. It seems that another component of the national consciousness, also noted by Hofstadter, won out: the tendency of we Americans to persuade ourselves that we are "among the best-behaved and best-regulated of peoples" (p. 6), icons of civility. Violence has remained repressed in the national imaginary as it had been for so long prior to the King and Kennedy assassinations, the urban riots and the antiwar consciousness of the 1960s. Perhaps we have arrived at another such testing moment, although the names are different and more numerous. Many are saying them. Meanwhile, we find ourselves being constantly reassured that "this is not who we are," that violence is un-American, even as this clearly *is* who many of us are. If civility rather than violence is really the national identity, why is there so much killing?

Published in the same year, and responding to some of the same pressing concerns about burning inner cities, mass protests and excessive policing, Richard Sennett's *The Uses of Disorder* argued that the modern state had gone too far in repressing aggressive instincts, to the point that they could emerge only as radical violence. Far better, he proposed, to forestall violence by encouraging the expression of social tensions that could be negotiated face-to-face and lead to conciliation. City life, he thought, provided the perfect site for such engagements, allowing people to undertake "meaningful conflict" and to "see the dimensions of that which they oppose." In cities, people need to have "some consciousness of themselves, they will continually be asking what it is in them that fails to be adequate for the social world they live in, what parts of their own lives are reconcilable or irreconcilable with the lives of the people around them."[2] Sennett does not use the word, but he is talking about what others have called civility, a taking account of events in ways that informally adjust and adjudicate outcomes toward nonviolence. In his conviction that this somewhat "anarchic" society can be comfortably combined with the preservation and positive contribution of "affluence" (p. 188), Sennett is veering toward another attribute of civility, a negative one for its critics: that it serves to prop up the status quo by suppressing any transformative energy and declaring all actual or potential violence to be unacceptable.

Hannah Arendt was also publishing on the subject of violence in 1969 and 1970, when she directed her animus against the student radicals who were, she thought, violently disrupting a process of inevitable reform and disseminating a culture of "theoretical helplessness."[3] She makes a clear distinction between power (*Macht*) and violence (*Gewalt*). Power is always a group possession and is the core of state control, whereas "no government exclusively based on the means of violence has ever existed" (p. 149). Power, one might say, includes the power of violence but is always primary: violence becomes primary only when power is lost. If not violence, what then assists us to positive change in the world? Arendt's answer is a familiar one: a "horizontally directed" series of federated units exercising mutually corrective functions (p. 230). Spontaneously evolving "council systems" (p. 231) are notably small-group formations, maybe "only ten of us," allowing for the dialogic emergence of "rational opinions" (p. 233). Here is civility rhetoric with all its possibilities and problems: a positive prognosis for a small number of people whose representative status must always be questionable as they inevitably find themselves acting and speaking for others in a proto-disciplinary manner.

A few years earlier, in 1967, Herbert Marcuse gave a lecture in which he avowed that there is both "violence of suppression and violence of liberation" and that "preaching nonviolence as principle reproduces the existing institutionalized violence."[4] Civility culture is all very well, then, but not when pursued to the point of disavowing a violence of resistance and response. How much violence do we allow, and how much civility? The latest mass-distributed effort to tell the story of the American constitution, Jill Lepore's *These Truths*, is bookended by a question posed by Alexander Hamilton in the first of his Federalist Papers: To what degree does good government emerge from "reflection and choice" rather than depending upon "accident and force?"[5] What forces are unleashed when a government promises to "insure domestic Tranquillity," as does the constitution of the United States? (p. xii). Can there be a civil society administering itself by civility, a *civil* civil society, or must the state impose its powers of violence to keep the peace?

Reading, teaching and discussing fine writing, what we call literature, is commonly held to subsist far away from violence, whose appearance in such literature often generates discomfort or outright disapproval. Few if any lines of English poetry have created as much pushback as those in the original (1937) version of W. H. Auden's "Spain," which invokes the violence of political action in referencing "the conscious acceptance of guilt in the necessary murder." George Orwell was an early objector, pointing out that this sort of talk came most easily to those who were nowhere near the fighting.[6] Auden demonstrated his own discomfort in his revision, getting rid of the self-righteous "necessary" in favor of the somewhat softer "fact of." But the awkwardness remains: we seem to be reading a bland justification or acceptance of fatal violence. Why should this be such a shock? Is it not reasonable to claim that, in the cause of resisting the fascist revolution, blood will have to be spilled, in response to that already spilled by the nationalist armies? Is this not a de facto truth in every recourse to military violence? Perhaps the impropriety consists in Auden's implicit justification of assassination, coolly plotted death administered according to rational calculation rather than resulting from punctilious impulses and open conflict. But also, I think, the shock emanates from the fact that this is *poetry* we are reading, the highest form of literature. Poetry, like much of what we receive as literature, has from the first been full of violent death—open almost any page of the *Iliad*—but it conventionally comes adorned with heroism, destiny, metaphysical explanation and high purpose. Or it is narrativized in ways that make its onset seem appropriate and somehow just, like the death of Macbeth. Shakespeare prepares the way by showing us that he who is losing his life at the end of the play has done bad things. But, if we accede to this persuasion, we are surely endorsing violence, so, as Adam Smith opines, "we detest Iago as much as we esteem Othello; and delight as much in the punishment of the one, as we are grieved at the distress of the other."[7] We can say that such a death is retributive and restorative, reestablishing a functioning social order. But it is still violence and requires at least a second thought. Obviously, the potential for a psychopathic reading is there in all fictions that represent violence, and even normally socialized readers can find violence appealing, as in the standard friend-enemy narrative. But the slow time of literary reading has, in its better applications, the potential to impede any relish in maiming and killing. Finding violence 'engaging' in the sense of appealing is an ever-present risk, one that tragedy often invites, but, again, it is not the sense of the word that I mean to emphasize in this study, even as it must be recognized. In Dickens's *Oliver Twist*, Fagin and Bill Sikes are both villains and deserve punishment, but there is little narrative relish in their demise; Dickens does not celebrate death, which he finds too grave and serious to generate pleasure. His juxtaposition of judicial and accidental hangings raises questions about the metaphysics of justice even as it withholds critique. We are to weigh the violence by which they have lived against that by which they die. Even Macbeth, among the worst of Shakespeare's villains, who may or may not die offstage according to a director's preference, is afforded some profound and unforgettable lines concerning fate, prophecy, good and evil. The necessity of violence is always up for questioning, something to be engaged *with*.

But the tenor of Auden's lines is not one of high tragedy or moral interiority; it is rather that of a committee meeting, where the necessary murder is just another item to be voted on as we move down the agenda. Part of the shock may well be that poetry is not supposed to embody the rhetoric of bureaucracy or the suppression of emotion and affect that bureaucracy so often demands. We are not comfortable when it makes bald statements like Auden's. Nonetheless, his is a complex line, and there is more to be pondered about the *conscious* acceptance of *guilt.* This is not retributive rage, like that expressed in Milton's sonnet on the Piedmont massacre. The speaker admits that a form of wrong is involved, something about which one will feel guilty. He admits also that he knows this, he is conscious of it, but he will endorse it anyway. One thinks forward to Himmler's notorious Posen speech, where the extermination of Jews is dramatized as a painful necessity, a harrowing event putting the well-being of the perpetrators themselves at risk, something they would never do unless for the most overpowering reasons. Genocide is rewritten as self-sacrifice, by blaming the victims. But Auden is no simple Himmler-in-the-making, because there is an escape clause. Anyone defending Auden's line can invoke the aesthetic alibi, insisting that we are reading literature, not the report of a real event.[8] Auden, in other words, is not expressing his own view but dramatizing a narrative voice, perhaps even with corrosive irony. Apparent avowal thus becomes disavowal, and the poet is off the hook. Instead of looking like an apologist for cold-blooded murder, he becomes an ingeniously critical transcriber of things he observes in the world around him. He becomes a 'real' writer, complex and elusive, pointing to a predicament but not solving it. The necessary extinction of barbarous customs by way of the murder of those persons practicing them was a common rationale for the culture of colonial settlement and imperialism. A famous fictional representation of this occurs in Conrad's *Heart of Darkness*, where Kurtz adds a postscript to his letter justifying the civilizing mission he has apparently embraced: "Exterminate all the brutes!"[9] Again, the aesthetic alibi figures here: this is not Conrad's voice but that of a character transcribed in the report of another character, Marlow, and thus doubly distanced from the author. This is 'literature.' In apartheid-era South Africa the censors were often themselves literature professors who allowed challenging work to be published if it could satisfy aesthetic criteria, if it could claim to be literature. In so doing they inevitably ran into all sorts of disputes about where literature stops.[10]

Conventionally, it has often been thought to stop where history starts. Literature has not commonly been held to a standard of objectivity, of reporting events as they 'really' are or were. But there are exceptions and blurred boundaries. Zola thought of the writer of novels as a scientist in pursuit of facts, while many historians, who are supposed to be truth oriented, accept that their research remains motivated even as it seeks to be objective and that their conclusions may be speculative.[11] Most readers of literature do not expect a factual record; they anticipate that different perspectives will be staged, different feelings educed, different conclusions suggested. Those looking for facts can find these assumptions threatening, as leading to a 'relativism' for which nothing is but as it is seen or felt. They feel themselves heading down a slippery slope to a point where 'anything goes.' And yet literature rubs up against history every time something is referenced, whether a punctual event (the Battle of Borodino, the Gordon Riots) or a long durational condition (the conditions of factory labor, life in a country house). Nonetheless, its principal questions are understood to be about how characters feel about their lives and how they enact those feelings rather than why or how they happen. A good deal of moralizing comes with this. There have been impassioned debates about whether, for example, 'the Holocaust' is a fitting subject for novels and films, but few seriously suggest that it should be beyond the remit of historians. Readers have asked whether a work of fiction is paying proper attention to what we know to have been going on around it. A famous case is the representation and/or displacement of plantation slavery in Austen's *Mansfield Park*. Is it adequate or not? According to what criteria? And, if it is not, do we attribute the fault to its characters or to its author? What do we expect a novel to perform or incite? The 'fiction' of W. G. Sebald presents a moving and rigorous engagement with the border between literature and history, one where we are constantly pushed to decide between fact and imagination, both in the written word and in the identification and authentication of photographs. There are no easy answers. Historians who write counterfactual histories, on the other hand, presume our acknowledgment that things did not happen in this way, though this does not make it simple to decide on what finally constitutes a fact.

The other Auden one-liner that comes to mind in discussions like this (as it does for David Bromwich) is from his poem on the death of W. B. Yeats: "poetry makes nothing happen." This is commonly taken as a statement that poetry is without real-world effects: whatever you write, the world will not change, an insight that can generate either permission (it's only poetry) or despair (wishing it were more consequential). Poetry may help us imagine what we might feel about something happening, and that is all it does. But I am not the first to read the line in another way: poetry creates an event out of nothing, makes nothing *happen* (or *nothing* happen), brings about something that was not there before and could not have been predicted. And once it has happened, we are stuck with it; it won't go away. The more memorable it is, the more it is circulated, the more it is thought about and the more ideas and emotions it generates (this is one argument of Shelley's *Defence of Poetry*). Auden's awkward line about violence, once published, remains with us, quotable over a cup of coffee or picked over in print and in classrooms. We are able to worry over it because we don't have a settled meaning for it; we are not sure how to convey its sense into the world we inhabit. This most unpoetic of lines has, in other words, now taken on the status of poetry, an inextinguishable fragment of thought that keeps on giving, or taking.

So Auden's line demonstrates that poetry makes *itself* happen, even as that happening does not occur as a conventional world event, a changing of things as they were before. This is where things get interesting, because poetry is language, and language is in the world, sometimes in ways we don't much ponder ("please pass the sugar") and at other times in ways that we ponder compulsively, as with the function of poetry and of literary language at large. Here we are quite often at sea. Are we being prompted to endorse the necessary murder, to critique its agents or simply to confront their existence? The violence that the poem references is open to each of these verifications, so what seems to ensue is an incentive to decide between them: a holding to account. Choosing only one and moving along would be the sort of reading that many teachers of literature regard as reductive or polemical. Being aware of more than one has become the mark of sophisticated reading, but it can also be uncomfortable, unless one resorts to a conviction that all ambiguity is a goal in itself. How ambiguous would one want to be about violence and its necessity? Are we *sure* that Auden is not approving it? What do we make of another famous line by Yeats in "Easter 1916" that a "terrible beauty is born," a claim that comes in a poem that appears also to sideline civility by dismissing, twice no less, all "polite meaningless words"?[12] What does Auden imply when he writes, again in "Spain 1937," of "poets exploding like bombs"?[13] That poets are not exempt from physical annihilation? That their works have explosive power? Both? Violence exists and must be confronted, but how and without ambiguity seems to be the question, in a culture that has "never been happy or good," driven "mad" and living in light of an "enlightenment driven away."[14] The time it has taken for me to write down these thoughts, like the time taken up by a classroom discussion about Auden's line, is a happening of nothing, and one that does not want to finish. Were the text being pondered that of a long novel, the happening would require an even greater commitment of time, certainly in the time of reading and potentially in that of discussion. One word for the protocol that enables such discussions is civility. We are thinking or talking about the nature and value of violence and thereby not enacting it, or not yet. We are hearing voices and countervoices and weighing up options and possibilities, perhaps moving to a decision, perhaps not. But to invoke civility is not simply to endorse peace, because civility, like literature, is caught between two stools; it can look like a necessary condition for positive social exchange (its most common sense) or be construed as a management technique for the silencing of dissident perspectives, a deferral of transformative agency. It is either a necessary suppression of violence or a suppression of violence that really is necessary (something like what John Lewis called "good trouble"). What if the peace that civility assures is the peace of injustice and unavowed violence? Reading and discussing literature enact and require civility; each works to slow us down, bid us listen, keep us from explosive response. In performing civility we suspend decisive judgment and final commitment in a way that is essentially unviolent, and we ask for time to consider and reflect. We extend, potentially, permission to differ. This is mostly deemed a good thing. But both literature and civility also generate a doubt about whether we ought to be doing something, enacting a change rather than standing back or standing by. Of course, reading, talking and teaching *are* a form of doing something, and there is a long tradition that values detachment as positive and necessary, a corrective to the more unreflective kinds of doing that dominate social life. But because talking about language is always a step away from unselfconscious enunciation, there is always some sense of a gap, even as philosophical argument can make that gap smaller or even irrelevant. Something like this happens with civil behavior (when it is not merely habit); acting civilly involves awareness of not acting uncivilly, or with violence. In both reading or speaking about literature and performing civility, we keep violence at a distance. This need not involve turning a blind eye or deceiving oneself about real violence, including the violence that can come with the inauguration of peace, whether personally and promptly or in the form of the impersonal slow violence that Rob Nixon writes about.[15] Both literature and civility conventionally position themselves at a distance from violence, whatever they may be in themselves; both entail a suspension of immediate response; and both have been invoked as exclusionary qualities that shore up hierarchies by designating categories of barbarism and what is not literature, or is bad literature. Both challenge and may even subvert a certain notion of sincerity; we do not need to really respect those whom we tolerate, nor do we fully or at all believe what we read in poetry or fiction. When civility is not being performed interpersonally, when it abstractly describes a way of life that is open to some and not to others, it becomes available as a rationale for precisely the violence against others (savages, barbarians) that its own core behavior claims to offset. Similarly literature, when it is not being read and discussed in living time, can be summoned by whomever to index a preferred category of social-educational identity that is performatively exclusionary. How can we learn to think civility and literature *with* violence as well as against it? Is such a state of attention achievable or sustainable? Is the deviousness of these terms always going to frustrate us?

Telling good from bad literature, advocating civil behavior, standing at a distance from violence—these are prominent topics in Jane Austen's *Northanger Abbey*. And deceiving himself about violence by overestimating the prevalence of civility is a particular shortcoming of its male hero, Henry Tilney. Henry likes a good gothic novel as much as anyone, but he is confident that its scenarios belong to a barbaric past that the modern world has left behind thanks to the progress of civility in two of its senses: refined manners and 'civilization' itself. A favorite moment in the novel has him patronizingly resolve a misunderstanding between his sister Eleanor and the heroine, Catherine Morland, over something "uncommonly dreadful" that is about to happen in London, involving "murder and every thing of the kind."[16] Eleanor, whose mind is on her other brother serving in the militia, imagines a "dreadful riot" that might put his life at risk (p.

92). Catherine, an avid reader of gothic novels, intends only reference to a new and exciting publication. It might seem that Henry is the voice of authorially endorsed good sense in pointing out the difference between "streets flowing with blood" and what comes out of a "circulating library" (p. 92). But, as so often, he is a little too self-satisfied in his perspicuity, and Austen has tipped us off a few lines earlier when his lecture to the ladies arrives at the subject of politics: "and from politics, it was an easy step to silence" (p. 91). Now, barely a page later, we are very much back with politics, albeit by way of the rhetoric of litotes: riots are *not* what Catherine means to conjure up. Henry's mockingly precise evocation of "three thousand men assembling in St. George's Fields" (p. 92) nonetheless signals that such things could happen, and most readers of Austen's own generation would have known that they did happen. A refutation becomes an affirmation.

Furthermore, while much of Henry's wit is expended in teasing Catherine about the differences between modern England and the long-vanished world of castles, dungeons and haunted mansions ruled by brutal male aristocrats, it gradually becomes clear that Henry's father is indeed a modern translation of the cruel gothic tyrant, albeit one almost comically corrupted by contemporary commodity culture. The violence that late eighteenth-century upper-middle-class life imagines itself as having transcended is still very much alive in the irascible temper of General Tilney, in his capacity to generate gothic gloom and repression and in his putting at risk the safety of the heroine in sending her home unattended by any servant. The General's homage to the memory of his dead wife does not extend to any chivalrous respect for the other women in his charge, and his desire to add to the family wealth is a classic baronial obsession. He is less boorish than the bullying John Thorpe, but he is cut from the same cloth. Henry is wrong to pooh-pooh Catherine's fears: "Remember the country and the age in which we live. Remember that we are English, that we are Christians" (p. 156). His jocular reference to the protective ubiquity of local gossip—"every man is surrounded by a neighbourhood of voluntary spies" (p. 157)—that makes it impossible to keep secrets signals also (though he may not mean it to) the existence of a Home Office domestic surveillance system that was put in place in the 1790s and would impact the lives of Wordsworth, Coleridge, Thelwall, Shelley and many others at the time.

Northanger Abbey is no simple-minded satire directed at a young girl's uneducated enthusiasm for sensational novels. It shows the various ways in which archaic violence still persists in modern life and perpetrates events that are no less cruel than their medieval precursors. Catherine is not consigned to a dungeon or sexually assaulted by a corrupted cleric, but she lapses into a "silence and sadness" that makes her "the very reverse of all that she had been before" (p. 189). She is rescued from this arguably life-threatening condition only by Henry's finding the courage to defy his father, as all good young adults in gothic novels must do. *Northanger Abbey* is itself the gothic novel it pretends to mock. The "midland counties of England" (p. 158) really do contain dangers, despite Henry's Whiggish assertions about the progress of civilization. Seeing the novel in this way encourages us to ponder further the implications of the language of terror and murder that is applied to both riots and gothic novels, "more horrible than anything we have met with yet" (p. 91). Henry is a zealot, indeed a pedant, in his obsession with the proper use of words, but words are not containable by proper usages. The fantasy violence that the gothic novel offers its readers does suggest that ordinary life happily fails to provide such strong stimuli, hence the appeal of reading vicariously and from a safe distance. But Austen's story blurs the boundaries by reinstating equally toxic forms of violence into the lives of her characters as they are living them in the book that we are reading. Does reading about long-vanished violence distract her young people from recognizing violence in their present world, or does it somehow help them prepare to engage with it when it happens? There is no simple answer.

Northanger Abbey is no *Clarissa*; it is not even *Evelina*. One cannot imagine General Tilney presiding over a betting ring that operates by making old working women who are barely mobile run races for the amusement of their betters, as happens in Fanny Burney's novel. But images of unconstrained male aggression afford plenty of troubling signs that in the world Austen does represent, civility alone is not enough, and it is *Clarissa*, as much as *Pamela*, that casts a shadow over her story. Richardson's less-optimistic novel is not a narrative of "virtue rewarded" (*Pamela*'s subtitle) but of rape and systemic violence designed to highlight the "general depravity" that the author saw around him in his own times.[17] The habit of writing (and writing and writing) that functions as a domesticating force in *Pamela*, heading off the violence it ponders and projects, works in *Clarissa* in almost the opposite way, as a stimulus and incitement, at least for Lovelace, the libertine figure whose facility in literary references does nothing to tamp down his cruel and destructive behavior. Writing works well enough for Clarissa herself—"while I *think* as I write, I cool, and my hurry of spirits is allayed" (1:387)—but the explicitly Satanic career of her seducer is not to be distracted by letters. Repeatedly nominated a "man of violence,"[18] he personifies uncontrolled sexual predation and a devotion to revenge. The greed and ambition of the heroine's family and most of those around her contribute to a comprehensive culture of violence, an experience of "terror" (another common word) that is located in the eighteenth-century reader's here and now some years before it will be reassigned to medieval Europe by the conventions of the gothic novel. Clarissa's death is the ending that Austen hints at for Catherine Morland just before she is rescued; Marianne Dashwood (in *Sense and Sensibility*) comes even closer to the same fate. A plethora of circumstantial violences well beyond a merely romantic disappointment makes the condition of women one of physical and mental oppression to the point of torture. That is one reason why Richardson refuses a happy ending.

Faced with this approximation to Balibar's "inconvertible violence" (to be discussed later) that Richardson finds in his own mid-eighteenth-century England, civility is able to present only the lamest of defenses. Punctilio, politeness, manners and civility are all brought up for analysis in the narrative. Gentlemen should be gentle, writes Clarissa, and "manners should be the essence of it" (2:73). But politeness is not always true politeness; it can be "studied" and employed to deceive people (2:26, 471, 486). Most of the time Clarissa behaves "civilly" to Lovelace, but he scorns mere "civil regards" as an inhibition on his passions and desires (2:58, 302). She wants justice, not mere civility, whose common forms, necessary as they are, are only the groundwork for true moral integrity (1:138, 143; 3:461). Characters struggle to understand and to practice civility as a way to navigate through life, but civility does not save them. It works best when it is least put to the test.

What's in a Word?

I have been thinking about civility since the early 1990s, when I became curious about the connection between its eighteenth- and late twentieth-century incarnations: the first seeking to assuage dissent and diminish violence without actually expanding the vote or changing the laws, and the second newly attached to an ideal of civil society as the one big thing whose absence had brought down the Soviet Empire and whose dissemination would secure a global democracy based on neoliberal principles. Eighteenth-century civility was seen as being enacted above all by literature; in the late twentieth century that connection seemed more attenuated though by no means extinct. The most popular model of civility was now to be found in political science, where it was proposed as the spontaneous energy sustaining liberal civil society. Both civility and civil society were being offered as healthy alternatives to state control of markets and of political life, on the assumption that self-monitoring groups, not governments, could be trusted to lead us all into a happy and prosperous future. But the case for a literary incarnation of civility had not completely disappeared; it continued to be assumed by many teachers at all levels of schooling that literary study generated civility, and novels were still being written in the same spirit. I found myself perplexed about how exactly to understand the links between the two centuries, how to explain the apparent durability of a concept of civility that had been rigorously thought through by 1800, and often found wanting, but that still survived as a ready-to-hand concept for addressing (and some thought solving) problems in modern life. Then, with 9/11, the pattern seemed to be broken, as terror and revenge, along with a renewed commitment to violence, came forward as needing all our attentions. If there were to be an effective way to argue against these dramatic developments, it did not seem likely that it would come from a conventional reversion to civility. But then again, a few years into the twenty-first century, civility was back on the rhetorical front burner, its absence from daily life and political culture now being lamented as destructive of the public good. This time there was less confidence about civility's likely incarnation in civil society and almost no confidence in governmental bodies. Civility seemed to be out there on its own, a lost attribute still shouting loudly for a hearing, even though it could not be coherently theorized or identified. And literature still figures as part of the discussion. Wai Chee Dimock imagines it as taking over some of the civil society functions of the 1990s in calling literature "an NGO of sorts . . . an unusually fine-grained as well as long-lasting one, operating on a scale both too small and too large to be fully policed by the nation-state."[19] Pheng Cheah proposes all political activity as "always already modeled on the incarnational power of culture," and culture as capable of "incarnating ends as objective works in the sensible world."[20] In a subsequent study, Cheah amplifies his idea of a "normative worldly force" to literature, a "force of making possible" through the deployment of an "incalculable gift of time" that can never be anticipated or preempted.[21] The civility function here becomes ontological, built into the constitution of the human mind and body. Alongside such initiatives there is another voice, well articulated by Achille Mbembe, who echoes Hofstadter (and Fanon) in arguing that violence and not peace is the hallmark of the Western democracies that were born out of "the colonial empire and the pro-slavery state." Instead of supplanting this violence, democracy is a strategy for ignoring it, deadening awareness that killing rather than caring is the protocol of its survival.[22] Bruce Robbins analogously asks "what is it that enables all this inflicting of pain on people outside our borders to go on and on?"[23] Must literature not reckon with this as part of its informal NGO (nongovernmental organization) function, find some means of evaluating both creative and uncreative forces?

What began in the 1990s as a question about civility and civil society—two concepts or one, and what sorts of concepts?—has for me in the meantime become more and more a question about literature, with which civility had from the first been associated in its opposition to violence. For civility took early form *as* and *in* literature, which was the privileged medium of its distribution. And not just in writing itself but in the literary pedagogy that began in the reviews and magazines and was then gradually adopted into the educational protocols of the schools and universities. Civility models an ideal form of private and public life—how we might actually live together—while literature presents (most comprehensively in the novel) representations of life that are without immediate consequences; we can pick up and put down a book with very little obvious effect on those around us. Literature thus takes a position against the violence that is always potential in real-time events that cannot be recalled, by allowing us to practice, in the imagination, decisions and responses that need not ever go public. Ever since Homer took the wrath of Achilles as his topic, literature has represented and even sometimes glorified violence; but in so doing it raises questions about the ethics of representation that instigate extended processes of deliberation. Civility and literature come together in the modern period as restraints, one declarative and the other imaginary, on destructive behavior.

But literature has not always been protected by its avowal of a merely imaginary life, nor has it always been happy to stay there. For much of the seventeenth and eighteenth centuries in Britain, licensing acts forbade the publication of any text without official approval, and transgressions could be subject to gruesome and even fatal punishment.[24] Within the modern anglophone world, literature has regularly been deemed politically or morally incendiary. From the *Pamela* controversy through the *Bovary*, *Ulysses* and *Chatterley* trials to the Rushdie *fatwa*, books have been received into the world as threats to law and order, and to someone's idea of civility, and have thus been deployed toward violences that they are generically set up to avoid. Sometimes writers have invited controversies that cannot promise to assure nonviolent resolutions: *Uncle Tom's Cabin*, one might say, deploys political disenfranchisement to encourage readers to at least ponder civil disobedience. Such outcomes remain possible for any book, sometimes predictably, sometimes not. Jean-Paul Sartre argued that every work of art creates an "absolute beginning," one dependent on the freedom of its reader or beholder and reactivated with every rereading or viewing.[25] That includes the attribution of endorsing or even performing violence, notwithstanding the conventional permissions that come with being called art or literature. Derek Attridge has similarly ascribed to literature a "singularity" whose formation cannot be predicted but is always to be experienced as an event. Publication is simply a "letting something happen" that triggers an "idiocultural" response in every reader that is different from that of every other reader. (This does not preclude the emergence of efficient consensus, but that consensus is never either absolute or guaranteed.)[26]

Meanwhile, there are other conditions that are modifying and perhaps changing (it is not easy to say which) the relations between literature and civility and of both to violence. Civility culture has always been modeled on small-group experiences, and one of the appeals of literature, especially in the age of print (first paper and now also digital), is that it can broadcast small-group narratives to unpredictably larger ones, even to a mass readership. In the 1740s the publication of *Pamela* generated disputes over, for example, male violence, the wedding contract, the virtues of politeness and prudence and class conflict. In its efforts to resolve such debates, the book reignited them. Many modern readers continue to respond in good faith to more recent best sellers, which range from topically urgent high-cultural texts like *Beloved* or *Midnight's Children* to even more popular examples in crime fiction, science fiction and romance. Sartre, in the 1940s, felt that French writers had lost their public, along with the bourgeois ideology that sustained the connection, leading him to recommend that writers become more adept in using the popular media—film, radio, newspaper—to gain attention.[27] But defenses and critiques of all kinds and degrees of literature continue to be made, and literature is still widely held to be making an important and perhaps unique contribution to a good life, especially in a world perceived more and more as turning away from the humanities. Many of these defenses have not moved very far (if they have moved at all) from those made by Kant and Schiller about the necessary freedom of aesthetic experience, which for Wordsworth, Coleridge, Shelley and Blake was envisaged as the agency driving all of human life. Even those more attuned to the power of ideology often reserve a space for the counter-hegemonic operations of art and for its incarnation as critique. For Bill Readings, what education should offer is not quite either freedom or critique but obligation and an awareness of dissensus.[28] Art and literature still matter to a lot of people, some of whom think long and hard about how and why they matter.

Writing in time means, of course, that one is never in time and always behind the times. Things can change quickly. The steady growth of the Me Too movement and the explosion of Black Lives Matter as both an interracial and global phenomenon, coming on the heels of a pandemic that has presented, for so many nonwhite persons as well as many whites, a devastating threat to physical and economic health, has made it possible to at least imagine the whole game changing. Suddenly, decades if not centuries of both gender and racial prejudices, and the violence they sponsor, are being denounced by record numbers of people and violently defended by others. We ask again about the play between civility and violence, with the policing apparatus finding it harder than ever before to dismiss protesters as nothing more than a bunch of rioters and looters. Literature will take its time with this, but a lot of literature is already there waiting to be read again: Zola, Dickens, Hugo and a huge list of twentieth-century fiction that sets out to assess the claims of both civility and violence and to give life and meaning to the faces in the crowd. Literature's representation of violence has been intermittent but persistent. Class antagonism was recognized as formative in nineteenth-century British literature, often conceived as the violence of white men against other white men. The repression of white women by white men has been on the literary agenda since at least the eighteenth century. American literature has from the first been more attuned to register racial violence, that of white people against nonwhite people. Still timely, and perhaps in time? My effort here is to reassess, for our present moment and foreseeable future, the balance of accounts between civility, literature and violence and the claims to attention that literature and civility can plausibly make in the recognition of and response to current violences.

And yet, can there be anything new to say about civility? Both its celebration and its critique are well established. They have been current for a long time and are regularly updated. But what is documented is not always remembered, and some of what is enunciated has not been documented. Students coming late to class, using their phones, marching and shouting instead of politely requesting; Washington politicians insulting one another and scorning compromise. These and similar laments about the decline of civility have been going on for a long while, but they continue to appear in newspapers and magazines as if for the first time. So too, though much less commonly, do defenses of incivility, recently embraced by the political right as well as by the countercultural left raised on readings of Fanon and Marcuse. The appearance of déjà vu in these invocations is not just the result of a failure of collective memory, for civility is one of those words whose very function lies in imprecision and obfuscation. It is a weak concept. It has never been precisely defined and has never been legislated, though corporations and universities habitually devise codes of civility that operate somewhere between persuasion and coercion. While widely regarded as a good thing, it has never settled into identification as a clear-cut moral virtue at the hands of the philosophers. John Rawls's effort to argue for a "duty of civility" in the face of the inevitable imperfections of a democratic justice system are themselves inevitably open to dispute.[29] For sociologists and political scientists, civility mostly functions within the sphere of civil society, another unstable term that has in recent times been understood as made up of voluntary formations counterposed to state-based bureaucracies, though this has not always been true. For one commentator, civility should be understood as "the most elemental expectation of American citizenship" and a core component of that civil society that is "a secret of our success as a nation."[30] Most commonly civility is produced in everyday speech as the property of the good people and what the not-so-good visibly lack. Meanwhile, among oppositional minorities it has been received as a hypocritical standard designed to insulate the powers that be from criticism and to preempt dissent.[31] To many ordinary language users, civility is another word for politeness, although politeness is only ever a part of civility and can sometimes even be taken to work against it.

Any complacency in our habitual recourse to civility as a known virtue or placebo should, however, have been shaken up by the publication of Étienne Balibar's *Violence and Civility*, which presents the challenging proposition that the two terms must be thought of in apposition rather than opposition.[32] Civility is not simply against violence but with it, each embedded in the other in ways that do not permit tidy segregation. This is more than just an acknowledgment that civility *can* involve forms of violence, a traditional enough understanding. It suggests that civility, our best word for the set of desires we have about nondestructive behavior, *cannot* be held apart from its own declared antithesis.[33] Balibar's account, which will require more detailed discussion later in this study, risks its own incoherence in order to unsettle any residual comfort we might take in keeping good things apart from bad things. In this it is congruent with Teresa Bejan's more locally historical argument about Roger Williams's investment in a pared-down model of civility that allows for the acknowledgment and preservation of a good measure of hostility.[34] For both, civility occupies a site—hardly a middle ground but a shifting and uncertain terrain—that is also a traditional environment for literature and the pedagogies deployed around it. Tobin Siebers, for example, has found in the work of Geoffrey Hartman a "desire to resolve conflict without either taming or identifying with it."[35] What such resolution might or might not be raises difficult questions and answers that may be less than fully satisfying but that are a major preoccupation of the rest of this book. They are formulated in the aftermath of the Trump presidency, which once again generated intense discussion about civility and incivility. The anonymous dissenter within the administration whose letter generated massive publicity in September 2018 noted that "we have sunk low with him and allowed our discourse to be stripped of civility": the author was merely the most visible among those who lamented the demise of public sociability.[36] At the same time there has been, in many parts of the world, a return to charismatic leader politics and a new appetite for strong government, as long as it pushes certain buttons: militarization, protectionism, anti-immigration, white supremacy. In places where an ethos of civility was habitually invoked to keep the peace, rampant incivility—whether as spontaneous expression or calculated political strategy—now shows itself without embarrassment. Among some groups it is positively celebrated. The acceptance of reasonable disagreement that has long characterized the self-image of liberal-center argumentation has seemed disturbingly weak in the face of anger, bigotry and prejudice. These tendencies are apparent both nationally and internationally. It is again timely to look at the uses and abuses of civility, as indeed it has always been throughout the roughly four hundred years that constitute its career in the long modern period.

As the old truths are still to be heard spoken, so they are, like civility itself, often seen to be wearing thin. Both national and international relations are under stress from migrations, themselves driven by climate change, pandemic, scarcity and war and by reaffirmations of nationalism that are upending the diplomacy of politeness and deference all over the world. The project of 'Europe' that has been increasing its scope and size since the post-1945 settlement is now more than ever under strain, while inherited global alliances in trade and defense are also breaking down. One result of this increasingly visible polarization of interests is a further strain on the vocabularies used by politicians and their (conscious and unconscious) allies in the media to manage social conflict and explain people to themselves. All cultures function by way of a set of ready-mades, words that circulate as unquestioned positives without being looked at too closely. In more than usually stressful times such terms tend to be worked harder and to be more aggressively defended from critical analysis. (The career of the word *terror* after 9/11 is a prime recent example.) Representative democracies must finesse the fact that most of their citizens have little or no effective power beyond registering a highly manipulable vote. One form of pacification is verbal. Anglophone democracies trade heavily in a legitimating vocabulary that includes civilization, freedom, security, civility and tolerance as their governing properties; terror and barbarism belong to others. But no political science that is in the business of defending democracy can afford to recommend repressing that degree of dissent and disturbance needed to generate progress of any kind. Thus, reform preempts revolution, and allowable dissent is marked off from violence. Most words that matter are contestable and have a history of use and misuse that can be mined, adapted or ignored as their users decide.[37] Terms that seem bland and self-explaining may have roots in violently polemical histories, even accumulating meanings that are on the face of things quite contradictory. These are accepted as ambiguous when ambiguity is not threatening but pressured into single senses when it is: Derrida's analysis of the Platonic *pharmakon* is the classic demonstration of this, and Raymond Williams's magisterial *Keywords* is an exemplary listing of words we should particularly not take for granted.[38]

Not taking words for granted, not accepting them at face value, takes time, as does the experience of the meditative reading or classroom discussion of literature. Those who seek to rule over others are generally in the business of cutting into that time and preventing the proliferation of alternative interpretations or understandings. The author of *Mein Kampf* writes a long book that argues against the value of any book as compared with the spoken word when the task is one of consolidating obedience. Great movements are made by "great speakers" rather than "great writers." The "great masses of a nation will always and only succumb to the force of the spoken word."[39] Hitler's idea of reading is explained as precisely and purposively antiliterary, aiming not at the exploration of complex alternatives but at the isolation of a single main idea repeated over and over again. Only this will provide the ready response demanded by critical events and stop people being mired in "the terrible muddle of things learned" (p. 48). The main idea, of course, is not something for hearer-readers to choose or deliberate; it is the one provided by the speaker. At the same time as I. A. Richards, for example, in *Science and Poetry* (1927), was devising a case for the complexities of poetic language as a force for nonviolence, Hitler was working in the other direction. His one big idea is the idea of the one big enemy, because two enemies would bring about "the division of the attention of a people" (p. 152). With malign ingenuity, that one enemy, who is of course the Jew, is a shapeless figure of cosmopolitan affiliation who can, like an artful teacher of literature, turn "truth into untruth" and disable the entire cognitive apparatus of a nation (p. 82). Such a figure must be the focus of an absolute violence because it threatens above all to undermine and complicate violence itself. Naziism has no place for critical philology.

This is not surprising, since critical philology itself is an important incarnation of the literature-civility complex. Nietzsche described the philologist as a "teacher of slow reading," one dedicated to frustrating anyone in a hurry. Philology requires us to "go aside, to take time, to become still, to become slow." Writing in 1886, he saw his own generation as too much given to "indecent and perspiring haste."[40] His lament and his injunction remain eerily timely for our own generation of texters and tweeters. Not infrequently philology has expressed a sense of something lost. Erich Auerbach saw himself facing the failure of cosmopolitan Europe and the onset of a standardization that would erode the complexity of its languages. Philology's task is to provide points of departure (*Ansatzpunkte*) with the potential for "centrifugal radiation."[41] These are concrete and precise, but not in such a way as to support a closed methodology or finished product. One must avoid the false positivism of one word one meaning, of the sort that is apparent in Hannah Arendt's complaint about political science having failed to connect its key terms to "distinct, different phenomena."[42] One could, for example, insist that civility has an exclusive meaning that should be understood as different from what is meant by politeness, manners, citizenship or civilization, and the world might be a tidier place if it did. But the record shows that all of these senses have been invoked and assumed and that making distinctions is often the last thing on the minds of their users, who are as often in the business of obfuscation as of clarification. Raymond Williams's *Keywords* captures this well, as does Reinhart Koselleck's concept history.[43] I. A. Richards's *How to Read a Page* is another keywords project, making clear the importance of recognizing and accepting confusion rather than simply lamenting a lack of clarity. To think that important words are *not* ambiguous is to miss the most important part of our education. Words support "necessary techniques of multiple representation."[44] Critical philology is not a plug-in operation.

This is made abundantly clear by the word *civility*, which has long been doing yeoman's work in the service of politicians and pundits, corporate and university administrators and just about anyone who is anxious to keep things calm and quiet in actually or potentially divisive situations. But there is little agreement about what civility is and about exactly when one crosses the line from honest dissent to a culpable undermining of the social order. The earliest uses in English specify having to do with the art of government, either in a relatively neutral sense (as in the Latin *civilis*) or indicating a secular rather than a religious orientation. It seems to have taken until the sixteenth century for the familiar modern association with positive attributes of peaceable politeness to accrue. At the same time civility came to overlap with civilization as a marker of propriety and proper behavior, something that some persons and groups possess while others do not. *OED*'s subentry 12c records a different sense: *civility-money* was, in the eighteenth and early nineteenth centuries, the term for a bribe or tip paid by prisoners to their jailers in hopes of receiving favors. Civility, in this sense, is fungible and unaccompanied by even a shred of moral or aesthetic probity; it has no inward attributes; it is just a matter of paying up. In our contemporary world the idea of civility as a murky, ambiguous and even deceitful quality has become much more familiar. An inspection of the record suggests that it was always there to be found.

In *Keywords* Williams mentions civility only in his entry on civilization, for which it often appeared as a synonym in eighteenth-century use. But it has never been hard to argue that an excess of civility, in its bad sense, can be at odds with a flourishing civilization; eighteenth-century commentators were particularly sensitive to the potential hypocrisy of good manners as a front for mere self-interest, although neither Samuel Johnson nor Noah Webster (in 1828) records any negative senses for civility. Williams died in 1988. In the latest, heavily revised and updated edition of *Keywords* the editors add *civil* into the list as a separate entry, speculating that its continued popularity has to do with a certain vagueness about exactly what it means, its ability to "articulate the individual and the social while bringing little additional semantic content to that articulation."[45] The great French encyclopedia project of the mid-eighteenth century was much more precise and rather more cynical about civility, which is grouped (in Louis de Jaucourt's article) with affability and politeness (*politesse*).[46] Affability is what the socially superior practice toward their inferiors and is often nothing more than an artificial virtue serving self-interest. Civility is only a part of politesse, but neither can be assumed to emanate from the heart; politesse belongs to persons of quality, civility to those others who are striving to be thought polite. It is thus an attribute of social climbers and can be annoyingly excessive as such; Jaucourt cites Montaigne on the phenomenon of being uncivil through too much civility, which then becomes both tiresome and useless.

Civility is a modern concept, albeit unevenly modern. Neither Greek nor Latin, the sources of so much of our ethical and political vocabulary, possesses terms that transfer into modern languages as the bearers of the full range of meanings and ambiguities that civility invokes. Latin comes closest, but *civilis* has only a late and rare figurative usage invoking good manners. The Greek terms used in scholarly translations as equivalents to civility either do not pass over at all or do so with quite different meanings (e.g., *philanthropia*). Cicero, who is widely invoked from the Renaissance onward as the exemplary classical theorist of politeness, gifts the word *decorum* to the world, but the terms he uses in his analysis (e.g., *honestum, utilis, mansuetudo, clementia*), though they do include a range of meanings from moral integrity to crude self-interest, have not been adopted into the modern languages, in the senses he designates, as central to the concept of civility.[47]

Among the modern languages it is French and Italian that historically set the pace; to this day German speakers have a traditionally negative reaction to *Zivil-* words because of an association with the French *civilisation*, received as a shallow and superficial category of mere manners or as a purely formal description of attributes, in contrast to the more profound and metaphysical German *Kultur*.[48] The ever-increasing spread of anglophone vocabularies is having an effect, however. Some present-day German speakers have found the "relative ahistoricity" of *Zivilität* to be an advantage for neutral conceptualization, and one writer proposes that it is now more suitable as a general term than the hitherto overused "civil society": we have come full circle, back to *civilis.*[49] English speakers were from the start more receptive to the appeal of civility. The explicit class coding that marks Jaucourt's article and fits readily into the courtier image that still dominated official French culture in the 1750s would also inform, in the Earl of Chesterfield's popular English work, the aspirations of those striving to upgrade themselves into (and perhaps out of) the middle class. There is still a residue of this effort at social mobility in modern invocations of civility, according to which manners (preferably sincere) maketh man (even as their adjudication is often assigned to women). It is common to see civility invoked as a measure of what is absent, with dire consequences for the general social order.

Jaucourt's understanding of civility, and its precise relations to words that might easily but should not be taken as synonyms, stands as a model of rational ambition for the proper uses of words, but it has not taken root in the common understanding, which continues to reproduce a confusion about what it is and is not: hence Thomas Hobbes opined that "a man that seeketh precise truth had need to remember what every name he uses stands for, and to place it accordingly, or else he will find himself entangled in words, as a bird in lime twigs, the more he struggles the more belimed."[50] Terms for the virtues and vices are especially prone to "*inconstant* signification" because they reflect little more than "the nature, interest and disposition of the speaker" (p. 24): one man's wisdom is another's fear; one man's justice is cruelty for another. Such words can never be the true grounds for "any ratiocination," and they are more dangerous than metaphors because they disguise rather than confess "their inconstancy" (p. 25). Absolutist as he may be in politics, Hobbes stops short of suggesting that exclusive or 'proper' meanings of words can be fixed by anybody. He knows that no king or emperor rules the language, whose slipperiness is indeed useful for the maintenance of the status quo by those whose interests it serves. The best we can manage is a critical philology, examining the "definitions of former authors" and attempting to correct them by offering our own (p. 21). This is the insight that leads to *Keywords* and to the German concept histories, and it accepts as a given the contested nature of words rather than seeking to establish fixed once-and-for-all significations as authoritative. Some philosophers and intellectual historians still adhere to the idea of one word for one clear idea, while concept theorists tend to uphold a normative range of ideas that must be observed if a concept is to persist *as* a concept. But some words will simply not settle down into readily manipulable shapes; they are the words that can mean radically different and even opposite things. Civility, which wanders between identifying a social virtue and something close to hypocrisy and deceit, is one of these. Its radical uncertainty or ambiguity devolves from its role in the early modern period (along with cognates like courtesy and politeness) as denoting how persons behave around monarchs and other authority figures at a time when explicit violence was being punished or discouraged. If nodding and smiling is a genuinely affable gesture, all may be well enough; if it is an effort to disguise or defer violent hostility with the appearance of good manners, things are not quite so simple. Literature too deals in fictions that can be taken for realities; it is also the medium in which civility's inconvertible violence can be represented.

Uncivil Times

The disappearance or marginalization of kings and princes does not diminish the complexities of civility's invocations, which recur as it takes its place in the vocabulary of bourgeois life. Norbert Elias has given us the standard thesis about the early stages of this process. The early modern state's priority, he surmised, was taking over the power of violence from the (dominantly male) aristocracy. As displays of impulsive aggression became punishable, "reflective detachment" came to be a feature of social subjectivity; this was then further encouraged by the demands of "bourgeois professional and commercial functions."[51] The process is historically cumulative and incrementally more and more reliant on displacement and repression. Reflective detachment is also exactly what would be encouraged as the preferred ethos of literary pedagogy. As society becomes more complex and differentiated, Elias argues, more people experience "ambivalence of interests" and motives, and more and more interactions are characterized by a lack of "decisive outcome" (pp. 395, 396). The resulting uncertainty proliferates the protocols of "self-constraint" in "pacified social spaces" that preempt violence but place considerable psychic and emotional pressures on their inhabitants (pp. 446, 448). The threat of critical violence is thus normally occluded and invisible, but always to be sensed. This habit of "vigilant self-control and perpetual observation of others" (p. 478) that marks Elias's model of civilization is especially hard on the middle classes, who always look both above and below themselves for contrasts and comparisons (p. 508). A preoccupation with civility—an indecisive, volatile and potentially deceptive standard that must always be specified in time, place and persons—is both a symptom of and an imagined cure for this predicament. Early modern civility culture was indeed the mark of an emergent bourgeoisie, but one that was simultaneously on the defensive as the very condition of its emergence. Latter-day invocations of civility follow the same logic: they are articulated as that which one possesses and that which the other person lacks, no positive without a negative and no sure standard for either. Civility and incivility require each other to subsist intelligibly.

So it is that we continue to encounter regular reminders of the loss of civility and the terrible consequences of its disappearance, along with arguments for the positive values of incivility: a refusal to allow important issues to be buried by social coercion or to accept a deflection of political argument or action by appeals to good manners. At times this resistance to civility has come from the left, who have the most to lose by acceding to unwritten codes of conduct that tend to favor the status quo. More recently it has come more stridently from the right, as a celebration of violent and rude behavior in itself, more confidently expressed now than at any other time since the heyday of European fascism, and visibly uninterested in the creation of any kind of consensus. In the United States since the 2016 election this behavior has become, consciously or otherwise, a charismatic strategy: the more abusive I am, the more authentic and counter-establishment I appear. Appeals to a supposedly traditional civility culture seemed at first unable to respond effectively to this development, although the purposively peaceable transracial constituents of Black Lives Matter are making a strong counterstatement.

While new circumstances clearly argue for critical attention to the rhetoric of civility and its long-term attributes and affiliations, they devolve from a long history of violence and nonviolence facing off in theory as well as on the streets.[52] A visible commitment to civility protocols underpins those peaceful demonstrations that give hope to the left in dark times: the worldwide peace marches of February 2003, the recent (since

2017) women's marches, the gathering at Standing Rock, and the Occupy movement are examples. So far—although Black Lives Matter may yet prove an exception—most of these have been either ignored (the United States went to war within weeks of the marches in 2003) or, when too threatening, violently repressed.[53] When the left's behavior has included attributable episodes of violence (Seattle in 1999, Geneva in 1998), they have been played up by the media to justify even more aggressive policing: Portland in 2020, where the 'security' argument was publicly challenged, may signal a new direction. While commitment to civility alone has not had notable political successes, those contemplating violence are all too aware of the sheer power and scope of the militarized state apparatus that faces them on the streets. Meanwhile, as social media and the virtual economy emerge as new environments for pursuing the struggle between left and right, between one faction and another, or among competitive individuals, civility continues to be part of the debate: flaming, stalking, hacking and trolling all identify actions deemed improper or uncivil. The technology has moved on, but the language for adjudicating its limits and opportunities remains noticeably familiar.

The Trump campaigns and presidency have recalibrated the balance between civility and incivility as approvable or effective political strategies. The events of 9/11 had similarly occasioned a shift in the prevailing rhetoric: the celebrations of civility and civil society as the soft-revolutionary agents of the West that had helped bring down the Soviet Empire took a back seat as rage and revenge called for a retributive and 'just' violence toward the enemy. Thereafter, President Barack Obama hewed relentlessly to a rhetoric of civility in the face of repeated rebuttals from an enraged, uncompromising and implicitly racialized opposition that calculated (correctly as it happens) that it had nothing to gain and much to lose from polite and respectful collaboration.[54] International relations moved significantly away from the middle ground where self-interest sees civility talk as its ally; intemperate and abusive language and punitive policies became more and more acceptable among heads of state, with a US president leading the way. How the idea of Europe will be remodeled by the British exit from the European Union and by the volatility of the North Atlantic Alliance remains to be seen, but displays of uncivil behavior are palpable, again most visibly in the form of right-wing nationalism.

The events of January 2021 in the United States gave yet more urgency to newly elected President Biden's call for an end to "uncivil wars." The long-term extent of global and domestic social disintegration resulting from the coronavirus pandemic remains impossible to predict, but there will almost certainly be serious crises.

Again, for all of these reasons, it is timely to revisit a topic that has been visited so many times before. The Elias thesis, which implies that we are living less violent lives now that the state controls most of the weapons and engaging peaceably in trade and commerce, continues to generate its advocates. Steven Pinker garnered widespread attention, much of it skeptical and critical, for his recent argument that violence has declined and is declining, for some of the same reasons that Elias had invoked.[55] A good few of Pinker's explanations for his proposed decline in violence have to do with the evolution of print culture and the expansion of readerships.[56] Many people continue to defend the idea that literature makes us better, less aggressive persons, although that view has not gone uncontested. In fact, the history of literature may be written as one of contestation. During the Cold War, the role of the aesthetic was taken very seriously by the rival power blocs. Communists and capitalists alike spent considerable time and money on attempting to direct the reading and listening habits of readers at home and abroad; a renegade poet or novelist was seen as a serious threat to thrones and altars. Sixty or so years on we may find this a quaint misconception, attuned as we are to the idea that the market drives everything. A few of us might also object, now as then, to the attempted instrumentalization of the aesthetic sphere, which needs to be protected as the last bastion of ambiguity and disinterest, a place where you can write whatever you like about anything. The circulation of what we have come to call a world literature, mostly in English, calls for a reexamination of literature's traditional positioning, deliberative and dialogic, within (what remains of) civility culture. Is it, for example, once again time to ponder the value of a literature of rage, and what would that look like? What directions emerge from literature's indirections? And, in the words of the old song, how long has this been going on?

It has been going on at least since the sixteenth century: Erasmus and Castiglione are founding figures for modern civility theory. Elias's "inbuilt self-control" and "reflective detachment" are exactly the forms of behavior instilled by reading, especially reading imaginative writing.[57] Marvin Becker has described the close alliance between civility and literature at the beginnings of the early modern period: "correlations were commonplace between poetry and civility."[58] This was no simple alliance, however. Castiglione was held by some to be a Machiavellian spirit, and his *Book of the Courtier* (1528), translated into English in 1561, was widely held to be a handbook of hypocrisy.[59] Civility, often under the name of *courtesy*, was open to the same concerns and critiques that would recur in the eighteenth century at the point when a transition to the modern mass readership was under way. Some scholars have identified courtesy with the Christian virtues, rendering it implicitly proto-theological, while others have pointed to its affinity with dissimulation and deceit.[60] In *The Faerie Queene* Spenser stages an extended analysis of courtesy, both as a thing in itself and in relation to violence, and his insights are by no means reassuring. The poet's letter to Raleigh makes a famous claim about the poem's purpose being "to fashion a gentleman or noble person in virtuous and gentle discipline."[61] But courtesy alone is no guarantee: the true courtesy of which "civilitie" is the agent (p. 147) has become "nought but forgerie" and "fayned shows" (p. 4).[62] Whether it subsists at the court of Elizabeth I is very much open to question, and even the good knight Calidore uses refined manners to attain dubious ends in courting Pastorella, thereby temporarily forgetting his mission, while the poet-figure himself seems to be living in the countryside, at a distance from the court. At the end of it all the Blatant Beast, an incarnation of all that is uncivil, still roams the land, uncontainable by the best of knightly efforts. Violence meanwhile escapes management by moral-metaphysical codes, most notably in the terrifying figure of Talus, who does much of Artegall's dirty work in Book Five. Here already the violence is that of settler colonialism, as the landscape over which Talus ranges is that of Ireland. While Artegall usually gets to slay the nobler sort of bad man, Talus, often called "yron man," lays about the commoner sort. He is invulnerable and incipiently uncontrollable, a weapon of mass destruction and incipiently of genocide operating without apparent emotion. Artegall has some claim to courtesy, but any wider civility that might ensue from his example is spread and maintained by brute and fatal force. It is not a pretty picture.

In other words, the entanglements of literature, civility and violence with which I am concerned are all there in Spenser's epic, written for a 'courtly' readership. Literature is taking on civility for its associations with violence, and violence already governs the inauguration of colony and empire. Similar questions become pervasive in the eighteenth century, when something that looks like a middle class articulates a code of behavior and a set of expectations for both self-advancement and peaceful coexistence that are not limited to court or salon culture. Lovelace indeed specifically adverts to Spenser in nominating Clarissa as "my Gloriana," and his performance of the violence of chivalric culture is a key element in Richardson's critique of masculine aggression, dueling included.[63] This is also the time that a globalization of European literature picks up, one that continues into the nineteenth century with the circulation, in translation, of authors like Goethe, Scott, Byron, Balzac and Dumas. At the turn of the eighteenth century much of the literary-aesthetic discussion was about the claims of ancients and moderns. Are we progressing or going backward? Can we assume that we understand the personalities and motivations of long-dead individuals, or must we arm ourselves with a detailed scholarly and philological apparatus to track the radical differences that history enacts? In the modern global era this question becomes not temporal but spatial: What if anything do we have in common with persons in the far-flung corners of the earth? How does the same book register among readers in Birmingham and Beijing? Whom may writers like Rushdie or Ondaatje be said to represent? Whom do they speak for and speak to? Is there a unitary world literature, and should there be? Is the 'masterpiece' a marketing ploy, a technique for the dissemination of ideology or a medium for the creation of global understanding and civility? And how much do any of these questions matter in the apparently all-conquering ambience of the new social media? Is literature just part of the legacy media, or can it be of use in mitigating or preempting the many forms of violence suffered by so many millions across the world?

The accepted narrative about the eighteenth century is that civility and literature worked together toward the diminishing of violence, not least through the virtual agency of fictional heroines (Pamela, Clarissa, Julie): arbiters of modern manners still tend to be women.[64] Nonviolent behavior was gendered feminine because the forms of violence it countered—rape, sexual harassment, dueling—were all distinctly male and register as such in, for example, the novels of Burney and Fielding. Insofar as males embraced civility, they opened themselves to accusations of foppery, enhancing the need to find a way of validating a robust, energized politeness that was open to both men and women. Sentiment and sensibility played into the same plot; in the nineteenth century, culture (*Bildung*) functioned very much as a remasculinization of nonviolent interiority. Mr. B's reformation, in *Pamela*, begins when he develops the habit of reading. People read books and discussed them at home, in salons and in coffee houses, in private and in public, and thereby cultivated the deliberative skills that would equip them to function as respectable citizens. This was a prepolitical or nonpolitical experience, one that allowed for adjudications that could substitute for a restricted franchise where most men (and all women) could not vote. On the one hand, it could seem to serve as a gradualist preparatory routine for a slowly emergent access to political recognition; on the other, it was a compensatory gratification offering sui generis pleasures that no one could take away because they were entirely virtual and without apparent consequence. Koselleck argues that bourgeois interiority evolved as an alternative source of agency in the face of political incapacity, taking form as both moral law and aesthetic taste.[65] While moral law aspired to a declarative clarity (something is wrong or right), taste (like civility) formed itself by eschewing absolute or coercive standards as the price of its own sustainability. These initiatives, along with the Masonic lodges and the socially organized republic of letters, would eventually, according to Koselleck, come to overturn the absolute state by which their members were denied recognition. Literature, it seems, might here be assisting in making something happen.

Fanon and/or Kant

In the early eighteenth century literary criticism functioned in the (albeit limited) public sphere, often along party lines and in relation to the theater, a site of visible disputation and even physical antagonism. After 1789 criticism increasingly recommends interior mental experience as its proper domain—Charles Lamb's essay on how much more one gains from reading rather than seeing *King Lear* is exemplary here—and emphasizes a distance from politics as the guarantor of its continued existence.[66] Already here we can see a privileging of slow time as the proper time of reading; the same slow time that would be proposed as the attribute of a future literary education.[67] The violence of ordinary life—often apparent in the riotous behavior of theater audiences—is now consigned (as by Schiller) to a sphere outside the aesthetic from which the aesthetic is immune. As schools and eventually universities seek to expand the educational franchise, the teaching of literature in particular emerges as a key component in the training of nonviolent and nonpolitical (or at most pre-political) responsiveness. Defending the absolute importance of what defines itself as seemingly without practical consequences becomes the defining attribute of literary studies. Civility, meanwhile, always belonged in the public sphere by way of its identification with manners, and while it was for a good part of the nineteenth century pushed aside in favor of an internalized model of culture (as *Bildung*), it has never been fully displaced and is if anything making a comeback, not just in the hortatory invocations of popular social commentary but in theory and scholarship alike.[68]

It does so as still very much in touch with its original formation as an analogue or instance of the protocols of literary reading, but the profile of that interaction has changed at both ends: a civility that is stretched to discursive breaking point by the work required of it on a scale well beyond its foundational small-group formations, and a literature that is at once competing with charismatic new social media and being projected and marketed as globally accessible only by way of translation and anglophone dominance. The forms of violence with which both literature and civility are inevitably entangled look different from what they were in the early imperial period, even though the contrasts are often more apparent than real. Readers of *Mansfield Park* or *Jane Eyre* were once able to ignore their authors' allusions to the economy of slavery, although the evidence was there to be picked up had anyone been motivated to do so, especially during the height of the abolition debates.[69] Now decolonization and its aftermaths, and the unresolved legacies of slavery and settler colonialism in the United States, have made the violence of race consciousness more or less unignorable in both past and contemporary literature: in how we read the past and in what we write for the moment. Two world wars and their attendant genocides had made it brutally clear that violence on an almost unimaginable scale was fully at home in the European heartland.[70] Sartre, in 1947, accordingly confirmed that evil is not just an "appearance," not "the effect of passions which might be cured, of a fear which might be overcome, of a passing aberration which might be excused, of an ignorance which might be enlightened." Nor can it be outfaced by a simple denial of violence, "because we are in a universe of violence."[71] Sometimes, as Marcuse would also suggest, violence is called forth as the only way to end violence. By the 1960s Sartre is introducing to a wider readership the work of Frantz Fanon, calling out Fanon's analysis of nonviolence as part of Western ideology, a screen covering over the foundational and ongoing operational violence of the entire settler-colonial enterprise. No country engaging in torture (as France was in Algeria) could get away with simply specifying its enemies as the only sources of violence. For Fanon, violence is the bond shared by colonizer and colonized, a legacy to be expunged only when the introverted aggression of the native population (generated by rape, torture, the scaffold and the lash) can express itself in wars of liberation.

Fanon's writings responding to the emergence of national liberation movements in the 1950s and 1960s remain key to an understanding of the ongoing relation of literature and violence and of the potentially eviscerated relation of literature to civility. For Fanon, courtesy and politeness (civility) properly belong only within emancipated groups of decolonizing or newly decolonized peoples: the world he imagined as beginning to take shape or still to come. Civility evolves among those within the new societies and is then indeed an agent of solidarity. Others outside those groups, especially former colonists, are treated at best with rudeness.[72] Literature, meanwhile, is for Fanon unlikely to be at the forefront of any revolutionary movement. Too many writers belong to the radically compromised class of intellectuals, which is never in the vanguard of historical change; and too many hold back from approving the violence that is for Fanon necessary to the creation of a revolutionary subject. The inherited cosmopolitanism of the writer will generally work against embracing the more local voice of the people, and when writers do come around to the cause, their messages will tend to be both belated and highly mediated. Thus, aesthetic detachment does not have a positive use in times of national liberation; it will be useful again only in the body of an established nation-state. Until then it will remain in the province of ideology. In Fanon's analysis, literature is spared an effective identification with violence only insofar as it misses the moment and fails to identify in any meaningful way with transformative events. Its nonviolent disposition is not enough to prevent revolutionary change, nor does it help the cause. Its innocence is preserved only by virtue of its writers being out of touch; its residual tendency to civility is out of place and out of time during a revolution. Only after a new nation is founded can reflective detachment again be useful in the service of a new internationalism.

Fanon here recapitulates some elements of Trotsky's argument in *Literature and Revolution* (1924). All culture develops after the events that bring about critical historical change: "mind limps after reality" and "in the rear of the historic advance."[73] Art "needs comfort, even abundance" for its development (p. 19), but life in revolution is "camp life" (p. 77), where everything is in motion. Efforts to capture this in literature will tend to privilege a "social hatred" (p. 230) that will seem out of place in the new society to come. No literature can free itself of the conditions in which it takes life: bourgeois art can never "make a breach in class solidarity" (p. 225). It cannot therefore assume a vanguard function in specifying the nature of a world that has yet to come into being. But it can claim a diagnostic function, representing the characteristics of the forms of violence that afflict the world that is about to disappear. This representation could presumably include some intuition of the violence that might be necessary to bring about radical change. If literature cannot model the new society, it can surely register the destructive lineaments of the old one. Fanon, in the same spirit, supposes that the literature and aesthetic theory of the colonizers must belong to ideology, as part of the apparatus justifying (white) rule over other peoples. How much of this has survived and lived on in the new nations has been an urgent concern for those who propose that decolonization is a process by no means to be thought finished. What is new does not fully emancipate itself from its pasts, neither in the sphere of culture nor in that of the social-economic formations that remain embedded in other sectors of the global framework, as well as in the new nations themselves. The world that Fanon saw coming has not, in other words, yet come fully into being. It has certainly not wiped clean the inherited cultural-economic slate.

Modern defenses of the aesthetic mode often continue to defend its immunity from the real and the literal, just as Schiller did, though they sometimes work harder to assure themselves that what results from this is some sort of positive agency or worldly address. Efforts to access or create the universality to which key Romantic writers aspired have been answered by a concern that 'properly' aesthetic responses were mostly open to the social and economic elite. This syndrome contains its own element of exclusionary violence, and that violence has become even more apparent thanks to the broadening consciousness of race and racism upon which, according to David Lloyd, the very construction of the modern aesthetic itself also depends. What then is the likelihood of rereading Kant and Schiller in ways that open some positive incentives for a better world to come? Do they endorse the violence we seek to discredit or somehow stage it for critical attention? Lloyd argues that race consciousness is, throughout modernity, from Kant to Adorno, constitutive of aesthetic theory rather than just contingent to it.[74] It is the "savage" who is consistently marked out as outside or at best on the threshold of an ability to deliver judgments of taste, because too doggedly dependent upon physical needs to be capable of disinterest. This same criterion has segregated out aesthetic judgment in class terms: neither the working class burdened by labor and scarcity nor the philistine obsessed with material desires and profits can readily develop an authentic taste. The proper demonstration of taste thus functions as a hazing ritual for entry into the elites.

Is it yet plausible to suggest that aesthetic judgment (along with the premised universality based upon it) can always potentially remain open for any and all of its current outsiders to experience? Taste can function as a mechanism of class mobility, whether actual, partial or merely imaginary (all captured, for example, in E. M. Forster's portrayal of Leonard Bast in *Howards End*): this is indeed its ideal role in the bourgeois imaginary. But it is much harder to enable this transformation in a racialized encounter where the physiological marking off of the other remains seemingly ineradicable: however deftly Kant's African or Carib learns to think and feel beyond being rooted in physical needs, she or he will remain marked as an African or Carib. Such persons may have a foot on the ladder that leads to what stadial theory calls civilization, but significant historical time, and presumably a time of colonization, must first pass before the individual attains it. Until then the person remains limited to an enjoyment of mere "charms," at best a candidate for future access to judgments of taste. Kant's narrative seems to render the aboriginal populations of Australia and Tierra del Fuego as yet more deeply abjected; they are parsed as barely human.[75] One must confirm Lloyd's verdict that there is no finessing the carefully calibrated racism that sustains such arguments: simply to invoke the crude state of eighteenth-century anthropology does not excuse the failure of an imagining of the humanity of the other that Montaigne, for example, seems to have managed long before.

So does this mean that there is nothing in Kant's aesthetics that is available to the racially abjected subject? Some recent commentators suggest otherwise, offering a reading of Kant that explores not the coherence of a 'Kantian' theory but the loose ends and incompletions in his texts. Howard Caygill has argued for the emergence in the third critique of an aporetic method that is more concerned to present problems than to pretend to solve them. In the final critique, Caygill suggests, Kant's propaedeutic method involves a clear admission of disjunctions and produces a position that "is always in anticipation, emerging momentarily among the fragments thrown up by the clash of the traditions."[76] This unstable syndrome cannot, presumably, preserve even its own racialized assumptions from future disturbance. They are foundational, but the foundations are not solid; they are threatened by the weight of possibility laid upon them. J. M. Bernstein goes as far as to argue that the Kantian model suggests that "art and politics are one." The theory of taste juxtaposes "appearances in their own right together with the concepts of communication, intersubjective agreement, and shared judgement that are constitutive for emphatic, autonomous political thinking."[77] Aesthetic thinking projects a community that is felt as lost and may therefore be still to come again (p. 65). In a similar spirit, Antony J. Cascardi has proposed that the aesthetic judgment is always pending, always unrealized, always to come. It cannot then function as the foundation of *any* current political order, even if it appears to be premised on the given, racialized state of ethnological understanding.[78] Nor, in principle, can it guarantee the exclusion of anyone from membership of an expanding category of the universal. Kant's racist presuppositions are thus not themselves immune from being questioned in the terms generated by his own arguments. I do not intend this as a strategy to 'save' Kant from Lloyd's critique but to suggest that Kant's apparatus, passed down through historical time, may exceed what a standard idea of coherence can handle. Marcuse had argued back in 1937 that the remit of bourgeois universalism was simultaneously *both* the maintenance of a social order that oppressed the bourgeoisie itself *and* an uncontainable force for liberation, generating a painfully "real longing alongside poor consolation and false consecration" in bourgeois life.[79] People are allowed to experience happiness only in the beauty of art, but that beauty "contains a dangerous violence that threatens the given form of existence" (p. 115). That given form includes not only the class systems of the European nations but also their global colonies and sites of exploitation. The colonial encounters that dominate the modern period, as well as the decolonizing processes that come along with and after them, can offer stringent testing sites for working through the tension between racial assumptions and universalist aspirations that mark Kant and Schiller's formulations of judgments of taste. The gradual acknowledging of the artfulness of 'primitive' art is just one component of that testing.

Lloyd repeatedly confirms that the denial of aesthetic judgment to the 'savage' is also a denial of any claim to "civility" or "civil society" and thus a banishment to the sphere of an implacable violence, even as Kant himself finds some illustrative virtue in the apparent necessity of a 'civilized' warfare.[80] Civility and taste arrive together, as they so often have done. In Simon Gikandi's work, civility figures again as that which is denied the black African in the elaboration of a European culture of taste.[81] Gikandi further notes that the aesthetic sphere was explicitly posited as a refuge from the negative psychological effects of commerce and that there was no bigger example of commerce than the trade in human bodies; the impulse to displacement was therefore a strong one. Homi Bhabha has also registered the coincidence of discourses of civility with the emergence of a Western modernity implicated in colonial exploitation.[82] And in identifying the significance of "sly civility," he has advanced our understanding of the concept to the point of explicit disjunction involving a "discursive doubleness," a "process of misrecognition" and "continual slippage" (pp. 95, 97, 99) that preempts the efficient operation of empire and casts both colonist and colonized into a no-man's-land of uncertainty and failing communication. Sly civility is not as much (or not only) an act of resistance as a withdrawing of all epistemological boundaries that license human subjects to function with some consistent sense of themselves. Here again, civility aligns itself with the literary and bumps up against a violence that is already on the record but, while momentarily held in abeyance, can always be about to occur again.

Aesthetic theory (and often 'theory' in general) is part of the modern mode of literariness, the 'literary absolute' that was first proposed by Friedrich Schlegel and has been further described by more recent scholars and critics.[83] That literariness is not simply or wholly contained by the liberal-humanist pedagogies that have been based upon Kant and Schiller; and Kant and Schiller themselves may contain possible applications beyond those of ideological liberalism, as is attested by the various commentators I have just been citing. I will return to this question in my final chapter, which will also take up the significance of the sublime and of the paradigm of subalternity that Bhabha's sly civility delineates and that Lloyd also explores. Arnold famously opts for acquiring a compensatory wholeness of spirit from the best literature of the past, but the self-undermining irony and reflexivity of the Jena Romantics always subsist along with the humanist consensus as at least countercurrents and at times objects of equal attention and attraction, leading to a model of *Bildung* that is always under stress. Literature and its pedagogies are both divided and dividing bodies, a besetting condition that has generated academic and sometimes public dispute.[84] Enormous pressure has been exercised upon literature and literary studies to contribute to the sorts of agency in the world that doctrines of aesthetic disinterest seem to deny them. And indeed, whether the task be imagined as preservationist (the best that has been known and thought in the world) or radically innovatory (unsettling the metaphysics of presence and the social orders that attach to it), the aesthetic project is an interventionist one, a solicitation (to use Sartre's term). As such it has always been open to accusations of or associations with forms of violence. Violence has, for example, been attributed to the 'theory' project, which often avows its commitment to imagining a new social justice, while the 'humanist' faction (I use these terms as inevitable shorthands) has largely thought of itself as resisting that violence. But it is not hard to accept that the defense of things as they are under the banner of preservation and tradition can, like Rawls's "duty of civility," entail a silent commitment to its own forms of violence; meanwhile, one of the besetting mantras coming from the side of theory has been Jacques Derrida's proclamation that deconstruction (a.k.a. theory) changes nothing; or, perhaps, makes nothing happen.[85]

All of which is to say that violence is other to civility and literature in exactly the way that so many things called 'other' are imagined—as the outside that is already inside, the stranger or foreigner who is disturbingly within or among us. It is not thus wholly surprising to read the response of Mikhail Suslov, on behalf of the Department of Agitation and Propaganda, to Vasily Grossman's request that his book *Life and Fate* be published in Russia: "Why should we add your book to the nuclear bombs that our enemies are getting ready for us? Its publication will only help our enemies."[86] Suslov does not say that the book *is* a bomb, just that it adds to the threat that the bomb represents; recall, again, Auden's line about "poets exploding like bombs." But the sense of weaponization is inescapable, especially in light of the long history of writers of literature, in Stalin's Russia and beyond, being imprisoned, exiled or put to death as instigators of a threatening (counter)violence.[87] Whether it be the solitary voice of lyric poetry or the social complexity of the long novel, there is in literature (i.e., in what is designated as literature) a potential to be taken beyond the boundaries of its own declared insularity within the aesthetic mode, its own identity as 'just' imagination, as 'mere' representation. There are surely a number of reasons for this. Any language offers itself for being made referential; fabulation itself stimulates a teleological mind-set (wanting to know what happens); pondering imaginary worlds lowers the barriers of repression in both writers and readers. The isolation of literature within the aesthetic sphere, even when self-avowed, is always under stress. The violence it keeps at bay is never finally banished; the civility it disseminates is provisional and fragile. Nor is it correct to assume that writers always aim at preserving aesthetic detachment, even when they or their defenders resort to it as a protective doctrine. Novelists who describe atrocities do not commonly set out to inspire disinterest: they seek to create a record and to extend the life of that record even as they slow down unmeditated response. The events have already occurred and cannot be changed. The question is how to respond in the aftermath. In *The Emigrants*, W. G. Sebald's narrator tells his own story of hearing other people's stories, creating a space-time in which "it truly seemed to me, and still does, as if the dead were coming back, or as if we were on the point of joining them," and where "once you are under the spell, you have to carry on to the finish, till your heart breaks."[88] Sebald has captured the imaginations of millions of readers with his accounts of what it is like to talk "for three whole days far into the night" (p. 180) with those whose lives are lived in the presence of history's horrors, events that no word can capture (certainly not *Holocaust*) but that are compulsively called up by an endless stream of words. This is not, or not only, an aesthetic alibi or the expression of a creative imagination but a witnessing. It asks us to consider whether and how we wake up sadder and wiser, and perhaps whether we can hope to wake at all.

It is, then, redundant for either writers or critics to pursue an ideal of absolute connectedness or unconnectedness between literature and violence, or civility and violence, because no one has control over the conditions in which texts will be received and circulated. Some authors urgently want to rectify injustice; others hope to avoid being identified as troublemakers. Neither has full control of the outcome. Lots of people will never read *The Emigrants*, but millions have and will. A single word or phrase might generate "a thousand unapprehended combinations of thought."[89] Or it might fall on deaf ears. One's own efforts at disinterestedness do not preempt the interests of others taking over what is written, nor do claims to a limiting interest (radical or conservative) impede being read in quite other ways (thus Balzac's monarchism was, for Engels, the least significant of his effects as a novelist). No one has a final say over the uses to which fabulations might be put, so the claim to immunity on the part of the aesthetic is somewhat supernumerary, more a matter of emphasis or a gesture of self-protection than a claim to an impermeable, defensible border. Schiller cannot keep at bay Fanon, nor can Fanon avoid the dynamics of play in Schillerian *Schein* (image, representation).[90] All statements are interpretable, but those declaring themselves as literary are implying that their *point* is to be interpretable, even when (as in the literature of witnessing) they are also claiming some communication of or relation to historical facts.[91] When Binjamin Wilkomirski's *Fragments* was proven not to be a credible Holocaust narrative, it nonetheless remained a novel; the questions it raises simply become different questions or the same ones differently weighted. Even if it were received as a 'true' memoir, questions about typicality and credibility would still arise: Did things happen just this way at just this time? Conversely, establishing the book as a fiction based upon a known historical situation leads us back to that situation, encouraged by the effect of the real. Either decision, leaning toward fact or toward fiction, puts the reader into the uncomfortable role of a bystander, one needing some sort of response. Primo Levi's unforgettable account of Hurbinek, a speechless, suffering child of the camps, stretches the imagination in the manner of magic realism, making us wonder whether he can possibly have existed as such. His coming back to life is indeed in the hands of the author: "Nothing remains of him: he bears witness through these words of mine."[92] He was 'real,' but his life barely began, and he lives on only in words that would compel the attention of most readers even if not imagined as 'true.' Meanwhile, a clearly fictional event like that depicted in Kafka's "In the Penal Colony" does not cease to disturb because it never happened. Fact and fiction become debatable and interactive, a complexity that has led some to declare that phenomena like the Holocaust should never be the subject of aesthetic representation, as if that were possible. Literary writing is (or declares itself) more than usually distant from evidential truth, but it can also claim the authority of witnessing something, however far it might seem from the rhetoric of reportage.[93] Its instabilities merely play up the predicament it shares with all language, one that it both celebrates and regrets. The preservation of play and pleasure in representation itself is what aligns literature with the project of civility; the inevitable breakdown of that moment (the moment of suspending distinctions between belief and disbelief) is what brings on an engagement with various forms of violence. It also, as Shelley argued long ago, opens a space for an experience of love. But that in turn opens the possibility of a recognition of love's insufficiency, a testimony to the persistence of inconvertible violence. The question is thus one of literature's reach: whether it can grasp what we want it to achieve; whether there can ever be a *we* without the assumption of a *them*; whether these questions themselves might not be a bit, or too much, of a reach.

2

Civil Beginnings

Crusoe Plays the Gentleman

There are various explanations one might advance for the extraordinary success of Defoe's *Robinson Crusoe* (1719), which went through five (arguably six) editions in its first year and has been selling steadily ever since both in English and in translation, making it one of the most widely disseminated British novels of all time. Few of its modern readers would number among its charms the empathic or charismatic appeal of the hero himself, who seems for page after page to have either no personality at all or a distinctly unlikeable one: a man fully prepared to sell into slavery the boy who has saved his life; an arbitrary killer of wild animals; a boring accountant who shares with us long lists of his livestock, crops, dry goods and financial investments, along with a detailed recipe for the making of bread; a morally unstable figure who recalls his religious observances mostly when his luck turns bad and forgets them as soon as prosperous times return. His career as a slave trader and slave owner seems to occasion no self-doubt, no complex introspection.

The mythic and historical fabric of the novel is, however, as profoundly developed as the dimension of character is (seemingly) underworked, and a great many of the prevalent questions governing what we recognize as modern life are rehearsed in telling detail. Does religious affiliation matter to the living of a happy and generous life? Is God watching us, or can we get away with less than admirable deeds on an occasional or even regular basis? How does one know when one has enough or too much to live on? What kind of world would we design if we were left to ourselves in a minimally provident environment? What circumstances govern, and what follows from, the suspension of sexual desire in a boy's own world? These are some of the questions that have presumably projected the novel into a transnational circulation wide enough to support Ian Watt's argument for the figure of Crusoe as one of the four fictional foundations of modern individualism.[1] They are, for thirty years or so, pondered by Crusoe in solitude. After the rescue and enslaving of Friday, they take on an intersubjective dimension, but hardly a dialogic one. The sight of a second shipwreck that has drowned his fellow Europeans had set him into a melancholy longing for the companionship of his own kind. But the subsequent acquisition of Friday is inspired only by his desire for a helper, a "servant" who will help him escape the island.[2] The pleasures of civility and of polite exchange are less urgent than the practical exercise of authority. Matters of civility would seem to have little significance for such a figure.

And yet, one of the less evident but emergent morality plots that the novel sustains is that of the idle gentleman who is obliged by events to become the self-sufficient man of industry. Shortly after the opening of the book, Crusoe remarks that it had been his choice to go on board ship "in the Habit of a Gentleman; and so I neither had any Business in the Ship, or learn'd to do any" (p. 15). Nonetheless, his narrative is punctuated with moments of self-aggrandizement, ironized to be sure but still noteworthy, when he refers to his kingdom, his estates, his castle and his country residence—making the point that all such worldly possessions are relative and unstable at the same time as contributing, we assume, to the veneer of self-respect or social grandiosity that Crusoe maintains in his island solitude. (The 'real' Crusoe, Alexander Selkirk, was not so lucky, having "so much forgot his Language for want of Use, that we could scarce understand him.")[3] And toward the end of the novel, the hero manages a cavalier gesture worthy of inclusion in the annals of chivalry, addressing three astonished sailors whom he has rescued from a group of mutineers: "Can you put a Stranger in the way how to help you, for you seem to me to be in some great Distress?" (p. 198). A man speaking thus deferentially while clad in goatskins and bearing two pistols, two guns and a sword (followed by a heavily armed Friday) must, we are to imagine, present quite a sight: enough so to moralize powerfully the fact that true civility is not to be judged by appearances, as the amazed ship's captain recognizes in "pulling off his Hat" and wondering whether he is being addressed by God or man.

It is congruent with Defoe's consistently masterful arraying of ambiguities that, like the rescued sailor, we cannot be quite sure how to read Crusoe. This display of polite concern and deference—"Can we serve you?"—emanates from one who is armed to the teeth, not the creature of courtly culture but the deviser and defender of a primitive civil society based on slavery and maintaining a foreign policy of militant vigilance from behind his stockade. Neither country gentleman nor primitive brigand, he is by origin a lapsed candidate for the bourgeois prosperity to which events will finally restore him. But Crusoe's demonstration of polite behavior is limited to those belonging to his own speech community and enabled by the possession of effectively massive force. The book seems never to represent an instance of peaceable contact without framing it by a prudent or necessary violence, mostly directed at the "savages." If it models peace at all, it is one dependent on possession and indeed ready deployment of the power of violence. While the novel incorporates a highly diversified vocabulary of fear words, it does not include the word *civility*, has no place for *civil society* and uses *civil* only three times, twice to signify polite behavior and once to specify a legal concept.[4] There are no usages at all of *polite*, *tolerance* or *tolerant*, key terms in the expansion of nonviolent behavior. It is as if Crusoe's clunky chivalry performed before the rescued sailors cannot quite find words for itself.

However, in *Farther Adventures of Robinson Crusoe*, the sequel that Defoe hurried out within a year, an inquiry into the nature of what we have come to call civil society makes up the largest part of the book. There is a more extended curiosity about how best to live together, but once again it is framed by violence. Crusoe returns to his island after an absence of several years, to encounter the epitome of civility in the Spaniards who still live there: "Their behaviour was to the last degree obliging and courteous, and yet mixed with a manly, majestic gravity, which very well became them; and, in short, they had so much more manners than I, that I scarce knew how to receive their civilities, much less to return them in kind."[5] The island proves to be a site for experimenting in the fashioning of a social world, as the Spaniards enact a policy of nonviolence that gradually wins over the brutish Englishmen with whom they share the land. Mutual need and the acquisition of women soften the dispositions of the English sailors; absolute religious toleration prevails. It is notable that religion plays no part in the evolution of this highly civil society: a working interdenominational faith accrues later, when all of the basic tensions have been resolved, only to solidify and rationalize the consensus that has already emerged.[6] By having the Spaniards take the lead, Defoe counters the popular Puritan image of decadent foreign Catholics hiding violent intentions beneath a veneer of fine manners. In the same spirit Crusoe's most extended encounter with authentic civility is with the French priest, whose "most obliging, gentleman-like behaviour" sponsors a perfect conversational climate "easily separated from disputes."[7] This ideal of "free conversation" (p. 121) sets the standard for social life (among the whites) on the island—the same ideal that Addison and Steele's *Spectator* had recently publicized for the readers of magazines.

This utopian space is not, however, the only incarnation of the civil society debate to be found in the novel. Later on, while at sea with his nephew, Crusoe reports on a cross-cultural event of the most brutal kind. On a visit to Madagascar, whose reputedly fierce inhabitants are actually behaving "very civilly" (p. 189), one of the sailors rapes a native woman and is put to death by the furious locals. This inspires a brutal massacre carried out by the English, whose cruelty impresses the narrator as "something beyond what was human" (p. 202). Crusoe is the only Englishman who stands aside and counsels against this slaughter, but he is quite unable to stop it. The peaceful paradigm that had governed life on the island does not seem able to restrain the violence of whites toward blacks. And when he is still further from its influence, heading home across Asiatic Russia, Crusoe himself proves vulnerable to the appeal of radical violence. Incensed at the sight of pagan idols worshipped by an unlettered populace, and moved by the story of a Russian killed for "affronting them in their worship," he tells his companions the story of what happened in Madagascar, "and how they burned and sacked the village there, and killed man, woman and child . . . and when I had done, I added that I thought we ought to do so to this village" (pp. 288–89). What he formerly rejected is now a model for imitation; toleration and civility now wear thin in competition with militant, righteous Christianity. Crusoe's narrative is emphatic about the need for "keeping an exceeding watch over our passions of every kind" (p. 21), but it also chronicles the constant falling away from such ideals under the influence of violent tendencies sponsored by both personal and culturally approved persuasions.

In its admission of the acceptability of ethno-genocidal violence in the name of some sort of justice or religious zeal, *The Farther Adventures* echoes the account of settler-colonial behavior in *The Faerie Queene*, as does Crusoe's slaughter of the cannibals in the first novel. There is indeed nothing here like the figure of Talus, who kills robotically and without reflection or remorse. More typically, Crusoe's narratives finesse the uglier side of colonialism by having him pitch up on an uninhabited island where there is no indigenous occupation to destroy or displace. The cannibals make use of the island, but only for their feasts, hardly a strong rationale for claiming property rights. One suspects that this fictional rendering of a true *terra nullius* corresponds to little if anything in the historical record outside the unexploitable polar surfaces. The sexual fantasies of settlement explored in Neville's *The Isle of Pines* and, along with hideous violence, in Behn's *Oroonoko*, are also absent from this prepubescent adventure story, as are the intergroup conflicts that make civility a defensively necessary recourse for the keeping of the peace.

The historical precedence of *Oroonoko*, published in 1688, suggests that the Crusoe stories are purposively (if perhaps unconsciously) laundering the evidence about the already well-developed economy of plantation slavery—which is actually the source of Crusoe's eventual wealth even as the profits are accruing in his absence and without his hands-on contributions. Behn's black hero has "all the Civility of a well-bred Great Man" and "nothing of Barbarity in his Nature."[8] He is far more exemplary in morals and manners than those white traders who deploy their own "finer sort of Address" (p. 82) to entrap him and sell him into slavery. It is fine manners that deceive Oroonoko, who believes that "*no Man of Wit*" could be a "*Knave or Villain*" (p. 88). Himself a slaveholder, he might indeed be forgiven for trusting to the bond of self-interest that connects him with his white betrayers. But race trumps everything, along with his value as a human commodity. In a prescient forecasting of the key event in Toni

Morrison's *Beloved*, he kills his own beloved Imoinda to prevent her entering a life of slavery and sexual violation, only to have his own suicide attempt impeded by the white plantation owners who thereby insist on their exclusive power over life and death. After Behn's story, the initial solitude of Crusoe's island could only have appealed all the more in its occluding so much of the historical record around racism and settler colonialism. Well into the modern period, learned men were still affirming that no black man could inherit or attain the marks of true civility.

The tension between violence and civility appears again in Defoe's anonymously published *Memoirs of a Cavalier* (1720), which reports on the life of an English soldier (fictional, but widely received as true) who fights in the European wars of the 1630s and then enlists on the king's side in the English Civil War. His travels in Europe educate the narrator about the gap between appearance and reality, protestation and performance, as when the finest "conversation" he has is with a courtesan and when French "civility" turns out to exclude simple charity.[9] But the major theme of the book is the horror of doctrinally driven violence against both civilians and other soldiers. Modest demeanor, by contrast, transcends dogma; it can be found in the "conversible temper of the King of Sweden" (p. 54) as well as in the amiable person of Sir Thomas Fairfax, "though I did not like his Cause" (p. 265). Good manners and moral virtue are, in the best of human beings, not at odds with one another; but in order to preserve the balance, moral virtue must remain tolerant and moderate.

Defoe himself was too young to remember the English Civil War, but he certainly lived through the Monmouth campaign and a prison sentence and was a regular witness to the injustices of religious intolerance directed at the dissenting community within which he grew up. His most famous fictional protagonist, Robinson Crusoe, manages to miss some of the most turbulent years in English politics by being away on his adventures from 1652 to 1687 (in the first volume) and 1695 to 1705 (in the second), which points up a sharp contrast between what is going on at home and what can be imagined in the experimental space of a remote tropical island. According to Clarendon no small part of the nation's troubles came from failed civility (his word), from the inability of politicians to govern themselves by "gentle applications, and moderate remedies" and from a court and parliamentary culture in which those in power proved unable to discriminate between realities and appearances, so "compliance and flattery gets the better of honesty and plain dealing."[10] The Duke of Buckingham is described as a mix of genuine "affability and courtesy" with "impetuous passions," unable to moderate his behavior or to make proper judgments about whom he should trust and reward (1:39, 42, 48). Clarendon's list of fateful political figures is a congeries of emotionally disordered character types whose acts cannot be restrained by any efficient culture of civility. Sir Richard Weston, Earl of Portland, is a mixture of "imperious nature" and "feminine temper" (1:64); Mandevill (*sic*) exploits his "natural civility, good manners, and good nature" only to advance the Commons against the Lords (1:243); while Hambden is figured as the complete Machiavellian courtier:

> He made so great a show of civility and modesty and humility, and always of mistrusting his own judgment and of esteeming his with whom he conferred for the present, that he seemed to have no opinions or resolutions but such as he contracted from the information and instruction he received upon the discourses of others, whom he had a wonderful art of governing and leading into his principles and inclinations whilst they believed that he wholly depended upon their counsel and advice. No man ever had a greater power over himself or was less the man that he seemed to be, which shortly after appeared to every body when he cared less to keep on the mask. (1:245–46)

In other words civility is a mask for hypocrisy and self-interest. Yet more critically Archbishop Laud is presented by Clarendon as *too* guileless, too willing to subsist "without the least condescension to the arts and stratagems of the Court" by way of his own "unpolished integrity" (1:82). He was also burdened with a querulous nature, "a sharpness of his language and expressions," making him easily manipulated into giving offense at the instigation of others like Cottington, himself "a master of temper, and of the most profound dissimulation" (1:132).

Clarendon portrays these ungoverned or hypergoverned personalities (and others like them) as subsisting in a world where civil manners and moral virtue are hopelessly and tragically disconnected and open to radical misrepresentation, with terrible consequences for the nation. For much of the following century the various commentators on and theorists of civility would attempt to juggle these two elements into some sort of working harmony, until the consensus again broke down completely in the controversy surrounding the publication of Chesterfield's *Letters.* Defoe, for one, is committed to a workable synthesis of manners and morals, as perhaps befits one who began life as Daniel Foe and renamed himself in more genteel style and who had been indicted at the Old Bailey as "a person of bad name, reputation, and Conversation."[11] Large sections of the *Serious Reflections of Robinson Crusoe* are given over to a discussion of the problems and possibilities of the culture of civility. Here it is argued that while solitude is to some degree our natural condition, and infinitely preferable to being in bad company, yet good company is the best of all and the most fully human condition. Good company can, however, exist as such only by way of a commitment to "honesty," for there is a "cunning" that is "so like honesty, that many a man has been deceived with it, and has taken one for t'other in the market."[12]

The medium of good company, the highest form of human sociability, is "conversation," here purified of its sexual connotations (as intercourse) that were still very much current in Defoe's time. Man is a "conversable creature," and conversation is the "brightest and most beautiful part of life." But the prerequisite for good conversation is self-control and predictability: a man must be "on all occasions the same, ever agreeable to others and to himself" (p. 71). Only a "good man" can manage this happy demeanor, for if a person be not of good character, "it is impossible but the disturbance will be discovered without" (p. 72). Composure of mind can come only from virtue and must always be visible as such: it is (or should be) "impossible effectually to counterfeit" (p. 74). Defoe, unlike Clarendon in his portrait of the politicians of the Civil War years, proposes that conversation *does* distinguish vice from virtue: the culture of civility (though *Serious Reflections* uses the word only once) can then function as an agent and analyst of social cohesion upon authentic principles. But there remain men who are "unconversable" (p. 77) and whose influence can be restrained and limited only by a new commitment on the part of court and gentry and, in the extreme case, by laws against lewdness, vice and irreligion. Like Robinson Crusoe, the state must back up its investment in civility by visibly deploying a few well-primed weapons.

The image of Crusoe playing the gentleman while armed to the teeth provides an appropriate icon for understanding the paradoxes of a civility culture that can never fully relax into trusting polite behavior either in itself or in relation to those forces and interests that enforce its limits or compensate for its failings. Notwithstanding Defoe's assurances about the ultimate transparency of a good nature, many pondered the potential deceptions of civility culture; nor can the person being civil be sure that some unconscious strategy of persuasion or ingratiation does not motivate his or her polite demeanor by putting it at the service of some form of self-interest. But at their best, civility and the conversational and conversable norms that sustain it bring a capacity to inhibit the violent confrontation of competitors or antagonists, thereby allowing space and time for circumspection, compromise, accommodation and mutual self-defense. The popular periodicals of the eighteenth century circulated as handbooks of good taste and good manners for the middle classes, so it is not surprising that they take up the topic of civility in a sustained way. The *Tatler* and the *Spectator* in particular were and are still commonly accepted as "exemplary instances of the discursive institution of the bourgeois public sphere" whose norms and traditions they sought to articulate and preserve by persuasion and example rather than by crude authority.[13] A comparable inquiry into the claims and consequences of polite behavior runs through all of the periodicals gathered up in multiple volumes and published from 1803 on as the collected *British Essayists*, which thus form an encyclopedia of taste and distinction for a later generation as well as an extended record of the variety of eighteenth-century attitudes to the culture of civility.

Robinson Crusoe, however, had little time for books and magazines and for the reading culture that would for many of Defoe's contemporaries constitute the best medium for an education into civility. One wonders how he learned his manners, produced so effortlessly after three decades of solitude followed by some years as a de facto absolute monarch. Books, along with pen and ink, are salvaged from the wreck only as an afterthought, among "several things of less Value."[14] The books are Bibles and prayer books, but months and years go by without any mention of opening any of them. (Crusoe hardly needs the Bible, as his memory is stored with apt citations to fit almost any occasion.) The first report of his so doing is, furthermore, hardly describable as reading. Somewhere around year fifteen, he opens a Bible in search of a random inspiration and is delighted to find a cheering message (p. 124).[15] Friday's education appears to be oral; it is not made clear that he is ever taught to read, although his master refers both of them to the authority of the scriptures (pp. 172–73). There is no book club on Crusoe's island. And no letting up on the supply of guns and bullets needed to keep the "savages" in line.

For most others aspiring to upward mobility in polite society, the printed word was crucial. Introducing the *Tatler*, the editor of the *British Essayists* finds that Steele and Addison have done more for the "national character" than any number of military and political achievements, operating on the "social mass" in undramatic but thoroughly pervasive ways: "Rudenesses were reformed, incivilities were checked; and a system of mutual urbanities and accommodation superseded the grossness of vulgar manner."[16] The weighty authority of Samuel Johnson himself is cited as an endorsement of the benign effects of these periodicals on the "loud, restless and violent" habits of the party system and in regulating "the practice of daily conversation" (1:vii–viii).[17] Wit was made to subsist with decency, and decency took on the habit of pleasing rather than intimidating others. An "English temper" naturally given to rudeness and defiance was taught good manners (5:15) without collapsing into "French fopperies" (6:216). The recommended conversational norm is a middling one, affecting neither "silence" nor "eloquence" (5:146), embodying the same worship of the middle register that Johnson preferred in diction and vocabulary, the happy medium between vulgarity and hyperbole that he found in the language of Dryden. Like Defoe, Steele looks to "simplicity of behaviour" as "the perfection of good breeding and good sense" and most fully approves "the honest countenance of him who utters what he really means" (5:5, 97). At the same time he projects a situation in which "the old English plainness and sincerity . . . is in a great measure lost amongst us" under pressure from a world full of "dissimulation and compliment" (7:189).

Such back-and-forth statements on the desirability and possibility of an authentic civility sustain an extended debate in the periodicals. Civility as performed is a matter of representation, of appearances, which aligns it with the fabulist essence of literature, while the discussion of books is itself projected as a training in civility. The golden rule of aesthetic response is not to confuse appearances with realities, representations with real things; poets do not lie because they never affirm. Civility *is* enacted in the world but also blurs the lines between image and identity: modesty can mask megalomania, and hypocrisy can hide behind the rhetoric of sincerity.

In both spheres, mistakes matter. Misreading civility can lead to consequential errors of judgment. Taking literature for reality, in the manner of a Don Quixote, can also cause trouble. But misunderstanding a book strictly within its aesthetic dimension (i.e., never taking it as real) mostly produces only amusement or recourse to statements about taste being not worth disputing. Both civility and literary taste can be learned, and both functioned to project and demonstrate the claims and possibilities of the newly monied classes to respect and distinction. Defoe's *Compleat English Gentleman*, written in 1728–29 though unpublished in the author's lifetime, perfectly caught this moment of emergent social confidence among the merchant classes in stressing that merit mattered more than birth in deserving the title of gentleman, with true civility consisting in what has been earned and learned rather than what has been inherited. The same spirit is evident in the popular magazines that followed in the wake of the *Tatler* and the *Spectator*. But those same publications register significant reservations about the sufficiency of civility as a reliable defense against a world of emulation and specialization. Civility is indeed most needed when most threatened, when it is least likely to be able to flourish. One of the most common concerns of the century was the proliferation of the division of labor, seen as necessary to the success of an increasingly complex economy but very dangerous for the well-being of the social whole. An observed increase in terminologies related to occupational specializations—the culture of expertise—made it harder for people to understand one another and to preserve openness of mind about the lives of others, at the same time as the widely noted creation of new wealth made its possessors more prone than ever before to the corruptions of the luxury cycle. These were the anxieties that led, among other things, to a polemical fascination with civic humanism (already nostalgic in Renaissance Italy), which looked to republican Rome for its political ideals. Such aspirations were under even more stress in an eighteenth-century environment undergoing rapid modernization on all fronts and less and less able to maintain even the illusion of a political culture governed by self-imposed restraint and dignified disinterest.[18] Civility appealed as one of the means by which the stresses of this rapidly evolving society might be eased and rendered livable, even as the pressures of that same society made civility more and more tenuous and open to hypocritical exploitation.

Thus it is that Johnson's *Rambler* reflects on the inevitable devolution of the "great community of mankind" into "smaller independent societies" of class, preference and habit, a tendency further exacerbated by occupational specialization and threatening to restrict us to "the jargon of a particular profession."[19] The ethic of civility, whereby "no man should give preference to himself," can work against this possibility (20:234). In a similar spirit *The Lounger*, published in 1785, looks back to a primitive social order in which behavior, law and morality were all roughly aligned, a condition long since lost to "a state of society so advanced as ours," which therefore has need of a more refined system of manners, albeit one that cannot be "precisely set down" (36:5–7). By this same logic, however, the social conditions that render civility culture so desirable are themselves developing in directions that make it harder and harder to maintain: modernization means more specialization, not less, and the very opening up of the class of gentlefolk to exemplary members of the up-and-coming classes also puts them further and further from the majority whose life situations will tend to consign them inevitably to the masses and to an identification with uncivil behavior. Within the upper middle class itself, where lies the best hope for modeling and maintaining civility culture, the increasing reliance of the professions upon an ever-increasing expertise will produce, in the words of Vicesimus Knox, "peculiar temptations which lead imperceptibly, without uncommon caution, to error, absurdity, and vice" (42:193). Such commentators are well aware that the new middle class is to some extent a revolutionary one wherein the energy required for its progress and consolidation is going to be potentially at odds with the mechanisms available for self-restraint. From the very first the *Spectator* had been concerned that what was recognized as civility was not so much a signal of ethical progress as a symptom of the mere vicissitudes of fashion. So it is that country dwellers always find themselves learning a set of manners and mannerisms that are already out of date in the towns. In the "nowadays" of 1711, Addison found that "one may now know a man that never conversed in the world, by his excess of good-breeding." Country folk are behaving with great formality while the fashionable metropolis holds the highest respect for "agreeable negligence" (7:256). Manners work not to unite society but precisely to segregate it. "Coarse uncivilized words" are now marks of good breeding in the towns and will infect the country at just the moment that they pass away in their current location (7:258). The group of Oxford dons who produced *Olla Podrida* in 1787 had an even more serious concern: that civil conversation works positively only among those who are already conversable, already predisposed to behave deferentially and considerately: "That conversation may answer the ends for which it was designed, the parties, who are to join in it, must come together with a determined resolution to please and to be pleased. . . . He, who is about to form a conversation party, should be careful to invite men of congenial minds, and of similar ideas" (41:36). Conversation, in other words, is not so much a conversion experience, drawing in the rude and uncivil and teaching them manners, but a replication of the already converted, an exchange whose harmony is guaranteed by the prior exclusion of unconversable elements. This may be the ultimate concession to a divided labor society, one wherein civility culture becomes the property of a few and only imaginatively or coercively a model for the many. Indeed, in its traditional function as a mark of distinction, it had always been just that. The high point of eighteenth-century optimism about the openness of civility culture to unfamiliar interlopers, and about its adequacy as a means of social modification and reform, is itself significantly qualified by a sense not only that it cannot perform that task but also that it was never meant to do so at all. And by 1787, when these Oxford dons are sequestering a space for "men of congenial minds," the debate about civility had breached the gender divide in an irreversible way. The role of women in the dissemination of polite culture had been more significant in early eighteenth-century France than in Britain, but that would change with Samuel Richardson's best seller.[20]

Publishing a Civil Tongue: The Pamela Debate

All sweetness? That is the approximate Greek root of *Pamela*, a name that figures in almost everyone's list of books enabling the oft-cited "rise of the novel." Unlike Crusoe, who roams all over the world, Richardson's Pamela stays very close to home, barely leaving the house to which she is consigned after leaving her parents. Crusoe's world is masculine and exotic, if short on society; Pamela's, claustral and feminine, though full of interactions. Two radically different theaters for the eighteenth-century novel yet not so different in outcomes and methods. Crusoe encounters strangers in foreign lands only to discover his bourgeois British virtues: prudence, godliness of a sort, tolerance (but only within limits)—the same virtues possessed by Pamela. The body of the man is protected by guns and swords, that of the young woman by piety, honesty and courage. Both turn out to be adequate to the challenges faced, whether at home or abroad. One major difference: Pamela learns to cope with her own sexuality and with the more potentially destructive male desire that threatens her, while Crusoe turns his back on sex as well as marriage. Crusoe's "conversation" is minimal and never of the bodily sort. Pamela learns and teaches the art of civil sexuality as well as good table manners and what best to read for social and self-improvement.

But Pamela stays housebound only in her plot line. Like *Robinson Crusoe*, Richardson's novel went all over the place. Within a few years of its 1741 publication, it had been translated into French, German, Dutch, Danish and Italian. Russian and Spanish editions appeared before the end of the century. Crusoe moved yet faster and further: into French, German and Dutch within a year; soon after into Italian, Swedish and Danish; and in the nineteenth century into Spanish, Arabic, Japanese and Persian, among others. What kind of global culture might this adumbrate? What would readers of the novel in translation have taken from it? Reading itself, the act of restful absorption (though not all reading is private reading), seems a peaceable enough habit. But the imagined content of Crusoe's life is not one that disseminates pure social harmony and hospitality. He encounters these things, to be sure, but does little to create them for others; self-interest is his primary motivator, backed up by violence whenever it seems necessary. Pamela, on the other hand, with much more limited local opportunities, founds a kingdom of kindness that all may enter—masters and servants, lords and laborers. The conversion of the dissolute and the taming of violence gradually come about, although it is a slow and hard-earned victory, and one depending on constant small-group interactions and reading groups where habit and familiarity instill mutual trust. The uppers have to learn that Pamela is not a "subtle, artful gypsey" using piety, good manners and sentimental effusions to scramble up the social ladder, while Pamela has to risk trusting that aristocratic violence will not carry her off or put her through a sham marriage.[21] Conversations between characters are frequently based upon the reading of Pamela's letters: private thoughts become public, and the public slowly expands around them. Reading is in itself a constraint on social violence; time passes between initial response and subsequent discussion, offering opportunities for reflection and moderating primary intensities. Reading, in this way, helps make us more civil, a common word in Richardson's text but one first used there in a sense that is ironic and unstable. Pamela has just had a letter from her parents warning her against trusting in appearances. In reply, she writes that Mrs. Jervis is "very civil" and that we should not assume that she is otherwise: "Sure they cannot all have designs against me, because they are civil!"[22] Pamela's hope that this particular civility is sincere turns out to be ill founded. It is up to her, in determining to "carry it civilly to everybody" (1:7), to model a version of civility that is to be trusted and that can serve as a socially bonding force. The novel's ongoing interrogation of civility in both its good and bad senses fits in with the critical etymology its heroine practices throughout, making her a "little equivocator" in her master's eyes (1:19, 211). Taking a lead from Thomas Hobbes's suspicion of abstract nouns, she tells Mrs. Jewkes: "I shall not at this time dispute with you about the words *ruin* and *honourable*; for I find we have quite different notions of both" (1:121). We have earlier been told that "the honour of the wicked is disgrace and shame to the virtuous" (1:109); Pamela's insights into the uses and misuses of words frustrates her master and deflects his sexual urges, but it is an important part of his education. Philology slows him down and makes him think.

In the second part of the novel Richardson elaborates in considerable detail what is entailed in Pamela's accession to the responsibilities of high life. She herself refers back to her incarceration and abuse as having been "in breach of all the laws of civil society" (2:40). This is telling. She is not claiming any breach of the law: that same law, after all, would have permitted a sham marriage. She is invoking a less precise but still authoritative standard: the body of protocols required for people to live together in respectful and nonviolent ways. The core element is reading and writing, and especially the informally effusive culture of letter writing. As the reformed Lady Davers avows: "We cannot receive from any body else the pleasure of sentiments flowing with that artless ease, which so much affects us when we read your letters" (2:33). The product of such pleasure is social levelling: "You see I put myself upon the same foot of correspondence with you" (2:25). Pamela's life story represents one of the high points in literary history for those who look to the written word as a civilizing force, a peace-making energy and a force for the good. Writing—the right sort of writing—can do no harm. But it can move great numbers of people. What are the limits on its effects? The extraordinary level of attention paid to Habermas's 1961 *Habilitationsschrift* (finally appearing in English in the portentous year of 1989) on the function of private reading and conversation as generative of the eighteenth-century public sphere perhaps reveals just how deep this fantasy is among humanists and social scientists. (It circulates most commonly now as the lament for the loss of critical attentiveness and authentic sociability that has accrued with the dominance of the electronic media.)[23] Pamela's command of language and literature helps position her as an agent of moral renovation, one based on virtue and desert rather than on kinship and class. But it is slow and gradual work, based not on widely available print but on the circulation of handwritten letters. The lucky few among the ambient poor might come in for an enhanced commitment to charity, and the occasional bright young local person might, given the right circumstances, find access to prosperity and even (like Pamela herself) to an exemplary pedagogic career. Given that the handwritten letters are put into mass-marketable print, we might say that the novel overcomes its own transcription of small-group interactions and broadcasts them as replicable in all families in all places. Or we might say that it insists on privileging the slow pace of one-at-a-time conversion of rudeness and violence into sociability: a very gradual revolution, if a revolution at all.

In this way *Pamela* is both retrograde (in content) and highly modern (in form). The heroine works entirely person to person and in manuscript. She reads neither novels, newspapers nor journals, all of which were widely available by the 1740s. And she shows herself rather disapproving of entertainments like masquerade and Italian opera, along with the racier examples of contemporary theater. The novel was a more licentious genre at the time than it became after Richardson's best seller, which imposed a strong incentive to domesticity and respectability on a tradition of miscellaneous tales, romances, translations and pornographies. The sorting of the novel genre into a pious and plain-speaking English norm was largely effected by *Pamela* itself, though even Richardson could not wholly exclude an element of titillation and prurience that satirists like Fielding were quick to notice. Sentiment, religious propriety and (only mildly qualified) chastity proved highly marketable; even the aggressively masculinized muscular Christianity evident in *Joseph Andrews* could not entirely steer away from Pamela's core values of charity and sympathetic concern. Absorptive novel reading now became respectable, no longer so obviously to be conducted with one hand.[24]

Richardson's claustral image of an upper-class rural Lincolnshire household is not completely without ventilation. Mr. B is, after all, mentioned as a member of parliament and one possibly to be made a lord:[25] he does go out into the world, even if his good wife mostly stays home. But it is still largely personal contact that spreads the updated civility gospel, even as it is documented in the most modern of media. The dense associational culture that was already in place and that would develop even more rapidly in the later eighteenth century, goes unmentioned in the novel.[26] No more is it the case that Pamela's rightness of mind and judgment come from her reading. Although she is—to her master—surprisingly well read and can go to bat with him on the lessons to be learned from the life of Lucretia, her exemplary identity comes from natural integrity more than from education. What we have here is a version of the Habermasian paradigm, according to which private reading becomes dialogic within the family and establishes the prototype of a public sphere, but a limited one.[27] Knowledge of literature gives Pamela enough cultural capital to alert Mr. B that she is to be taken seriously as an equal, but it is not the core content of her appeal. It is as if Richardson is tightening the screws on an emergent print culture whose power he must recognize but whose departure from a containable pastoralism he must challenge or inhibit. So his story slows down the speed with which messages pass from the private to the public sphere, supplanting print with epistolary communication and face-to-face conversation. The fact that the reading public proved so responsive to his conduct book circulating as a novel shows what an appetite there was for nostalgia for a premodern world; but the limited dialogic scene of the plot is magnified exponentially in the famous controversy that followed the novel's publication.[28]

Any emergent cosmopolitanism is emphatically refuted in the plot, which constantly upholds plainspoken British (and mostly English) good sense and dismisses foreign manners (especially Frenchified ones) as corrupt or ridiculous; Richardson and Fielding, who differ on so much else, both endorse this linguistic nationalism. But it is countered by the printed book's popularity in languages other than its own. European translations of *Pamela* have been studied by Mary Helen McMurran, who argues that Richardson's (successful) efforts to ensure the literalness of the French translation, printed in London under his supervision, were unusual at the time, when mostly unfaithful translations, reverse translations and pseudo-translations dominated the market in fiction.[29] James Raven has shown that a high proportion of the "English" novels published in the eighteenth century were translations of this sort, at first mostly from the French and thereafter also from the German.[30] *Pamela* went into the wider world as an icon of Englishness but did so in ways that inevitably passed beyond the control that its author was able to achieve with the first French edition. But the book's primary message was still that English civility was a distinctly national thing, worthy of imitation by others but not likely to be found elsewhere. It thus had much to do with the dissemination of what Srinavas Aravamudan calls the "national realist enclosure" that has been received as normative by far too many critics and readers of the novel.[31] Insofar as it marked out typicality, it also nudged readers away from paying attention to the variety and ethnographic miscellany of fables, oriental tales and travel stories that were available in the marketplace and thus contributed significantly, as Aravamudan shows, to a provincializing of the national imagination, indeed rendering it precisely *as* national, the property of us and not them. To what extent the legacies of this inheritance have constituted an encumbrance on both the world novel and its capacity to disseminate global civility remains a matter for further discussion. Even more radical exclusions become apparent when one considers the case famously made by Marx that the financial preconditions for a British middle class were dependent upon a colonial violence set going by around 1700.[32] But Richardson (in *Clarissa*) manages only the slightest of references to plantation slavery in noting, very much in passing, Uncle Anthony Harlowe's "vast fortune obtained in the Indies."[33] By now (in the 2020s) the best-selling status of novels from what is often called the global *periphery* (for want of a better word) has certainly challenged what remains of the image of peaceful sociability governing the manners of places like rural Lincolnshire, and it has also insisted on confronting many more and greater kinds of violence than those enacted by Mr. B and his dissolute relatives. In the novel's own century, Fielding's attempt to retain the fictional appeal of fistfights and male harassment of women within the mode of comedy is already undercut by, for example, Burney's *Evelina*, as well as by Richardson's own *Clarissa*, where violence, and especially violence toward women, figures as a serious problem for English culture. William Earle's *Obi*, only recently rediscovered and made available as a text for teaching, negotiates an even more fraught relation between (sentimental) narration and violence, in this case that of plantation slavery. Crusoe's world already presents challenges to Pamela's model of a civility to be imagined as an outcome of writing and reading fictional narratives in the national spirit.

The Chesterfield Controversy: Inspiring Artful Conduct?

Pamela's letters were not the only ones to capture the attention of those seeking guidance in the ways of a world seemingly more open than before to new social and economic input. The posthumous (in 1774) publication of Chesterfield's *Letters to His Son* brought to a head all the anxieties attending what William Warner has aptly called "the century's attempt to represent honest feeling honestly."[34] Chesterfield was, as we have seen, by no means the first to raise doubts about civility culture, but he raised them at a time and in a way that persuaded a lot of people to take them seriously all over again. Politeness and civility had already been opened to a rigorous interrogation by a wide range of moralists and writers, including Richardson. Indeed, critical alertness about the substance and effect of approved or fine manners appears well before the eighteenth century. Anna Bryson has shown at length that both Puritans and libertines stood against accepting the evolving consensus about civil behavior, the former suspicious that good manners were just a cover for hypocrisy, the latter hostile to any form of constraint applied to their own excessive way of life.[35] Both factions were expressing varieties of class hostility: the Puritans and their kind regarded civility as a set of pastiche aristocratic conventions designed to hide the true soul and to intimidate others, while the libertines sought to hang on to the traditional privileges of good living and uninhibited self-indulgence in the face of an evolving bourgeois consensus that called them into question. The bourgeoisie itself, those in the middle, found themselves all over the map, wanting some elements of civility culture but highly wary of others, just as one would expect given the tensions of adapting a self-declared courtly code of behavior to a largely middle-class environment.

Pamela did this from the bottom of the social ladder, from the servant class, and imaged a critical role for women. Chesterfield comes at things from the other end, from the aristocracy, and parallels his reassertion of upper-class control over manners with a vigorous remasculinization of the conduct book. The reception of the *Letters* indeed replicates the career of Castiglione's *Book of the Courtier*, whose popularity was indeed on the rise in early eighteenth-century England, although at that time the approved literature on manners was dominantly French.[36] By the end of the century, Britain had its own cause célèbre generated by the publication of Chesterfield's *Letters*. In the late eighteenth and early nineteenth centuries, Chesterfield, who is now remembered largely as the unfortunate object of one of Samuel Johnson's most famous letters, was everywhere. Tens of thousands of readers encountered him in his own words, published and pirated, translated, parodied or in one of the numerous abridged and selected spin-offs edited by people like John Trusler, whose *Principles of Politeness* was a best seller in its own right.[37] Defenses and refutations—mostly refutations—came hot from the presses. The second edition, advertised for June 16, 1774, only two months after the first (and there had in the meantime been one authorized and one pirated Dublin reprint),[38] already contained a "Postscript to the Advertisement" defending the book against the attacks it had received: that it was "calculated to inspire distrust, and an artful conduct," and that it recommended "gallantry with married women."[39] Above all it parsed civility as cynical self-interest: "Have a real reserve with almost every body; and have a seeming reserve with almost nobody; for it is very disagreeable to seem reserved, and very dangerous not to be so" (1:279).

Perhaps the first thing to point out is that the *Letters* were best sellers and as such reached indeterminate numbers of readers whose nature and social status could neither be exactly predicted nor controlled. Moreover, the son himself is a natural son and not a fully entitled heir, thus one who cannot assume that life will offer him the traditional aristocratic silver spoon. He thus becomes a middle-class man in the making.[40] Chesterfield is willing to advance the idea that "virtue is its own reward" (1:166), but this is not his last word on the matter; it is not even his usual opinion. Most of the book supports the opposite position and argues that merit is completely ineffective unless it is backed up by attributes that are more superficially ingratiating: good manners, fine clothes, good speech and general affability. Truth and good sense convince no one without being ingratiatingly delivered. This sort of cynicism might have been acceptable enough among a secure and self-contained patrician readership, but such were not in the majority of those who read Chesterfield. There is commonplace weak theology behind the argument: we live in a fallen world, to which "the golden age of native simplicity will never return," so the "ornamental parts of character" are but an elaborated version of the fig leaves of the primal couple. "People know very little of the world, and talk nonsense, when they talk of plainness and solidity unadorned; they will do in nothing . . . plain manners, plain dress, and plain diction, would do as little in life as acorns, herbage, and the water of the neighbouring spring, would do at table" (4:32). The affront to the Puritan virtues is at once behavioral, sartorial and linguistic: even Pamela, the icon of modesty, could prove alluring and sharply witty. The message is at once a fantasy relief from the stringencies of contemporary bourgeois self-discipline and self-abasement that were the vigorous legacy of the Puritan moment and a distinct threat to any personality that has absorbed and internalized those same values.

Coming after *Pamela*, Chesterfield offers a less exigent and more permissive prescription for self-advancement. He succeeds in part because of his habit of having things both ways. One does not become a scoundrel just because one resorts to dissimulation and conscious ingratiation: "A man of the world must, like the Cameleon, be able to take every different hue; which is by no means a criminal or abject, but a necessary complaisance, for it relates only to Manners, and not to Morals" (2:91). This blithe dissociation of manners from morals—the same dissociation that modern popular moralists like Stephen Carter are trying to overcome—assures the man of the world that he can dissemble without fearing any loss of moral self-respect.[41] The *Spectator* (no. 75) had made the argument that virtue led naturally to gentility and agreeableness: being good leads to seeming good. Chesterfield proposed a disjunction of being and seeming, suggesting that one cannot judge inner identity from appearance; and while this is a conventional enough attitude, it went to the heart of the recently confirmed mid-eighteenth-century sentimental community, wherein one *could*, it was thought, do just that. Adam Smith's *Theory of Moral Sentiments* (1759) argued that our deep and foundationally human desire to earn the approval of others led us to genuinely sociable behavior: we learn a common standard by watching others and imitating them and thereby discipline ourselves into both culture and community. Chesterfield's version of this same "taking the tone of the company that you are in" (1:282) seems to have more to do with how to get on in the world at the expense of others. Hugh Blair called this "complaisance" or habit of falling in with "the opinions and manners of others" a vice, and "the parent of many vices," leading to a "sinful conformity with the world which taints the whole character."[42] More routinely, no one wanted to do business, emotional or commercial, with those who could not be trusted. The modern analogue of this component of Chesterfield's *Letters* is probably the corporate strategy manual.

But the *Letters* is much more than this, much more than an expression of a crisis about being and seeming, albeit this crisis is the most important explanation of its celebrity. It is also and significantly a homeschooling and self-help encyclopedia for those denied access to the life of the upper-class gentleman but hoping to make the most of their more limited middle-class lives. It celebrates, for example, the value of bourgeois time management in a demotic diction that seems to cross the very class and gender boundaries that the *Letters* proposes to uphold: "How precious every moment of time is to you now. The more you apply to your business, the more you will taste your pleasures" (2:193); "I wish you would immediately begin to be a man of method; nothing contributing more to facilitate and dispatch business, than method and order" (4:58–59). Such homilies could be taken for those of Pamela or Crusoe, or of their common prototype, John Bunyan. For the busy man of affairs (and perhaps woman of the house) who has neither the time nor the money for the grand tour,

Chesterfield also offers the experience of imaginary travel. His letters follow his son all over Europe, and along the way they give us a guide to faraway places, in a manner somewhere between the dogged utilitarianism of an Arthur Young, the names and facts of the geography lesson (or of *Robinson Crusoe*) and the meditative travelogue of the educated voyager. "The world is the book" to which the son must apply himself (3:311), and one element of the chameleon personality is its absorption of the identities of others: "By frequenting good company in every country; he is no longer an Englishman, a Frenchman, or an Italian; but he is an European: he adopts, respectively, the best manners of every country; and is a Frenchman at Paris, an Italian at Rome, an Englishman at London" (3:353).

This aristocratic cosmopolitan ideal is very different from the trenchant nativism of *Pamela* and from the self-image of John Bull and militant Englishness and sits oddly with the informal homilectic language elsewhere in the *Letters*. It magnifies Crusoe's tentative and well-defended steps toward a transnational sociability, if not globally then at least into an idea of European citizenship. Chesterfield's very first letter is written in French (with a translation following), so a diligent reader can acquire a few words and phrases of the language.

A similar educational shorthand goes on with the classics, which were in the eighteenth century one of the major mechanisms of social and educational segregation. The extraordinary market for facing-page translations of the classics, as well as of monolingual English versions, could have been sustained only by a culture made up of persons attempting to acquire what they thought "everybody" ought to have. And if thorough knowledge of a language could not be had, then command of a few words, phrases, names and references would go some way toward providing the desired distinction. Chesterfield's *Letters* play their part in satisfying this appetite. Passages of Latin and Greek populate his pages, mostly with handy translations, showing a shrewd awareness that education provides a marketable social capital: "If you improve and grow learned, every one will be fond of you, and desirous of your company; whereas ignorant people are shunned and despised" (1:11). Also included are scansion exercises in English poetry (1:135), paying homage to an emerging pedagogy of English literature that was already beginning to substitute for the classics among the "illiterate" classes.[43] Here he is very much in line with the project of *Pamela*, prophetically sensitive to the use of literary criticism as a means of generating habits of self-determination and independence of mind, approved Protestant virtues that seem to have little to do with making friends and influencing people, although of course they can and do also have that effect. Anticipating generations of English teachers, he tells his son to test out all the claims of poetic diction against his own sense of the world, to "reflect a little" in order not to get into the habit of taking things simply "upon trust" (1:147–48). This is Elias's reflective detachment at work, and young Philip Stanhope is here exhorted to learn the habits that came more naturally to Pamela (who was, however, always ready to credit the importance of her own proper parenting) and to cultivate a personality that is "modest without being bashful, and steady without being impudent" (1:234).

And yet there is something eclectic and unstable in Chesterfield's language, evident in its proclivity for the attraction to French locutions that Johnson and Richardson criticized and in its tendency to disobey its own admonitions. The kind of literary pedagogy that is on offer is a long way from what would later emerge as modern criticism. Take, for example, the use of proverbs. Proverbs are deemed vulgar, and to use them is to give the impression that "you had never kept company with any body above footmen and housemaids" (1:181). "A man of fashion never has recourse to proverbs, and vulgar aphorisms" (2:225). It is tempting to suspect some irony here, in the manner of Swift's satirical dialogues, *Polite Conversation*, which largely subsist by way of proverbs, commonplace one-liners and formulaic repartee, of exactly the kind that their author, with false solemnity, has cautioned against. Proverbs are to be distinguished from "those polite speeches which beautify conversation." Swift allows that he might have reproduced a few sayings "of a proverbial air," but these are not to be taken as mere proverbs but as "the genuine productions of superior wits," from whom they were stolen by the vulgar![44] Chesterfield's *Letters*, despite his own apparent disclaimers, are peppered with proverbial phrases that seem closer to *Pilgrim's Progress* than to the fashionable master of ceremonies, phrases like "virtue is its own reward" and "do as you would be done by" (1:166, 281). At times this seems self-conscious: "Wherever you are, have (as the low, vulgar expression is) your ears and your eyes about you" (1:290); or "but (if I may use a vulgarism) one swallow makes no summer"

(4:281). We are instructed that the usage is vulgar but entertained with it nonetheless—the censure is hardly absolute nor, presumably, meant to be so. And indeed, there were many reprints of *Lord Chesterfield's Maxims*, a hundred pages or so of sententious passages and epitomes drawn from the *Letters*, on the model of La Rochefoucauld, and published separately and to popular acclaim.[45] The abbreviated and portable morality that proverbs provide is recognized as going against the spirit of the polite speaker, who should avoid overemphatic closure and tendentious opinion at all costs. But the same disavowed proverbial phrases are an aid to memory, a concession to the uneducated reader and an appealing rhetorical contrast with so much else in the book. The very coexistence of the negative estimate of proverbs with their constant use seems to embody the broad reach of Chesterfield's readership, which included both kinds of person, those in need of proverbial summary as well as those disdaining it. Proverbs are also habitually ambivalent and thus might seem to fit very well into the culture of evasion that Chesterfield examines and to some degree defends. There is a proverb for every occasion, and for completely different estimations of the same occasion: "He who hesitates is lost," for example, might serve one man's purpose, while "more haste less speed" can be applied to the same event by another. As Blake knew well in writing his "Proverbs of Hell," the same proverb can be read in quite opposite ways. A similar opportunism governs some modern proverbs: "A rolling stone gathers no moss" can be invoked to approve either rolling or staying still. The usefulness of proverbial expressions for endorsing any position that happens to suit the occasion and its audience makes them peculiarly congruous with the art of "complaisance" that Chesterfield was taken to be defending. They are perfect examples of the exercise of a certain sort of civility.

The recourse to pseudo-conclusive and opportunistic one-liners is completely at odds with the extended, meditative analysis that the discipline of literary criticism will seek to inculcate in its practitioners, prototypically apparent in Pamela's reading groups. The experience of reading Chesterfield can thus be disconcerting: one never quite knows where one stands. And this in turn is the predicament of the would-be polite person who resorts to a series of manners and mannerisms in hopes of being well-received and respected but who cannot control or fully predict what others may think, unless he or she is confident of consorting only with those who have agreed to play by the same rules. Indeed, the task of defining and expounding such terms as civility, politeness, manners, etiquette and others like them leads to a sense of vertigo. Where does one end and another begin? Are they different terms for the same thing, or slightly different aspects of a general category or radically different so that, for example, one would approve of civility but not of manners? Chesterfield plays into this with some energy as he tests our own tolerance for the *je ne sais quoi*, the fine line between "good breeding" and "troublesome ceremony."[46] The *Mirror* would note the bizarre terminological sublime whereby "it may often be the *fashion* to be *unfashionable*, and *decorum* to act against all propriety; *good-breeding* may consist in *rudeness*, and *politeness* in being very *impertinent*."[47]

These etymological acrobatics reflect a new historical sensitivity to the identification and confusion of nature with culture, of social ranks with sociable habits. *Robinson Crusoe* includes no mention at all of the word *polite*. The first volume of *Pamela* scarcely employs it: Pamela herself prefers *civil* for describing polite behavior. *Polite* appears in her vocabulary only after she is married, and it becomes more common still in the third and fourth volumes, published in 1742. Who knows what subtle inflections Richardson might here be proposing? Is politeness restricted to the rank Pamela now formally occupies, while civility was open to servants and to the language of servants? Does achieved politeness now keep at bay the possibility of cunning hypocrisy that civility might conceal? Is Pamela now firmly ensconced as among Jaucourt's persons of quality? The vagueness around words suggesting various kinds of nonviolent behavior made them useful for all kinds of purposes and rendered them open to variously minute distinctions, including even the hidden possibility of violence itself. All the more remarkable, then, that the matter of civility and its attributes, cognates and antonyms should preoccupy not only the diplomat and the novelist but also the philosophers of the time, those whose professional disposition was declared by Hobbes to be against loose terms and vague abstractions. These philosophers were still part of a humanist consensus that did not draw clear disciplinary boundaries between philosophy, literature, rhetoric and belles lettres. They invited a general educated readership and thus may be seen to be at work well within the reach of literature as it was then imagined.

3

Philosophy Polite and Politic

Shaftesbury's "Inmate Controller"

> All politeness is owing to liberty. We polish one another and rub off our corners and rough sides by a sort of amicable collision. To restrain this, is inevitably to bring a rust upon men's understandings. 'Tis a destroying of civility, good breeding, and even charity itself, under pretence of maintaining it.
>
> —Shaftesbury, *Characteristics*[1]

Some fifty years on from the Civil War and a mere twenty or so from the events of 1688 that have come down to generations of schoolchildren in their Whig incarnation as a nonviolent "Glorious Revolution," Shaftesbury, the most prominent eighteenth-century philosopher of politeness and one for whom indeed "to philosophise, in a just signification, is but to carry good-breeding a step higher" (2:255), feels able to acknowledge the paradox that has remained at the heart of all endorsements of civility in the modern anglophone democracies and beyond: that while polite restraint is the basic ingredient of a bearable and pleasurable life, too much mutual deference threatens us with a state of entrepreneurial and imaginative inertia. If it is liberty that has afforded us the realm of choice and discretion that makes politeness a genuine gesture, freely chosen and authentic, then that same politeness must not degenerate into a stale replication of passively repeated rules and conventions, at which point we would be an inert people vulnerable to losing the very freedoms that made polite interactions necessary in the first place. Shaftesbury reactivates the Latin root of polite, *politos*, meaning polished: that is, enhanced and burnished but still robust, not worn down to the point of fragility. Polite politics has a backbone. Liberty, in the Whig narrative that Shaftesbury espouses, has given us the opportunity to develop a social and economic world in which trade and commerce offer rewards to those engaged with others in a civility culture that is both emotionally and aesthetically pleasing and economically prudent and profitable. In that world some must rise as others fall, lest the engines of progress cease to hum along altogether and consign us to a stagnant premodern existence. There must be change and movement: civility can thus only subsist as a self-correcting and continually exploratory disposition that never knows in advance the limits of its own capacity and its own tolerance. The world becomes uncivil when it passes into barbarism or fanaticism but also when it is under the sway of excessive restraint and rule. Tyranny and anarchy alike preclude the culture of true civility, which must seek to sustain itself by "amicable collision."

Amicable collision is still collision, however, and bears within it the seeds of a possibly explosive confrontation. Civility thus rubs up against the edge of violence; it must make room for a measure of conflict that somehow does not exceed what can be contained by good nature. Shaftesbury seems to feel that the moment of fanaticism has largely passed. The French Protestants who arrived from the Cevennes in 1707 full of the "spirit of martyrdom" (1:20) were, he supposes, much disappointed by the "tolerating Englishmen" (1:21) who took little notice of them except by way of gentle and occasional ridicule (he glosses over the fact of their occasional persecution). The "spirit of bigotry" that ruined the ancient world (2:206) and more recently threatened the English state, whether in the shape of Catholics or Puritans, seems to be now held at a safe distance. With only a mildly self-mocking hyperbole, our author can promote Christianity itself as "in the main a witty and good-humoured religion" (2:217). The current enemy, he says, is foreign. England itself enjoys a "happy balance of power," but the French threaten to return us to "a universal monarchy and a new abyss of ignorance and superstition" (1:141). This very English balance of power is also a psychic one, bestowed upon every right-minded individual who has no further need to pass through the cycle of extremes represented by Puritan sobriety and Restoration libertinism. Richardson's *Pamela* sets forth a similar project. We have historically superseded the hegemony of either the "persecuting spirit" or the "bantering one" (1:50) and, as long as we can keep the French at bay, can now look forward to a happy life lived in the middle zones of the emotional and political spectrum. Shaftesbury lived a little too soon to have to face up to the challenges of a rampantly expansive capitalist economy in which the sheer accumulation and redistribution of wealth reintroduced social tensions that many would deem uncontrollable and destructive. The culture of luxury and desire had not yet been fully born. So the temptations he perceives facing the exemplary personality are seen as largely retrospective: rigid self-opinion, zealotry, tyranny, extreme religious orthodoxy. This is a sunny view of the state of the nation around 1710, of course, but it allows him to propose a twofold model of self-discipline and small-group testing out as a viable mechanism for assuring a happy and peaceful life.[2] Shaftesbury's image of the gentleman is completely unshadowed by the darker strategies of self-interest and vulgar prudence that will arouse concerns among some readers of *Pamela* and many of Chesterfield's *Letters* some sixty years later.

Shaftesbury's properly attentive individual contains a society within himself, albeit a small society. He draws from the sociable world an experience of give and take, checking and balancing, trying and testing that becomes the dynamic of an interior life whose findings are, thus processed, pitched back into the public domain as a further moderating influence upon the lives of others. (Adam Smith's better-known theory of sociability operates to the same end.) Neither private reason, understood as a monologic following through of deductive argument, nor public declamation, which merely bullies or oppresses us (even when it delights), can function as the agent of positive exchange. That agent can only be free conversation, unencumbered dialogue, "a liberty in decent language to question everything, and an allowance of unravelling or refuting any argument, without offence to the arguer," whereby "in matter of reason, more can be done in a minute or two, by way of question and reply, than by a continued discourse of whole hours" (1:49). The experience of such conversation with others trains the individual to replicate its mechanisms by way of interior dialogue or "soliloquy," sometimes called "self-converse" (1:110), whereby one becomes "two distinct persons" (1:105). These procedures should never be revealed because their integrity would be inhibited by any appeal to public approbation. They belong to "close retirement and inward recess"

(1:115), and they are properly preparatory to making any statement, since all statements are prone to disruptive excess, "for company is an extreme provocative to fancy, and, like a hot bed in gardening, is apt to make our imaginations sprout too fast" (1:106).

Shaftesbury's "self-converse" is one version of the trait that Elias called reflective detachment. It is also closely akin to what later critics will affirm as the core experience of reading literature: becoming other to one's self, exploring pseudo-statements (I. A. Richards), exercising the fancy and cultivating empathy. These are all peaceable activities. But Shaftesbury's metaphors for describing this inwardly dialogic self-discipline are militaristic and violent, and thereby emphatically masculinized, albeit in what could be the mode of irony. So "two formed parties will erect themselves within" and dispute the landscape of the mind (1:123), and there can be "no truce, no suspension of arms" between a person and his own rebellious subjects, his "fancies," for "if the fancies are left to themselves, the government must of course be theirs" (1:208). Each person must make a "necessary campaign" within himself, "set afoot the powerfullest faculties of his mind, and assemble the best forces of his wit and judgment, in order to make a formal descent on the territories of the heart; resolving to decline no combat, nor hearken to any terms, till he had pierced into its inmost provinces and reached the seat of empire" (1:228–29). If this is irony—and irony is most successful when we are unsure about it—then there are various ways to receive it. Are we being offered an undercutting of the importance of reflective detachment, which is ridiculed by being afforded the significance of a military encounter? Or are we to consider that detachment really is that important, because it is able to head off the terrible results of actual warfare by staging a virtual conflict within the individual mind? Both the military conflicts of the mid-seventeenth century and the contentious party politics that followed them are here imaged as energies to be absorbed into the single psyche and resolved there into a form that can be safely made public for the approval and imitation of others. Only after such strenuous self-monitoring and interior action can one hope that conversation with others can be something other than the rehearsal of vested interests and unbridled passions. It is this action of the "inmate controller" that no monarch or tyrant can expect to experience, having no incentive to "the privilege of becoming plural" in himself (1:138). The model of apt behavior here belongs to the writer.

This process of becoming plural is not merely self-generating: a person can be led toward exigent self-examination by two habits, "polite reading, and converse with mankind of the better sort" (1:234). One of these is private, with potential to be made public; one is already public. It is the pleasure of benevolent and peaceful exchange with others that makes us feel the value of working to make ourselves presentable and conversable. Reading books gives us something to say to others that is not likely to generate any more-than-amicable collisions. The encounter with literature accustoms us to the dramatic mode, wherein we are shown rather than told what to think and made to work out for ourselves the disposition of blame and approval among protagonists and events. Homer's poems are "an artful series or chain of dialogues" wherein characters "show themselves" and offer us models for self-examination (1:129). Homer prefigures Plato, the "divine philosopher" who "writ wholly in that manner of dialogue" (1:130). Poet and philosophers are masters of self-effacement and therefore of unopinionated writing: the author "makes hardly any figure at all, and is scarce discoverable in his poem" (1:130). Very different are the modern writers who talk only about themselves, for whom everything becomes a "sort of memoir-writing" (1:132), an array of vanities modeled on the French. Dialogue inhibits any tendency to self-display: "The author is annihilated, and the reader, being nowhere applied to, stands for nobody. The self-interesting parties both vanish at once" (1:132). Later critics would come to celebrate Shakespeare above all for similarly abdicating any didactic manner and purpose, although Shaftesbury, like many of his contemporaries, has reservations about the propriety of Shakespeare's plays. But he is at the leading edge of an eighteenth-century predilection for the dialogue form as an expression of the situated nature of knowledge and belief, of a pragmatist model of their application and sometimes of an artful recourse to the aesthetic alibi that allows for the publication of potentially dangerous opinions.[3]

Is this dialogic, self-monitoring experience open to all, or is it more restrictive and thus another example of the small-group disposition of so much civility theory? Is the masculine bent of Shaftesbury's language deliberately exclusive, or is it just an example (ironic or otherwise) of the generic gendering of everybody as male? Shaftesbury's system of self-cultivation is premised on the positive reinforcement provided by participation in polite social circles and on good reading habits. It cannot then be for everyone. Self-monitoring is in theory available to all, but it is harder for those who cannot see it modeled for them in Homer and embodied in the sociable subculture of gentlemen who can read him, just as it is hard or impossible for monarchs who are unaccustomed to being challenged at all. The culture of politeness is loosely elitist: at one point Shaftesbury assures his critics that the freedom of wit and humor is nondestructive and without risk as long as it appears only in "the liberty of *the club*, and of that sort of freedom which is taken amongst gentlemen and friends who know one another perfectly well" (1:53). In principle, however, the club is always open to new members, and in this way it is the perfect fantasy incarnation of the needs of an expanding social and cultural franchise offering to absorb as many as possible of the benefactors and beneficiaries of the new commercial economy. Men only, it appears. Furthermore, the exclusionary rituals and regimes are significant enough to guarantee that there will be no hasty extension of membership to those who cannot sustain the disciplines of literary reading and social scrutiny and those who cannot keep their voices down. The Puritan commitment to self-examination is respected and indeed made primary, but it is softened, regendered as male, and cannot function positively without the test of constant socialization among the better sort.[4] In this way Shaftesbury's theory of polite sociability is a perfect instance of how and why the *quoi* in the *je ne sais quoi* cannot be made the object of a rational-methodical treatise that might be accessible to all who possess basic literacy skills. Unlike Pamela or Chesterfield, he makes no lists of portable maxims. Unlike Kant in his account of judgments of taste, he is in no hurry to play up the potential universality that emanates from assumption that everyone will agree about what is beautiful.

The style and manner in which the best philosophy is written are, according to Shaftesbury, themselves an embodiment of the values of a "real simplicity" that is identified not with the diction of *Pamela* but with Greek comedy (1:169). As such it lies at an imprecise point—another *je ne sais quoi*—between the browbeating of the sublime and the dry precision of a rational method that can only be tiresome and dull:

The way of form and method, the didactive or perceptive manner, as it has been usually practised amongst us, and as our ears have been long accustomed, has so little force towards the winning our attention, that it is apter to tire us than the metre of an old ballad. We no sooner hear the theme propounded, the subject divided and subdivided (with first of the first and so forth, as order requires), than instantly we begin a strife with Nature, who otherwise might surprise us in the soft fetters of sleep, to the great disgrace of the orator and scandal of the audience. (1:169)

Method, of course, had a politics, one that impinged on the seventeenth century most frequently by way of Ramism and its Puritan affiliates and that would arise again after the French Revolution as a dangerously leveling component of the new democratism.[5] There was throughout the eighteenth century a vigorous debate about the status and effects of scholarship itself in relation to the difficult adjudication of what was historical and what was universal in human expression and experience. Its modern inheritance is apparent in the 'theory wars' of the 1970s and 1980s. The primary implication of a methodical presentation of evidence and argument is its proposed legibility, its attempt to minimize the effects of prior knowledge and customary understandings and to expose the incremental connection between things. Shaftesbury mocks the rage for categorization carried to the point of an absurdly minute philosophy that can no longer see the wood for the trees and the trees for the twigs and branches: a sublimity of ramification. But he finesses the degree to which his own preferred model of nature requires prior socialization and self-confidence, an *effort* at the natural. Claiming as one's own the territory of 'nature' was then and has remained the basic strategy in the political appropriation of style and the imagining of a common reader who is always a good deal more than common. In the eighteenth century the path runs from Shaftesbury to Hume and on to the so-called commonsense philosophy of James Beattie and Thomas Brown. It is attached to a model of sociability whereby true knowledge can be attained only by those who are not poisoned by being silent and solitary: "For whoever is unsociable, and voluntarily shuns society or commerce with the world, must of necessity be morose and ill-natured" (1:315). Being so, he cannot see straight, having lost not only the whole purpose of inquiry itself, "that natural affection by which he is prompted to the good and interest of his species and community" (1:315), but the very sanity and clear-sightedness that would enable him to form correct conclusions in the first place. The panic over specialization occurs in the context of a burgeoning debate about the pros and cons of the division of labor that would come fully into focus for the Scottish economists and their successors in both Marxist and liberal sociology. Specialization becomes increasingly necessary as the means for moving forward a scientific and technological culture whose declared project is to make the world a better place, while the fruits of that same specialization afflict us all with limited vision, deadening workplace routines and a life driven by a play between torpor and insatiable desire. The classic statement of the importance of art in this diminished world comes at the end of the century in Schiller's 1794 *Letters on the Aesthetic Education*. By that time, art and literature have once again to deal with the incidence of enormous constraints and expectations generated by another shattering political event: the French Revolution. This would generate further cycles of efforts to counterpoise aesthetic response to social, civil and national violence.

Shaftesbury, like Addison and Steele, is looking for a middle ground—the same middle ground that preoccupied critics like Dryden and Johnson as a principle of diction and the liberal political theorists as a principle of social organization. So between the pedantry of the scholars and the pure uneducated intuition of all-too-many English "gentlemen" there is the middle place occupied by the *virtuosi*. The range and flexibility of this term is somewhat lost to us now: we tend to apply it to those who, like violinists and painters, do things hugely beyond the normal in some technical sense. Around 1700 it had several senses, ranging from the approved general interest in lots of things at a reasonable but not excessive level of expertise, to the more disparaged, quirky and spendthrift obsession with something hopelessly arcane and useless, and thus visibly uncivil. This very slippage is evident in what Shaftesbury says about the virtuoso. Being a virtuoso in the approved sense of the connoisseur—one who has a more than superficial knowledge of a number of topics—is far better than being a scholar or pedant who has exhaustive knowledge of only one (1:214) and certainly better than reposing within the merely "fashionable illiterate world" of the familiar gentleman (1:215) who is proud to know nothing about anything beyond the chase and the bottle, the personality that Fielding's *Tom Jones* would so memorably enshrine in the figure of Squire Western. Properly cultivated, and holding together the sociable, moral and aesthetic life in happy harmony, the persona of the virtuoso is close to that of virtue itself (1:217) and expresses an ideal that would come down through the centuries as the epitome of a liberal arts education whose value is so often enhanced by its declared disappearance. Shaftesbury himself is not sanguine about the likelihood of the true virtuoso ever becoming a common phenomenon.[6] Human talents are too much steered by the division of labor, so the "sprightly arts and sciences are severed from philosophy," which must become "dronish, insipid, pedantic" and "useless," and offer no temptation to the lively youth (1:215).

The sprightly arts notably include literature, which keeps youths lively but not too disruptive; literature is the best model for philosophy as a whole. Without it there is a real threat that the psychic economy of modern life will pressure the virtuoso toward the merely curious, the "contemplation of the insect life, the conveniences, habitations, and economy of a race of shell-fish" (2:253), and thus toward the same obsession with minuscule distinctions that marks the philosopher: "cockle-shell abounds with each" (2:255).[7] At best one should be able to inhabit both the "fashionable" and the "learned" world at the same time (2:3); this was exactly the ethos of the recently founded Royal Society, whose procedures have been deemed as much social and conversable as they were empirical-scientific.[8] But the pressures threatening this middle, best-of- both-worlds condition were seen as increasing rather than diminishing, not only in the sphere of work conditions but also in the panic about gender roles that coded too much delicacy as "effeminate" and found modern conversation too lacking in the "male feature and natural roughness" that come with the "masculine helps of learning and sound reading" (2:6). The ideal middle state between the rough and the delicate would come to be identified as that of the true-born Englishman, a figment already opened to satirical representation by Swift but later reinvented by Burke and others as an icon against social and political Francophilia and radical politics in general. Modern literary pedagogy has also defended itself against accusations of effeminacy and excessive interest in things French while at the same time fending off investing too heavily in the dry masculinities associated with philology and textual scholarship.

Shaftesbury's virtuosity, like civility, is the product of work, and not the simple emanation of a given personality and place in the world.

Perhaps no traveler goes to Rome to view the treasures of antique sculpture without having to work at it: "However antiquated, rough or dismal they may appear to him at first sight, he resolves to view them over and over, till he has brought himself to relish them, and finds their hidden graces and perfections" (1:218). This does not happen by the exercise of mere "wantonness and humour. . . . The art itself is severe, the rules rigid" (1:219). Whatever natural inclination we might have for admiring the best things, what matters most is not innate: "Use, practice, and culture must precede the understanding and wit of such an advanced size and growth as this. A legitimate and just taste can neither be begotten, made, conceived, or produced without the antecedent labour and pains of criticism" (2:257). Over the next two hundred years the labor and pains of criticism would be built into the primary, secondary and higher education systems, wherein they still more or less subsist. The emphasis upon effort allows us to at least suggest a token or imaginary participation from the ranks of ordinary people. It also underpins Shaftesbury's larger project of stitching together the beautiful and the good as essentially identical and mutually entailed, in a gesture that briefly synthesized ethics and aesthetics just at the point that any such synthesis would be seen as lost to modern life and thereafter produced as the object of nostalgia—as it arguably was for Shaftesbury himself in his backward glance at Plato as his model—or as a contested analogy, as it was for Kant. What holds together truth, beauty and the good is a natural proclivity toward an admiration of symmetry, of the harmonious relation of parts and wholes (1:92). Because this appreciation of symmetry also requires, for all its naturalness, some effort—"'Tis we ourselves create and form our taste" (2:271)—it is a fundamentally social faculty, cultivated not by solitary meditation but by the experience of adjusting oneself to the standards and expectations of others. Poets and painters are "afraid of singularity" (1:96) and strive for ideal form because they do not wish to represent what distinguishes us from one another but what unites us in a consensual recognition of unity in diversity. Virtue similarly consists in what is "compatible with human society and civil life" (1:255); our natural inclinations toward accommodating others lead us to polish and develop those behavioral patterns that produce approval and imitation. In this way we come to understand that "the proportionate and regular state is the truly prosperous and natural in every subject" (2:267), whether in politics, aesthetics or ethics or in the simple manners that, in this exalted company, turn out to be not so simple.

The primary threat to this consortium of faculties and habits is that of singularity, of not being accepted or standing apart from others. This would seem to offer an endorsement of a comparative rather than a national literature. But Shaftesbury can also imagine a world wherein the power of "a contrary habit and custom (a second nature)" could produce a different and more negative sociability that would threaten all sound distinctions between right and wrong (1:260). This awareness is behind his ambivalent attitude to cosmopolitanism—on the one hand necessary to the social cultivation of the self, on the other prone to wander off into undesirable identifications with the monstrous forms of alternative cultures. As with almost all projects in which civility plays a role, questions arise about how large or small the preferred group can be. This same threat would become a feature of the debate about the condition of England itself, where divisions of labor and interest were seen to produce states of sociability that were radically deficient and different from one another (the class system) and experiences of singularity that were enforced rather than diminished by social life. But for the time being, the time and place of the Whig spokesperson of the early eighteenth century, civil sociability can be proposed as holding everything together in a nondestructive and progressive alliance. A gradually expanding circle of polite persons can ideally contain all of the tensions and maximize all of the opportunities that come with political and economic change. This is a "liberal individual" model, in that it seems to give everyone the chance to sign on, but it is also a check on the potentially divisive energies of that same individualism and its tendencies toward the worship of singularity and obsessive or extreme virtuosity. The work done by the up-and-coming middle-class person must be recognized by the arbiters of polite taste as deserving of the rank of gentleman: merit must earn rank, while inherited rank must demonstrate real merit, as Defoe had insisted. Vicesimus Knox would make the same case even more passionately in the aftermath of 1789, directing his concern at an aristocracy now more than ever at risk: Only "*personal merit* is a claim to superiority, which the most clamorous leveller cannot dispute." Without it, "the people will trample coronets under their feet" and "wipe off armorial bearings from the coach doors."[9] The scenes of riot and rebellion figured here as the signs of a world turned upside down make clear that in such a world the credibility of polite sociability would have more or less vanished. Civility would no longer ensure survival, because the violence now loosed exceeds all merely amicable collisions, and all the gentler persuasions of literary dialogism.

The appeal of literary models for imparting the most important kinds of sociable knowledge was enhanced by their not being part of the university curriculum. The visible involvement of the universities in the plots and counterplots that fueled the English Civil War (or Rebellion, or Revolution, according to one's choice of terms) ensured that the scholarly class would be the object of close and critical inspection in its aftermath. Locke, in recommending the sort of tutor one should be employing for the education of one's children, placed the highest premium on "Politeness of Manners, and Knowledge of the World . . . worn into him by Use, and Conversation, and a long forming himself by what he has observed to be practised and allowed in the best Company."[10] Learning is necessary, of course, "yet not the chief business . . . but in the second place, as subservient only to greater Qualities" (p. 255). The first place belongs to "*Civility*" (p. 249), entailing the overcoming of any impolitic "spirit of Contradiction" (p. 248) in order to cultivate "a care not to shew any slighting, or contempt, of any one in Conversation" (p. 250). What you know matters less than how you get across what you know, and without the art of pleasing no mere knowledge or information can gain credit. Prefiguring the argument that Chesterfield would later make so controversial, Locke opines that a "becoming Decency . . . with some civil Preface of Deference and Respect to the Opinions of others" will always fare better than "the sharpest Wit, or profoundest Science, with a rough, insolent, or noisy Management" even when such wit or science possesses the stronger argument (p. 252). Rude learning goes nowhere without polite assistance. Rough singularity will always place second to competent conversability.

In this spirit Horace, for Vicesimus Knox, becomes "the poet of gentlemen, and men of the world," rather than the object of the scholarly curiosity of "a Burman and a Bentley," and Cicero "a model, almost perfect, for an English nobleman."[11] Defoe's *Compleat English Gentleman* finds, on the other hand, too much emphasis placed upon classical education. Philologists are especially despised—"they seem to be form'd in a school on purpose to dye in a school" (p. 201)—but the entire preference for Greek and Latin as yardsticks of intellectual accomplishment is found wanting.[12] Most of what matters can and should be taught in English, and experimental science need never be carried on in anything other than the vernacular (pp. 195–222). Addison's *Spectator* had lobbied prophetically against the "violent . . . labour of the brain" that came with not employing the native language.[13] Doing things in English becomes not only a patriotic and democratic impulse but a countering of the specialization taking root in the workplace at large. A hundred years later, the battle against the belief that "nothing but classic reading is call'd litterature" (p. 222) would have been substantially won.

The polite distaste for specialized knowledge had the effect of making women more central to the transmission of a positive nonviolence. Women were traditionally figured as the softer sex and the repositories of a lifestyle of conversational leisure that could function as a refuge of polite interaction in the face of the uncivil demands of modern life, though they were also burdened with the counteraccusation of being, as Steele put it in the *Guardian*, "frightened at the name of argument" and "sooner convinced by a happy turn, or witty expression, than by demonstration."[14] At least by the middle of the century women too were not unfamiliar in the ranks of scholarship (though they figured much less often in experimental science). The author of the *Rambler* found that "there is no longer any danger lest the scholar should want an adequate audience at the tea table."[15] But the persona of the female scholar was seldom admired or fully accepted, as the notoriety of the late eighteenth-century "bluestockings" makes clear.[16] Women were of course major participants in both the production and consumption of culture, as the critical response to Habermas's male-oriented thesis about the emergence of the public sphere has by now made apparent.[17] But they were seldom received with full approbation even when apparently welcomed. The spiteful intensity of, for example, Pope's presentation of Eliza Haywood in Book 2 of *The Dunciad* and the responses of the male characters in Fanny Burney's *Evelina* to the redoubtable Mrs. Selwyn, speak for a culture within which outrageously sexualized slurs were far from unacceptable. The more favorably inclined essayist in *The World* who wants to include women in the circle of sociable knowledge pastoralizes them as closer than men to the "genuine simplicity of uncorrupted nature" and thus makes them emblems of an ideal that is threatened by the incumbent division of intellectual labor: "They are not fettered . . . by principles and systems, nor confined to the particular modes of thinking, that prevail in colleges and schools."[18] It is at best a backhanded compliment, but it does ally women with the newly valued common informality that made civility and literature into such persuasive disciplinary forces.

A Game of Backgammon: Hume's Conversable Philosophy

At first (and indeed second) glance Hume's early philosophical work, *A Treatise of Human Nature* (1739), would seem to be an exception to any developing alliance between philosophy and literature. The words are simple and sprightly enough, but the argumentation is taxing even to those assisted by reading it in "colleges and schools," and it is to this day among professional philosophers probably the most cherished of his books. Hume begins by boldly speaking out his ambition to produce a philosophical description of "human nature itself," the "science of MAN" that is the foundation upon which all our disciplinary knowledges are built and to which they must all ultimately refer.[19] The method is to be experimental and parsimonious with hypotheses, the foundation "almost entirely new" and unique in its comprehensiveness (p. xvi). But while our ignorance of the essences of "external bodies" (objects) does not hinder us from conducting controlled experiments, our approach to the human mind, whose ultimate nature is similarly unknown, is compromised by the recording mind's complicity in what it claims to be observing: we are at once the beings that reason and the objects upon which we reason (p. xv). The equivalent of an "experiment" here can then only be "a cautious observation of human life" derived from things "as they appear in the common course of the world," in "men's behaviour in company, in affairs, and in their pleasures" (p. xix). The object of inquiry is a society, and a self in society, that is reflexively constituted and situationally variable. With this daunting and prophetic recognition, the source of so much future anxiety for the human sciences, Hume sets going his inquiry.

The first of the *Treatise*'s three books culminates in an account of "personal identity" that is perhaps the most famously thorny passage of all in this generally demanding work. Identity, whether of objects or selves in the world, is predictably an unstable and difficult topic in a world where all assumptions of continuity now need to be explained, where all that is solid seems to melt into air, while at the same time conventions of recognition and legal personhood depend upon strong assumptions of that same continuity. Hume has already established that a powerful and "almost" universal "fiction of the imagination" is at work in allowing us to imagine the identity of objects through "a suppos'd variation of time" (p. 201), and he takes up the idea of the self as governed by similar processes. After much tough analysis, questions of personal identity are finally to be "regarded rather as grammatical than philosophical difficulties," for there is "no just standard" beyond the "merely verbal" whereby we can decide whether either objects or selves "acquire or lose a title to the name of identity" (p. 262). Following this admission he relates how the immensity of philosophy's task fills him with "melancholy" and a state of "forelorn [*sic*] solitude" akin to that of a mariner about to set out to sea in a leaky vessel that has already let him down in the past (pp. 263–64). Hume has cast himself into a condition of extreme singularity, the state most dreaded by Shaftesbury and by the theorists of polite culture: his peers hate him for demolishing their systems, and within himself he finds only "doubt and ignorance" (p. 264). He is here rewriting the narrative of Descartes's *Discourse on Method*, where the experience of radical isolation and the method of doubt lead to the apparent certainty of the *cogito*. But Hume's reflective detachment brings no such comfort, no recourse to a single first principle, only the understanding that most if not all of our operational certitudes are an "illusion of the imagination" and result from states of "experience" and "habit," things that he had hoped to connect to deep foundations but turn out to be themselves all that we have, thereby giving evidence of a faculty of understanding that "entirely subverts itself" (p. 267).

How if at all can this be resolved? We cannot say with the lazier apologists of polite culture that "refin'd reasoning" (p. 268) is not important, especially if we are ourselves of a philosophical disposition. So it is nature that comes to the rescue:

> Most fortunately it happens, that since reason is incapable of dispelling these clouds, nature herself suffices to that purpose, and cures me of this philosophical melancholy and delirium, either by relaxing this bent of mind, or by some avocation, and lively impression of my senses, which obliterate all these chimeras. I dine, I play a game of back-gammon, I converse, and am merry with my friends; and when after three or four hours' amusement, I wou'd return to these speculations, they appear so cold, and strain'd, and ridiculous, that I cannot find in my heart to enter into them any farther. (p. 269)

Yet he can and he does. The urge to abstruse inquiry does not go away, for the narrative is cyclic. After a round or two of civil sociability philosophy makes a comeback, and pleasure itself comes to depend again upon a commitment to the "learned world." Philosophy is superior to the mere daily rituals of "daily conversation and action" (p. 271), but it must remain the philosophy of a "true sceptic" who is "diffident of his philosophical doubts, as well as of his philosophical conviction" (p. 273), diffident of everything except the commitment to a rigorous effort at the avoidance of such phrases as "*'tis evident, 'tis certain, 'tis undeniable,* which a due deference to the public ought, perhaps, to prevent" (p. 274). Hume here brilliantly packages his skepticism about firm philosophical assertions as a component of the culture of civility: just as we do not offend others by denying their values and points of view to their faces, inhibiting the flow of good conversation, so in philosophical arguments we do not claim as certitudes matters that are, properly understood, very unclear. Hume advises against any unfortunate appearance of "assurance" and apologizes for any such mistake on his own part, pleading the pressure of "the present view of the object" as allowing him to get carried away (p. 274). If it is good manners not to impose your views on your fellow citizen, then the same tolerance must be extended to you, even if you are a radical philosopher. Hume is a specialist after all and not ashamed to show it in public, but he knows when to stop.

"Nature" is thus what steps in when philosophy (Hume's kind of work) threatens to get the upper hand and lead him to deviate forever from the give and take of ordinary life. Analogously, the doubt and discomfort he confesses to feeling when he is obliged to contradict rival theories are the product of a "weakness" coming from feeling "unsupported by the approbation of others" (pp. 264–65), in other words, from thwarted sociability. Nature is then a condition of dependency upon other people, whether expressed positively as sympathy or negatively as fear of singularity. As such, it cycles back into precisely the system of "habit" and "experience" it might have seemed to counteract. We might propose that the need to eat, to sleep, to make love and to converse with one's fellows is foundational, but then we can produce exceptions that radically modify every one of these inclinations. Or we might read these instances of "nature" as entirely without philosophical status, contingent upon who we are, where we are and when we are there, and differing for different people in completely value-free ways. Hume's decision to narrate the conclusion to the first book of the *Treatise* in his own voice, as if it is the story of his own life, only further emphasizes the question of authority and replicability. Is this everyman, or just David Hume? And if it is not everyman, who might be expected to share the Hume position and under what conditions? Descartes's *Discourse on Method* had raised similar questions, but Hume is much more emphatic about raising the question of replicability that puts in doubt any transportable summaries and conclusions.

It is no surprise that the disciplinary heir of Hobbes and Shaftesbury among others would find himself thinking in great depth and detail about the conditions of abstruse speculation in a culture of civility. His posthumously published autobiography briefly reports on the life of a man almost untroubled by destructive passions, an icon of stoicism and polite sociability: "a man of mild dispositions, of command of temper, of an open, social, and cheerful humour, capable of attachment, but little susceptible of enmity, and of great moderation in all my passions."[20] Here is the genial participant in dinners and games of backgammon, who worked as hard on his exit from life as he had worked on his conduct of it. But, as Thomas Reid reminded everyone in 1764, the *Treatise* had been received as waging "open war with common sense" and certainly seemed to have been "not written in company."[21] Hume himself would famously lament that the book fell "dead born from the press"; the first edition had indeed not sold through by 1756, although his biographer has argued that it was noticed by all those who had most need to notice.[22] Hume's early essay "Of Essay Writing," published in 1742 but never reprinted in his own lifetime, sets up a dialectic between the "learned" and the "conversible [*sic*]" worlds, the first premised on hard thinking in solitude and the second on "Company and Conversation."[23] The disease of the "last Age," he proposes, was the radical distance separating the "moaping recluse Method of Study" from the easeful routines of "common Life and Conversation." The promise of the present is the coming together of the two: the essay is the ideal form for this union, and Hume offers himself as a willing "Ambassador from the Dominions of Learning to those of Conversation" (pp. 534–35). Women especially are his projected readers, but even in this whimsical and humorously self-serving essay there is a sting in the tail: women are not to be trusted in judging works of "Gallantry and Devotion," both of which depend upon exploiting the warmer passions at the expense of reason (p. 537). It is Hume himself, in the apparent last analysis, who is the proper arbiter of the relation between the learned and the conversable, and it is the learned world that must provide its foundation.

Hume's own management of this relation has been much commented upon. His nineteenth-century editor, L. A. Selby-Bigge, noted that "the *Enquiries* [Hume's later effort] are an easy book and the *Treatise* is a very hard one," but he prefers the "first-rate philosophic importance" of the early work to the "elegance, lucidity and proportion" of the later.[24] He wants real philosophy, not literature. Both of the *Enquiries* were first published as part of a gathering of *Essays and Treatises*, suggesting that their author was anxious to mitigate any appearance of challenging his reader too directly. The first of them opens with an explicit discussion of the choices to be made between literary and ratiocinative methods, the one "borrowing all helps from poetry and eloquence," the other appealing more to the "understanding" (pp. 5–6). Casting the options as a choice between the "easy and obvious" and the "accurate and abstruse" (p. 6) styles, Hume seems to hope to have things both ways, carrying on a "mixed kind of life" that allows "none of these biases to *draw* too much" (p. 9). He is not willing to follow those who have no tolerance for the "accurate scrutiny" (p. 13) of metaphysics and no respect for the difficult labors of serious inquiry; nor does he have any patience with the use of sheer obscurity to beguile the public into error and superstition. Better to aim at "reconciling profound enquiry with clearness, and truth with novelty" (p. 16); to bring together, in other words, philosophy and literature in a spirit of civility.

Sociability and civility are evident not just in the style and manner of the *Enquiries* but also in its doctrines. A proper respect for the "social virtues" is at once "antecedent to all precept or education" and fundamental to "public utility." These virtues are not merely the product of social management, "invented, and afterwards encouraged, by the art of politicians, in order to render men tractable" (p. 214), but generated spontaneously by an "intercourse of sentiments . . . in society and conversation" that operates against our own tendencies to mere self-interest and leads to the formation of a "general unalterable standard" or approved behavior (p. 229). This reliance upon flexible urbanity reflects, as John Mullan has explained, a shift in Hume's thinking. In the *Treatise* he gave considerable importance to sympathy as a primary agent in social bonding; this is sidelined in the *Enquiries*.[25] A model of instinctive, universal response is replaced by a mediated and constructed environment as largely responsible for making us what we are. Hume asks the question that preoccupies all claims for the virtues of civility: "Why, in the greater society or confederacy of mankind, should not the case be the same as in particular clubs and companies?" (p. 281). Loyalties and affections are felt more strongly toward those close to us and are stronger (for example) among those who share a national culture than between foreigners, but this is the nearest we can get, Hume thinks, to the mechanism of a truly "general interest of mankind" (p. 225). Prospects for a global civility are thus not promising, and here again small-group and in-group interactions provide the strongest bonding agents. National and subcultural solidarity is admitted as the overriding tendency of the social instincts: it does not extend to all persons everywhere to the same degree. But the process of expanding our horizons beyond ourselves is still a positive one and leads to more actual good deeds than could come from a set of "loose and determinate views to the good of a species" (p. 225): Burke and thereafter Coleridge would recycle this view as part of the case against Jacobin "theory." The line separating those included in the circle of sociability and those left outside it is not to be firmly drawn, but there nonetheless comes a point at which 'we' stand against 'them.' Hume's sketch of the culture of polite exchange thus confronts its own exclusivity and justifies it on empirical grounds: we cannot be as involved in the lives and sympathies of distant persons to the same degree as we are in those closer to us. He does not profess the explicit nationalism apparent in *Pamela*, and there is nothing essentially restrictive about the "rules of Good Manners or Politeness" as facilitating "the intercourse of minds, and an undisturbed commerce and conversation." Indeed, in disguising "contempt of others" and performing "mutual deference" (p. 261), one might suppose that the circle of inclusion could expand indefinitely. But these polite attributes catch our "affection" instantly because they are face-to-face, witnessed in the round, and as such powerful enough to become "part of ethics" (p. 267). We are more likely to respond to those whose polite culture we recognize than to those whose we don't: the Spaniard who exits his house before his guest as a gesture of trust and respect (as if leaving him in charge of the household) might be misunderstood by one whose native manners habituate him to hold the door open for the other.

But if Hume includes the example of the Spanish host in his book (as he does here on p. 262), he can explain the event without misunderstanding, and he can also broadcast it in print form well beyond the limits of face-to-face encounters. The highly localized events of Pamela's life became the subject of a best seller. The image of coterie society can thus circulate globally, ironically generating its own localism as a worldwide motif for inspection and discussion. And Hume was certainly interested in attracting a wide readership. As early as 1740 he declared his desire to appeal to "ordinary readers" in publishing the third part of the work, "Of Morals."[26] The *Treatise* did not contain very many hard words or technical terms; it is a long way from the language of scholastic philosophy. What *is* hard is working out how these ordinary words are used and how they compose powerful and extended arguments of the most closely reasoned kind. Hume thus exposes as a "fundamental mistake . . . the insistence on the rhetorical transparency of common sense embodied in ordinary language."[27] Common sense is not the refuge of the lazy and the anti-intellectual (though Reid and Beattie and the eighteenth-century critics of Hume would push it in that direction) but a highly complicated state of mind and being that takes uncommon intelligence to unravel, as Hume's descendants in twentieth-century analytical philosophy have made clear all over again. The vocabulary of the *Enquiries* and the *Essays* is no more or less simple than that of the *Treatise*; what disappears is the journey through the thornier thickets of philosophical argument, which are avoided or finessed. Approximate and nonexclusive taxonomies replace categorical distinctions, in what seems to be a turn toward Shaftesbury's model of pleasurable accessibility: a turn toward literature. In his powerful study of Hume's career Jerome Christensen finds there an overarching commitment to forms of "self-restraint" governing passion, reason, rhetoric and self-presentation, and coincident with the professional persona of the man of letters working in a print culture that allows him to refigure and reauthorize his own works over and over again in different and differently profitable forms.[28] The effect is to "reinscribe the disturbing within the customary" (p. 15) in exactly the same way that commercial culture, which is the motive and the enabling condition of Hume's career, adjusts potentially violent differences to conversable norms. Scarcity turns to plenty in the reproductive process, treatise to essay to inquiry, aiming to cycle though the reading population in a decidedly unrevolutionary flow (p. 124) whose basic task is to keep on going, mirroring thereby the incrementally accumulating economy in which print culture participates: commerce as ongoing civil conversation.

To range across and between Hume's essays, in their variously published, republished and rearranged formats, is indeed to sense the deferral of ultimate meaning as the energy of the philosopher's lifework, and the life of his style, just as it had seemed to be in the famous recourse to dining and backgammon at the end of Book 1 of the *Treatise.* Polite refusal of final verdicts keeps the conversation going, much like a literary seminar. The essay form itself was associated with incompletion and experiment, pitching itself as a proto-conversational alternative to the rigors of deductive method and architectonic rationalism.[29] In the essay one could, precisely, *essay* or try out a position that need not be final. An assemblage of essays, like Hume's, makes the gathering of perspectives even more manifold and the exact fixing of an author's position even more difficult. This accords not simply with the commercial imperative, whereby one edition begets another by the addition, subtraction or local revision of its component parts, but also with the urge toward anonymity or self-protection that Hume definitely experienced (the *Treatise* was published anonymously) and that the notoriety of his career rendered at the very least prudent and perhaps even a necessary strategy for survival as an independent thinker.[30] A life and style of argument in which nothing stands still accords well with both the need to make a living out of reassembled books and with the uncomfortable exigencies of a legal preoccupation with fixed identity as the basis for possible proscription or prosecution. It is also the hallmark of intellectual civility.

The essay form in this sense might be said to project the life and thought of David Hume fully into the mode of temporality, imaging both as products of and participants in history. The intellectual crises and dramas resulting from the increasing recognition of the temporality of everything were also convertible to profit in the writing of histories, which were by the end of the century almost a necessary part of the portfolio of the practicing writer—Smollett, Goldsmith, Gibbon and Hume himself all wrote histories.[31] In Hume's *Essays* one can trace the lineaments of a developing historical consciousness that makes most of its findings themselves subject to the passage of time and the influence of place. Thus, republics are most favorable to the growth of the sciences, and monarchies to the cultivation of the polite arts.[32] France is more monarchical than England and therefore the seat of civility culture, the "art of society and conversation" (p. 91). England can learn from this but must also foster its own national culture. Civility is progressive, and we have more of it than any of the ancients did (p. 128), but it is also unstable, liable to "run often into affectation and foppery, disguise and insincerity" (pp. 130–31). Any achieved perfection in either the arts or the sciences is by definition at the point of decline, after which they "*seldom or never revive in that nation, where they formerly flourished*" (p. 135). But we also read that civility is progressive, part of the power of a national character that is transmitted from one generation to the next, one that must "imbibe a deeper tincture of the same dye" than its predecessor (p. 203). Civility is a northern, European accomplishment, not open to those unfortunate inhabitants of the "torrid zone" whose climate spares them the need for "industry and invention" (p. 267). For an implicitly more fortunate Europe, Hume's most positive arguments propose nothing less than an integrated theory of progressive culture based on the exercise of the civil virtues and the circulation of a knowledge that is both rational-scientific and literary-aesthetic:

The more these refined arts advance, the more sociable men become: nor is it possible, that, when enriched with science, and possessed of a fund of conversation, they should be contented to remain in solitude, or live with their fellow citizens in that distant manner, which is peculiar to ignorant and barbarous nations. They flock into cities; love to receive and communicate knowledge; to show their wit or their breeding; their taste in conversation or living, in clothes or furniture. Curiosity allures the wise; vanity the foolish; and pleasure both. Particular clubs and societies are everywhere formed: Both sexes meet in an easy and sociable manner and the tempers of men, as well as their behaviour, refine apace. So that, besides the improvements which they receive from knowledge and the liberal arts, it is impossible but that they must feel an encrease of humanity, from the very habit of conversing together, and contributing to each other's pleasure and entertainment. Thus *industry, knowledge,* and *humanity,* are linked together by an indissoluble chain, and are found, from experience as well as reason, to be peculiar to the more polished, and, what are commonly denominated, the more luxurious ages. (p. 271)

It would be hard to imagine a grander projection of the benefits of consumer culture and its contribution to positive civility than this of Hume's. But the very mention of *luxury* at the end of the paragraph alludes to the furious eighteenth-century debate about the pros and cons of production beyond need, for some the principle of progress and civilization as it is here for Hume, for others the sign of an irreversible alienation produced by the division of labor itself and by the consequences of a surplus economy generating destructive and fantastic desires among all classes, rich and poor, redrawing the boundary between need and fantasy and sending the state into inevitable decline.[33] Hume, looking only on the bright side, seems here to have done away with the existence of rude knowledge in a whirlwind of conversing, exchanging and let us not forget reading (including those women who read essays). His ideal project is the dissolution of conflict itself: here he anticipates the civility theorists of the late twentieth century. So "factions" become "less inveterate, revolutions less tragical, authority less severe, and seditions less frequent" (p. 274).

But do they disappear? If all moments of perfection are also moments of incipient decline, and decline, moreover, apparently beyond rescue—the best things seldom reviving in nations where they formerly flourished (p. 135)—then what are Britain's prospects? The English, Hume writes, have less of a national character than other nations, because they are a "mixture of monarchy, aristocracy, and democracy," religiously tolerant and therefore pluralistic (p. 207). They might therefore be imagined to have more defenses against corruption and decline than those nations that have invested in one single mode of government that, when it goes wrong, ruins everything. England's prosperity then depends upon its willingness to do away with factions and party politics—the very things that Hobbes and Clarendon had witnessed and worried about and that Hume himself acknowledges as "an animosity which broke out sometimes into civil war" (p. 493)—in a general commitment to the culture of civil conversation. There is, he writes, no better way of proceeding than "to encourage moderate opinions, to find the proper medium in all disputes, to persuade each that its antagonist may possibly be sometimes in the right, and to keep a balance in the praise and blame, which we bestow on either side" (p. 494). This model of a peaceable kingdom extending the culture of civility across the world was as current in the eighteenth century, as the British empire was beginning to be imagined (though it was very far from being in place), as it became in the aftermath of 1989 in the hands of the apologists of a new Euro-American imperium. Here, much more than in 1989, it is coded as analogous to and even a consequence of literary reading. We should not forget Hume's reservations, expressed in other essays and parts of essays and in the *Enquiries*, that the power of sympathy and therefore civility is greatest among people who are most like one another and that the bonding function of reasonable conversation is thus most efficient where least required. But when such paradigms appear in print, their reception is potentially much more extensive. Whether delivered in print or in person, Hume's prospectus for a culture of industry, knowledge and humanity, each begetting the others in an upward spiral of perfectibility, is shadowed not just by living memory—the wars and the demise of party politics—but by the onset of powerful theories of time and change that made any single statement of faith or belief inevitably contingent and disputable. Philosophy's ideal community, fixed in time and place and therefore out of time and place, was coming to be part of a reckoning with historical time. Civility culture could no longer be assumed as either transportable from place to place or perdurable in one place through time. Both historical inquiry and literary representation took up the question in mutually implicated ways.

Economies of Manners

Merchant, tutor, lawyer, philosopher, man of letters, aide-de-camp and private secretary: all careers attempted at various times by David

Hume. Also historian. *History of England* was his longest and perhaps most popular work and the basis of whatever prosperity he achieved in life.[34] The six volumes published serially between 1754 and 1762 were slow to make their way in the face of accusations of atheism, Jacobitism and both Toryism and Whiggery, but they finally won through to a wide readership. Hume's preferences as a historian were definitely with the ancients, as explained in his *Enquiry concerning the Principles of Morals*. Random empirical details of what happened in the "small cities of Greece" or the "harmless wars of Pisa" are of little interest unless enlivened by the fundamental human passions that "excite compassion" or "move terror and anxiety." History works only when "our hearts beat with correspondent movements to those which are described by the historian."[35] Hume assumes a universality of basic emotions of which "there is none, of which every man has not, within him, at least the seeds and first principles" (p. 222). It is the "constant and universal principles of human nature" that afford the historian the same reliability and accuracy as the "physician or natural philosopher" (pp. 83–84). There are indeed deviations resulting from the "great force of custom and education" and from a "diversity of characters, prejudices, and opinions" (pp. 85–86), but these are relatively superficial phenomena emerging from the "secret operation of contrary causes" (p. 87). They should not distract us from acknowledging the universal functions of the elementary passions. For Hume, reading history is very like reading a novel. And doing so, it seems, can move us beyond identification with small groups.

Elementary passions are not, however, enough to produce a uniform human society or sociability. When Hume commences his *History*, he can hardly wait to get through his brief discussion of the Britons (barely four pages), which can "afford little or no entertainment to men born in a more cultivated age."[36] Barbarism is violent and tedious and has nothing to show us. Laws, peace and "civility" come only thanks to the Romans (1:9–10). The Britons in southeast England had only, in establishing agriculture, taken "the first and most requisite step towards a civil settlement" (1:3). No interesting history is yet to be told. Civilized societies, preferable as they are for those who enjoy a game of backgammon and a good bottle, have never been universal. A long-durational group in a geographically limited space—that of modern Europe is the assumed norm—can hope for some continuity in its habits and expectations, but as long as the "barbarian" other appears in the record, other possibilities must be remembered and perhaps even anticipated. The policing of boundaries becomes urgent not only because of the threat of incursions by foreigners but also because the dynamics of temporal change produce imaginings of internal devolution and decline, as various cyclic theories of history affirmed. The stadial models of the political economists were optimistic inasmuch as they argued for a progress through primitive and intermediate phases (hunter-gathering, pasturing, agriculture) toward the world we have; but those same methods raised the possibility that civilization might begin to undo itself. Most often it was the highly developed metropolitan economies, with their complex divided labor systems, their consumerist cultures and their distance from the land, that were projected as the likely agents of decline and fall even as they purveyed the highest degree of cultivated pleasure.

This story has been often told, but it has implications for the understanding of civility, which is open to a double impediment.[37] First, it is not a permanent fixture of human societies. For most political economists, it developed only when peoples became sedentary, more numerous and modern. What had once not existed could also pass away: peace is always threatened by a relapse into violence. Second, civility is not simply to be admired for itself, because either there is no 'in itself' or we cannot be sure that we are seeing it if there is. Even if it were an indestructible element of social life, we should not trust it. It could be the signature of a well-disposedness to others, innate or acquired, or a hypocritical mask overlying sheer self-interest. Shaftesbury came as close as one could to making it into a virtue, but only against a tide of significant opposition. His contemporary Bernard Mandeville was sure that all the important components of "flourishing" societies emanate from the "violent and most hateful Qualities"; politeness comes from "Shame and Education," not from anything noble in humankind.[38] Civility and sociability depend on nothing other than hypocrisy: "In all civil societies men are taught insensibly to be Hypocrites from their Cradle" (p. 351). They are not even wholly beneficial, since "conversable People" will always opt for "inoffensive mediocrity" over "honest ability" (p. 245). The loss of civility culture need not, in this view of things, be subject to much regret. Such an event should be positively celebrated according to the logic of Rousseau's first *Discourse*, which attributes the loss of transparency to the onset of civilization and its investments in civility and politeness: "Suspicions, offenses, fears, coldness, reserve, hate, betrayal, will hide constantly under that uniform and false veil of politeness, under that much vaunted urbanity which we owe to the enlightenment of our century."[39]

Is our species naturally sociable and civil or naturally selfish and violent? Suppose we are both? Adam Ferguson submits that we have indeed evolved or progressed from "rudeness to civilization" and that we are also predisposed toward a group consciousness, a subsistence "in troops or companies."[40] Sociability itself is foundational, but the forms of that sociability are not. Social bonds are in play whether we have "agreed or quarreled," whether we are objects of "fear" or of "love" (p. 16). Our "mutual compassion" comes along with our tendency for "war and dissension" (p. 21). Sociability is neutral, in other words, and underlies the operations of both good and bad qualities, friendship and enmity (pp. 29, 33). This means that place and time play a vital part in nurturing one or the other side of this dual personality: we are "united by instinct" (p. 34) but open to influence and persuasion in deploying that instinct. We possess enough of an "amicable disposition" to provide the "foundations of a moral apprehension" (p. 35), and "love and compassion" seem to be the *most* powerful feelings we evince (p. 36). But that does not make them ubiquitous or all-conquering. Touching on the major debates of his time, Ferguson's mode is paradox. Wealth and luxury may corrupt but do not necessarily do so. Division of labor may threaten the integrity of society but does not alone bring about decline. A "feeble spirit" (p. 259) can infect any form of government, if the delicate balance of determining forces that operate in all societies is radically disturbed. The crucial binding component is "personal elevation and virtue" (p. 254) and a functional "spirit of society" (p. 218). No single factor—wealth, commerce, luxury, penury and so on—either creates or destroys this, though some are more difficult to control than others. The "subdivisions of arts and professions," for example, are positive only up to a point and should never extend to "the arts which form the citizen and the statesman" (p. 230). Because societies do become more complex through history, the task of managing relations between their parts and tendencies becomes harder. Thus, the "supposed condition of accomplished civility" (p. 209) that characterizes modern times calls for unprecedented scrutiny and vigilance, but civility itself is morally neutral: only a failure of "personal vigour" (p. 224) will bring about decline. The civic virtue that Ferguson espouses as the necessary core component of social integrity is most vulnerable to despotism and over-administration, typified in the standing army that removes citizens from the commitment to defending themselves. Proper citizenship thus entails embracing conflict rather than seeking to eliminate it under the guise of politeness: civility understood as duty to the whole must accept a level of confrontation—"disputes of party, and . . . noise of dissension" (p. 256)—that politeness alone will always misunderstand and reject.

In resuscitating and once again masculinizing the sense of civility as rigorous duty to the whole, Ferguson imagines virtue as *virtú*, as incorporating a measure of turbulence and even of necessary violence.[41] It cannot hold back the effects of time and change, but it is our best chance of mitigating their worst effects. No one system or culture has solved all of its problems, but smaller groups do better than large ones in deploying the required checks and balances. The larger the territory, the harder it is to unite people "in the execution of any national, or even of any factious, designs" (p. 271), and the more likely it is that they will be deprived of the independent agency that is essential to political health. But where are the functioning small groups, and how small must they be to operate at their best? The high points in the histories of Athens, Sparta and Rome are available as models, but they are premodern and extinct. Rousseau chose Geneva as his model, and before 1798 the Swiss Confederacy provided at least one possible example of the small-group ideal. But by the middle of the eighteenth century Britain was visibly embarked upon a massive extension of its territories across the globe, exactly the thing that Ferguson (and many others) found most dangerous for national integrity. What options, if any, are there for predicting something other than disaster? Is global civility a plausible ideal?

Recall that sociability was, for Ferguson, prone to express itself not only as amity and deference but also as violence: "Our species is disposed to opposition, as well as to concert" (p. 21). We are indeed so disposed to opposition that we enter into quarrels even "without any material subject of controversy." This aversive instinct can be managed, "fostered by its continued direction to its particular object." Ordinary language assists in this process: to speak positively of our own fellow citizens necessarily introduces the idea of aliens and foreigners as negative. One tool for the creation of social or national solidarity is therefore the invocation of the enemy other, as has been the practice of even the smallest groups (p. 22). The aversive instinct potentially threatens the war of every group or subgroup against every other, depending on the local-temporal definition of who is "us." Thus, the potential for "civil discord" inside the national group is deflected by focusing on the sense of a "common danger" that can be described as foreign. Local rivalries and distinctions are subsumed into an imagining of a greater whole. Along with most of his contemporaries, Ferguson regards it as natural that one has stronger loyalties to what is local and familiar than to what is remote. To the modern reader, it is all too apparent how easily such patriotism can be "fostered" into nationalism and intolerance.

Ferguson does not deny the conditions that make warfare seemingly inevitable. There is, for example, no paean to commerce as the harbinger of global peace and prosperity. What there is, instead, is a special plea for the status of northern Europe as the 'best of kind' in the history of violence. It starts with the familiar argument for the preferred location of "political wisdom and civil arts" in the "temperate zone" (p. 108). The torrid zone, whether because of geographical determination or the inferior quality of its minds, has "few materials for history" (p. 110), and its peoples are suitable only for "servitude" (p. 112). Ferguson's often compulsive evenhandedness here collapses into overt racism. The exceptionalism of Europe is further argued through its innovations in the culture of warfare, which has indeed almost become an expression of the "civilities of peace" (p. 198): "We have mingled politeness with the use of the sword; we have learned to make war under the stipulations of treaties and cartels, and trust to the faith of an enemy whose ruin we meditate" (pp. 199–200). The "manners of Europe," generated by the culture of chivalry, have taught us to eschew "artifice and surprise" in favor of an honest confrontation (pp. 200–201). Even the Greeks, who had not been educated into chivalry, observed no such standards.

It might be tempting to speculate that before the Europe-wide carnage of the Napoleonic Wars, such a view of things would have been plausible. But Ferguson has managed perfectly well to ignore the estimated eight million deaths from war, famine and plague that came about as a result of the Thirty Years' War, to take just the most spectacular example. Small armies fighting face-to-face in the open had characterized some recent conflicts, to be sure, and the conflicts of the recent Seven Years' War were fought significantly in North America and in those faraway "torrid zones" where there was deemed to be no interesting history. Culloden, for all its significance and traumatic aftermath, was a small affair in military terms. But the War of the Spanish Succession (1701–14) was land-based in Europe and had been extremely violent. Even the relatively contained Battle of Blenheim (1704) had produced an estimated fifty thousand or more casualties. Nonetheless, Ferguson holds to his case, which is nowhere qualified, for a north European synthesis of violence and civility that transcends national borders. The generic alien in this schema is that same inhabitant of the torrid zones who impinges, if at all, only at the very margins of Kant's theory of taste.

A number of Ferguson's insights are taken over and more casually rendered in Kames's *Sketches of the History of Man*, published a few years later (1774). Here too hostility toward other groups and kinds is deemed natural: "There is no propensity in human nature more general than aversion from strangers."[42] This time, however, the torrid zones provide a counterexample needing some finessing: the inhabitants of the Society Islands are "extremely civil" and seem to "have no aversion to strangers" (1:37). This is adduced as the result of an alternative "national character" (1:38), which in turn leads to the conclusion that they must be of a different "species" (1:20) or "race" (1:40). As for our European aggression toward and suspicion of strangers, Kames envisions a progressive and cyclic evolutionary sequence. Larger national groups generate softer manners, and violent passions subside. But then wealth and luxury erode the social passions and self-interest comes to rule, so "men end as they began" (1:348). Here "selfishness at last prevails as it did originally" (1:401), different only in that it is now "smooth, refined, and covered with a veil" (1:414). Whether or not this is progress seems open to question: the choice seems to be between violence with or without civility. The second has given us a regrettable tolerance of dueling, "no slight symptom of degeneracy" (1:414).

Nevertheless, for Kames, a general disposition toward benevolence disseminates through the modern world; our philosophers have persuaded us that "man is a social being, upon whom benevolence has a more powerful influence than fear" (1:373). Modern war is more humane because it is waged not against individuals but against the state, which "mitigates resentment" (1:352, 385). This must not come at the expense of patriotism, which is at best "a vigorous principle among the English, and makes them extremely averse to naturalize foreigners" (2:189). It is "connected with every social virtue" (2:249) and stands "at the head of social affections" (2:319). It is not simply love of one's place of origin—all persons have that—but a cultured and socialized passion, founded on sensing the value of a "strict union for the common interest" (2:323) itself affiliated with government, husbandry and commerce (2:318). It is most at home when a people is "in a train of prosperity" (2:330) and each has equal access to self-improvement; it perishes as soon as it is surrounded by "opulence" and smothered by "sensuality and selfishness" (2:335). Such, Kames fears, is the immediate prospect for Britain, and among the necessary remedies, one supposes (though this is never said) must be a restriction upon the ministrations of women, who have "less bitterness [than men] against the enemies of their country" (2:5).

In the final analysis Kames comes out somewhere close to the position argued by Ferguson. Fear and aversion to strangers are an innate human disposition, but we do have a social appetite, at first limited to our familiars but open to extension by personal experience and historical circumstances, even to the point of making possible a "hospitality to strangers" (2:189). Between ferocity and civility there is a middle ground, but it is always under threat because social-historical development does not stand still. We are impelled by our passions to "action without intermission" (2:209), and this is fortunate, since extended experience of "universal peace, concord, and security" could only make us "rival a hare or a mouse in timidity" (2:213). Human life becomes a matter of contesting the dangers we engineer for ourselves and accepting the inevitable degree of turbulence that ensues. Civility, in this world, becomes not so much or not just a habit of deference and disinterest but a vigorous ethic of engagement that must sometimes embrace dissent and even violence: we are already at the point that will become unignorable at the turn of the twenty-first century, where civility must be somehow imagined *with* violence instead of preserving a pure opposition to it. No simple ethic of deferential behavior is recommended by either Kames or Ferguson, nor does conviviality alone, pleasurable as it may be, serve as an adequate foundation for social well-being or security. Hospitality to strangers is all very well, but a measure of hostility may be necessary to preserve patriotism. Any positive estimate of civility must be open to rigorous critique, whether as mere good manners (which can be genuine or a mask for hypocrisy) or as the keystone for a comprehensive model of civil society.

Following the path forged by Shaftesbury and Hume, Adam Smith proposes a particularly close alliance between philosophical and literary method in the argument of *The Theory of Moral Sentiments*, a text first published in 1759 but worked over by the author right up to his death in 1790: the final version is even able to include references to the French Revolution. According to Smith, interacting with others is just like reading a novel: we 'know' what they are feeling only by using our "imagination," putting ourselves into their situation and "changing places in fancy." It is only this that creates a sense of "fellow-feeling," not any direct access to the sense impressions of others, which is impossible.[43] From this we are led to imagine ourselves as seen by others and to wonder how they see us. In this way, Smith suggests, "I divide myself, as it were, into two persons," the "spectator" and the "agent" (p. 113). Here again is Elias's reflective detachment. The spectator, variously called (echoing Shaftesbury) the "impartial spectator," "the man within the breast" and the "great inmate" (pp. 130, 147), acts to modify our tendency to extreme behavior, and especially violent behavior, pushing us to a shareable "mediocrity" that makes the imaginative identification with us by others more likely (p. 27). All of this goes on in the imagination, with no guarantee that our reading of the exact state of minds and hearts in other people is fully reliable, just like reading about characters in a book. Civility and politeness are referenced as in themselves fairly lightweight routines, but upon their observance "depends the very existence of human society" (p. 163). Their origins are, implicitly, hardwired into human nature, which evinces an "original desire to please" and "an original aversion to offend" (p. 116). If they are not themselves fully fledged moral virtues, they are the basis of "a real love of virtue" because we desire not only to receive but to actually deserve the approbation of others (p. 117).

Smith downplays more than most the aversive drive in human nature with his emphasis upon sympathy and benevolence as the dominant human personality traits. Divisive behavior is upsetting not only to its object and to its observers but also to the person displaying it, who loathes himself (p. 243). This disadvantage to the "rougher and more unamiable emotions" is so marked that it must be "the intention of Nature" (p. 37) to render them unappealing. Knowing or sensing this, anyone suffering extreme pain seeks to project it as less extreme in order to more easily earn the sympathy of bystanders. Our imagined recreation of suffering always "falls . . . short of the violence of what is naturally felt by the person principally concerned" (p. 45), but without it no identification at all is possible. Persons are engaged in a constant process of self-norming, presenting themselves in such a manner as to encourage rather than discourage the sympathy of others. The "perfection of human nature" consists in a natural civility that restrains selfish and cultivates benevolent behavior; this alone can "produce among mankind that harmony of sentiments and passions in which consists their whole grace and propriety" (p. 25).

Smith, Hume and Shaftesbury emphasize the positive kinds of sociability and thus leave most room for valuing the potential of civility; Ferguson and Kames are more skeptical and more aware of the paradoxes governing all human attributes. Mandeville occupies the extreme of cynicism in arguing for the positive benefits of bad things. All, however, are of one mind about the spatial restrictions on social bonding: we evince our strongest loyalties to those closest to us—families, friends and small groups united by interests of some sort—and the further we get away from our own subgroup or sector, the more indifferent we are to others. The same syndrome has continued to inform and afflict the postwar twentieth-century project of Europe (the topic of Chapter 5). At some point along the way, indifference turns (or can be turned) into hostility. Wars are not civil undertakings, Smith argues, precisely because the "partial" takes over from the "impartial" spectator, and moral vigilance is relaxed: anything goes as long as it succeeds (pp. 154–55). The order of intensity governing positive affiliations decreases with every extension of the social sphere, from children to complete strangers (pp. 227–34), finally producing complete dissonance: "The mean principle of national prejudice is often founded upon the noble one of the love of our own country"

(p. 228). Smith, with an almost grateful insouciance, is happy to consign mankind to what he can hope to manage: local solidarities. The matter of "universal happiness" is "the business of God and not of man" (p. 237). Whatever trade and commerce can do for the globalization of peace, tolerance and good feeling, it cannot finally seem to overcome an intransigent parochialism in the human disposition. Smith claims that we are more prone to self-restraint in our interactions with strangers because we expect less from them and acknowledge the existence of more unknowns (p. 23). One might expect this observation to turn into an endorsement of civility as more naturally apposite to situations going *beyond* small-group encounters. But that claim is not developed, except to the point that a rather shallow and prudential model of civility is in play. Our strongest concerns are with those nearest to us: to sequence family, close friends, neighbors, fellow nationals and so on is to register a diminishing intensity of affiliation. First loyalties are to our own "little department" (p. 292).

But how natural is this natural disposition toward benevolence and sympathy? To render it remarkable at all, it must be something "beyond what is possessed by the rude vulgar of mankind"; otherwise, we would not call it out for any attention (p. 24). It would remain an unnoticed component of the lifeworld. The class coding of proper 'human' behavior is never entirely dissolved into the concept of the 'natural.' Similarly, stadial theory was always set up to ignore not only the primitive national past—as Hume ignored the Britons—but the present-day inhabitants of the "torrid zones" who would either stay as they are or gratefully recognize the benefits of becoming gradually more like Europeans. Smith runs into problems and even contradictions when he sets out to estimate the relative functions of nature and culture in governing human behavior. Aesthetic judgments are more open to social determination than moral ones, but even different occupations in a single society can create different personality types, and "custom" acknowledges this: what best befits a clergyman does not work so well for a soldier (pp. 202–3). What we call "politeness" is very much a matter of cultural practice, and among "civilized nations" the stoical virtues are less at home than they are in "rude and barbarous nations." Self-denial is not as important in "ages of civility and politeness" where the abstinence from pleasure is not imposed upon us as necessity. Those Smith calls "savages" are too absorbed in basic survival to "give much attention" to the needs of others: what we call "humanity and politeness" appears to them as "unpardonable effeminacy" (pp. 204–5). Civility, then, is presented as both natural and cultural, and the scale is adjusted variously in Smith's exposition. Moral sentiments are least open to circumstantial modification (p. 211), but they are modified nonetheless. Savages, in Smith's world, are barely capable of what we call civility. If it is indeed a preexisting natural disposition deriving from the benevolence compulsion, it is hardly to be seen in some corners of the globe. And, if it belongs more habitually to "civilized" nations, how efficient or desirable is it that they seek to extend it to those called savages? Are they perhaps too far down the social-evolutionary ladder to be reachable? These matters, says Smith, are best left to God's dispensations.

Civility, meanwhile, threatens to seem most efficient when it is least required. The more widely it seeks to extend itself beyond those who already care most about each other, the less effective it becomes. As war became for the first time both 'total' and patriotic, with the conscription of citizen armies in France and Prussia in the 1790s, the small-group aspirations of civility were placed under new stress. Literature reciprocally found itself more and more the object of our best hopes for diminishing violence. Kames played a large part in preparing the way for a literary pedagogy that could work to protect throne and altar from the prospects of an uncivil world. His *Elements of Criticism* (1761), destined to become a well-used college textbook, made its case for the fine arts (his phrase) as moral, managerial and physiological in their capacity to dispel violence:

> By uniting different ranks in the same elegant pleasures, they promote benevolence; by cherishing love of order, they enforce submission to government; and by inspiring delicacy of feeling, they make regular government a double blessing.[44]

In other words, Kames proposes, sharing aesthetic pleasure softens conflict and sponsors mental health, leading to an enjoyment of good government. But these are still besettingly local conditions, not cosmopolitan incentives. Some 250 years on, we are still not sure what to make of the relation between politics, violence and the fine arts. In the nineteenth century this was often solved by dispensing with or sidelining civility as a useful term, although the needs that it described were by no means less critical as the project of literary pedagogy began to be newly formalized.

Kames's *Sketches* also summarizes long-held assumptions that the progress of society can be measured by examining its treatment of women. Women, being "delicate and timid," require protection, which is exercised more and more as the species evolves from "savage" to civilized states.[45] Savage nations treat women badly. A "glimmering of civility" (understood as civilization; p. 39) begins when some attention is paid to dress. The Crusades provided a crucial corrective to "the fierce manners of our ancestors" by forging the "bonds of chivalry" and a culture of "courtesy" (pp. 82–83), albeit along with an incentive to "gallantry" that has often gone too far. (Others saw them as little more than an opportunity for plunder and rapine.) This fetishization of women is exactly what is vigorously contested by Mary Wollstonecraft, whose *Thoughts on the Education of Daughters* (1787) and *A Vindication of the Rights of Men* (1790) both take issue with "the equivocal idiom of politeness" and a culture wherein manners may be "a painted substitute for morals."[46] The case is most fully developed in *A Vindication of the Rights of Woman* (1792), which critiques the whole apparatus of "gothic manners" that renders woman "either a slave, or a despot" who is thoroughly "*localized* . . . by *courtesy*."[47] That Wollstonecraft still brings up the example of the courtier as "eating away the sincerity and humanity natural to man" (5:201) indicates how current the early modern legacy of ambivalence about civility and politeness remains in the wake of the French Revolution. This came partly from the impact of Chesterfield, and more immediately from Edmund Burke's notorious effort to resuscitate a positive estimate of chivalry as what had been lost after 1789, with what he saw as dire consequences for civilization and in particular for the persecuted French queen Marie Antoinette.

It is all the more surprising, then, that Burke himself is not otherwise much given to positive invocations of civility or politeness. *Civility* does not occur in the *Reflections on the Revolution in France*; *politeness* appears once only as a sarcastic description of revolutionary manners; *polite* does not appear at all. The word *civil* is quite common, but never in its sense of polite deference. Burke's uses all hew closely to the Latin *civilis*, indicating citizens' assumed secular rights, claims or aspirations: hence civil is often opposed to legal, military or religious and allied with such terms as social, society, political and government.[48] This must seem surprising in an author who is so commonly invoked as the exemplary apologist of tradition and aristocracy, and it may be taken as striking evidence of just how radically the French Revolution refigured the profile of the inherited vocabularies. Paine's *Rights of Man*, so often cited as antithetical to Burke's text, shares the same emphasis: roughly thirty uses of civil, none of which have anything to do with politeness, itself a word that does not occur in Paine's text. Wollstonecraft's *Vindication of the Rights of Woman* (1792) uses civility only once, and in its sense as politeness, but of her eighteen uses of civil, only one has this sense. Further, of her six uses of politeness and four of polite, all but one are negative (e.g., "polite simper," the "insinuating nothings" of politeness). Refinement is (with one exception) similarly cast as false or superficial. On both left and right of the culture wars of the 1790s, there seems to be little patience with the words that so many earlier commentators had worked so hard to authenticate.

4

The Displacement of Civility

Violence in a Widening World

Civility Laid Bare

There is a striking moment in Matthew's Arnold's *Culture and Anarchy* (1869) when the author takes issue with Thomas Carlyle's inclination to "give rule to the aristocracy, mainly because of its dignity and politeness."[1] Arnold protests that the "manners and dignity" of an aristocracy are not what is needed now, useful as such "refinement" might be as a rebuke of the very worst of "middle-class" habits (pp. 83–84). The ordinary young upper-class Englishman is in fact singularly unqualified to respond to the national crisis evident in the "movement of ideas" typical of an "epoch of expansion" (p. 86).[2] So too, unassisted, is the utilitarian middle class. In the face of an incumbent anarchy, it is culture alone that can save us, an enriched notion of culture that is not merely a "toying with poetry and aesthetics" (p. 96) but a path to a "*best self*" that is "united, impersonal, at harmony" (p. 95). Aristocratic politeness may be a "kind of image or shadow of sweetness"—sweetness and light being Arnold's desiderata for a good life—but it is not the thing itself (p. 102). It lacks both energy and generality, along with the kind of inwardness that can preempt any possible deployment of good manners in the service of hypocrisy and self-interest. Where class, manners and religion divide us, only culture can unite. Culture is "the great help out of our present difficulties," our way "not only to perfection, but even to safety" (pp. 6, 202).

Arnold's attention to culture is a redirection of and turn away from the interest in civility that had dominated throughout the preceding century. It is plausible to suggest that the Chesterfield debate might have exhausted the inherited terms available for describing self-management in modern society. But, as is made clear by the twenty-first-century interest in civility, no one ever gives up on discussion just because there may be nothing new to say. Ready-made words work perfectly well until it seems that they are unable either to encompass emergent conditions or to attract the kind of attention needed to announce a new idea. Culture was such an idea. But how could such a concept offer both safety and perfection? What kind of perfection, and safety from what? Arnold's intent here is famously managerial. To preserve culture, a "firm and settled course of public order" (p. 204) is essential, and culture in turn teaches us to appreciate the state and to refuse "violent revolution and change": exactly the function of an education in the fine arts as Kames had described it. There must be a path "between despondency and violence" (p. 207), and that path is now called culture. Culture in turn is fostered through education (p. 209), and education depends on whether one reads and what one reads (p. 6). Newspapers will not do the job; not even the Bible will do the job. But literature, the best literature, will. Culture is "of like spirit with poetry, follows one law with poetry," and poetry will "transform and govern" religion itself (p. 54). Eschewing "fierceness" and "abstract system," assailing all "stock notions" and "stock habits," working only for "harmonious perfection" and "many-sidedness" (pp. 66, 197, 22), eroding the spirit of bigotry and provincialism, poetry can save us. Its progress is obscure and far removed from "direct political action" (p. 40), but it is as inevitable as it is gradual, operating "decisively and certainly for the immediate future" (p. 202). Ten years later, in "The Study of Poetry," Arnold was even more outspoken about the collapse of inherited beliefs and traditions and the unique capacity of poetry to provide "an ever surer and surer stay."[3]

Notwithstanding his critique of Carlyle's admiration for an aristocracy, there is far more that unites than divides these two prominent commentators on nineteenth-century British society. Carlyle was even more scathing than Arnold about the limits of politeness and civility for dealing with the challenges of the modern, material-mechanical age. He rebukes those who find that Goethe does not write "in the style of those we call gentlemen" and fail thereby to understand his "whole harmonious manhood."[4] He chastises those who retreated "behind the outmost breastwork of Gentility" in disparaging Robert Burns's nativist vigor; in Voltaire he sees the limits of a writer too directed toward "the politer part of the world" in an age of "polish."[5] English authors, he complains, are far too anxious to project "gentility," to be seen as "Literary Gentlemen" who are expert in "Dapperism and Dilettantism," and who can thus "be tied hand and foot by a spinster's thread" while being "unable to stand, save in stays."[6] Carlyle is defending the rough masculinity that was anathema to Arnold and endorsing the Saxonist, Hebraic patriotism that Arnold saw as a sworn enemy to Hellenism's sweetness and light. But they agree in their verdict on the inadequacies of politeness. More important, they agree in their high estimate of the poet as dwelling properly in what Carlyle calls the "spiritual life," where one is "not in the habit of yielding to violent emotions of any kind."[7] This high estimation of the literary aesthetic as a force for peace and good order carries over from eighteenth-century civility to nineteenth-century culture, even as culture displaces civility itself as a preferred term. Schiller and Goethe belong for Carlyle to a select group of writers, mostly German, who are setting the pattern of a "new era in the spiritual intercourse of Europe," even of a "World Literature." Now "all Intellect has fused itself into Literature," and literature "is fast becoming all in all to us."[8]

The congealing of the humanistic proto-disciplines around a literary model is thus now detached from its previously strong affiliations with vocabularies of civility and politeness. By the mid-nineteenth century the word *civility* is barely used in any conceptually rich manner, and *politeness* frequently takes on a marginal or negative connotation. Civility tends to be found as subsumed within civilization (as it still was, along with "civil," by Raymond Williams in *Keywords*) and thus rendered a secondary attribute rather than an entity. Culture and spirit now describe together not only the humanities but the entire project of rational-scientific knowledge that in German goes by the name of *Wissenschaft*. What is this culture, and why does civility seem to have so little to contribute to it? As Raymond Williams spent much of his career pointing out, *culture* is one of the most complex and contested words in the English language.[9] Only in the nineteenth century does it commonly appear as a free-standing noun of portentous significance, designating something much more profound than civility, and only late in the same century is it invoked as an overarching identity governing a nation or large group.[10] Williams explains that its range of senses "indicates a complex argument about the relations between general human development and a particular way of life, and between both and the works and practices of art and intelligence."[11] Arnold's use of the word is made even more complex by his adoption of its conceptual inflections in German, where the etymological field is arguably even more unsettled than it is in English. What Arnold means by culture, for example, is much closer to *Bildung* than to *Kultur*, and both are in competition with *Zivilisation*. *Bildung*, by common consensus, is one of those words that simply cannot be rendered into English, requiring an extensive critical-historical archive for its elucidation. While not of much importance to Kant, it receives major attention in, among others, Herder, Fichte, Humboldt, Hegel, Schelling and Goethe. Closely identified with classical philology (and somewhat resembling the Greek *paideia* in its conceptual profile), and drawing also upon a tradition of mystical (Christian) inwardness, it suggests bodily and mental perfectibility, union of the singular and the general, of the self with a community, and a coming to self-knowledge by overcoming the experience of division. It is lived in body and mind, not just passively acquired. Above all it eschews anything frivolous; it can have little to do with mere manners or with how one positions oneself in relation to others, which any association with *Zivilität* must inevitably introduce.[12] It is deeper and more inward than *Kultur*, which can (if understood as mere technological progress) actually inhibit the emergence of *Bildung*.[13] When it emerges in the genre of the *Bildungsroman*, nothing less than an entire long novel is required for its adequate demonstration.[14]

Arnold's German-inspired culture, then, is deep and serious, and its primary components are literature and criticism, the one very occasionally producing the best that is known and thought in the world, and the other telling us how to recognize and read it. Criticism for Arnold takes on a new seriousness, one that had been incubating throughout the eighteenth century as designating dispassionate rather than negative judgment, a sense further intensified by the paradigm of Kantian *Kritik*. The best of literature is rare enough that it would perish without preservation by criticism, which also sets the standard for the evaluation of any future literature. When literary genius does emerge from the often unpromising conditions of time and place, criticism is what makes sure that its raw materials and necessary prototypes are "ready to hand."[15] Disinterestedness, free play of the mind and aloofness from practice qualify the purveyors of true criticism for a secular priesthood, and certainly for a core role in the education system. Arnoldian criticism is all about affirmation, albeit by the negative way, since much of the literary record does not make the cut and remains useful principally for showing us what it lacks. But the Arnoldian model, which famously populated the school system, was not the only legacy of Romanticism.

A more subversive option was the so-called literary absolute described by Lacoue-Labarthe and Nancy, whereby, as civility recedes from any formative power, *theory* appears for the first time: "the inaugural moment of literature as *production of its own theory*—and of theory that thinks itself as literature." Here the pieties and holistic aspirations of culture are undermined. Literature and theory, and each as the other, are both the symptom of and the cure for a new historical crisis that now fully confronts the aporias of Hume's science of man; fragment and dialogue are its formal emanations.[16] The provocative incompletion of the fragment indeed finds its narrative in the exploratory evolution of conversational method, with its image of embeddedness in bodily space and time, but the mood is no longer one of easeful communication. Difficulty becomes unavoidable, meaning hard to find and defend, and the production of knowledge more stressful. The space once occupied by civility is, beginning in the 1790s, taken over not only by culture but also by theory and *Kritik*; civility is again nudged into a parodic role as at best mere good manners, at worst class-coded affectation. But the case for the common reader of the sort generated by *Pamela*, one who knows no language but English and resists the temptations of all abstractions that seem to threaten the ready alliance of head and heart, would not go away. Its exponents also claim the literary mode, but without the theory and the difficulty. The controversies generated around the exemplary career of Paul de Man as the touchstone for the functions of theory in the modern academy are merely the most dramatic recent instance of this ongoing competition for possession of authentic literariness.[17] But Arnoldian culture and 'theory' share one priority even as they decry one another: the negative estimate of civility.

Lacoue-Labarthe and Nancy take Friedrich Schlegel, especially, as their talisman for the emergence of literature as theory, and it is he who gives Romanticism its most challenging (and initially atheistic) spin. But Schlegel was not well-known to anglophone readers in the nineteenth century and perhaps too much marked by both personal and intellectual scandal to emerge as an icon of pan-European spiritual regeneration. That role belonged to others writing at the same time as Schlegel, above all to Goethe and Humboldt, and to Schiller, who gave Kantian aesthetics its turn toward social application and made it appealing to the likes of Carlyle and Arnold. *Bildung*, not irony, would take the preferred role in modeling a Romantic legacy, although irony remained in contention. Schlegel had indeed projected a disruptive idea of *Bildung* as a "continuing train of the most monstrous revolutions," but it also encompassed a paradigm of self-consolidation, one able to comfortably accommodate the minor frictions of the mind in ways that literary studies could turn to for keeping at bay the challenges that would resurface in late twentieth-century 'theory.'[18] Schiller is among the first to devise a role for the aesthetic that directs it explicitly away from social intervention and historical practice, and he does so by developing what Arnold would call (as did Schiller himself) the disinterested, free play of the mind. He is responding, in 1794, to the popular demand that putting into practice the ideals of the French Revolution must be the most important task of his generation. Schiller disagrees. Only the *Spieltrieb* (play drive) can avoid the violence that ensues from the antagonism between the feelings and the intellect, each seeking to defeat the other, but in order to do so it must remain without content or application, both a zero point in time through which the other drives move but do not colonize and an intuition of abstract form and harmony in the realm of aesthetic judgments of taste that, for Kant, relied for their assumption of communicability on being utterly unrelated to worldly interests. "All other forms of communication divide society. . . . Only the aesthetic mode . . . unites society, because it relates to that which is common to all."[19] Even animals have it in them to take pleasure in play. Schiller's model, furthermore, does not discriminate against the so-called idols and ornaments of non-Western cultures that Kant had relegated to the category of the primitive: they too are instances of the urge toward making and shaping for its own sake (*Bilden*).[20]

Schiller's emphasis falls upon the plastic rather than the literary arts, but otherwise his case for the importance of the aesthetic is very close to Arnold's. He too fears the violence of the masses, even as he allows for a necessary turbulence in the progress of human life, without which the species as a whole would stagnate. He too sets a very long timetable for the dissemination of the aesthetic into ordinary life; it will take more than one century for the "quiet [*ruhige*] rhythm of time" to do its work. Like Shelley's unacknowledged legislation by poetry, the process works "unnoticed."[21] Schiller seems to have little interest in imposing any sort of pedagogy of the aesthetic, recommending neither the informal imitation of persons of taste (as Hume and others had done) nor the protocols of an organized school system (on which Arnold spent much of his professional energy). The play drive is instinctual and universal, so always latent in human experience, even as for so many of us it is submerged by the business of practical life. How exactly it is to be generally liberated is not clear, beyond a recommendation that we immerse ourselves in the Greeks.

Arnold and Schiller also share a subjectivist priority; their model of the aesthetic is not based on sociable instincts like empathy or sympathy but on a cultivation of the self that, properly conducted, will make us socially benign by default. We are not earnestly bidden to enter into the lives of others but to develop our own ability to live above the world rather than just in it. (Nor are we encouraged to supplant sympathy by an exclusive adoption of theory or *Kritik*, both of which have afforded alternative, analytic options for attention to the social.) Civility, as an outwardly directed gesture, is not at issue here: it has no role in spiritual culture. Arnold does, however, make one concession to the language of politeness, if only by an impersonal etymological catchment that he may not have fully intended: he recommends the cultivation of *tact*. *Takt* (touch) for Schiller remained a lesser thing than the senses of sight and hearing, both of which remove us from material objects, while touch depends upon it.[22] Arnold, more positively, specifies "tact" as what is needed to apprehend a "touchstone," reactivating the sense of a body feeling another body; it is a faculty possessed by the Greeks and also by the French.[23] Tact toward touchstones plays up the physicality of the aesthetic also apparent in Arnold's proclivity for "concrete examples";[24] this invocation of the concrete would become a besetting recourse for anglophone literary criticism. But tact also has another meaning, the one we more commonly now intend, denoting polite discrimination and self-restraint: something, in fact, part and parcel of what we might call civility. This is a late sense in English, appearing (from the French) around 1800, and aptly described by *OED*'s citation of Dugald Stewart in 1801 as "that delicate sense of propriety which enables a man to feel his way in the difficult intercourse of polished society."[25] Jenny Davidson has argued that during the nineteenth century tact comes to occupy a primary place in the rhetoric of female conduct especially, as a mediator between managed feelings and socially generous instincts; as such it had been approved by both Burke and Wollstonecraft, who agreed about very little else in the lexicon.[26] It could thus occupy some of the verbal territory left open by civility and politeness as they ceased to embody acceptably weighty ideas and became indices of mere behavior. And indeed tact, though not a keyword for Jane Austen, appears in Edgeworth and reappears later in Eliot, Dickens and Gaskell. Adorno locates *Takt* as central to Goethe's *Wilhelm Meister*, where it is offered as "the saving accommodation between alienated human beings" and therein "inseparable from renunciation [*Entsagung*]" although in modern times living on only in its eviscerated form as etiquette or as "mere lying."[27] Tact, it seems, works briefly as a placeholder for what used to be endorsed as civility but can no longer, in the modern world, bear the weight it is asked to carry.[28]

It is much the same with politeness. William Godwin works hard to discriminate a "true politeness" that is a "branch of virtue" rather than a cloak for hypocrisy. One must not forget that "the greater part of human virtue consists in self-government"; to banish all politeness would be to do just that.[29] True politeness emanates from kindness, and the world that we have had better not try to do without it. This politeness would be a positive civility, a holding together of sociable relations in situations where absolute honesty is neither needed nor productive: hence, a minor virtue. But when politeness becomes obligatory or covers over conflicts that really deserve to see the light of day, it is bound to be repressive. In a world where public confrontation is seen as likely to lead to violence, it makes sense to do as much disciplinary work as possible by informal and self-administered means. One is more likely to revolt against a law than against a habit of good behavior. This is why Burke was just as worried about a revolution in manners as one against kings and princes.

Godwin's sustained etymological effort to carve out a place for positive politeness as virtue and urbanity rather than hypocrisy is something of a rearguard effort to resist a shifting language register in which politeness and civility increasingly find themselves tainted by bad histories and changing times. Carlyle, despite his critique, does not give up completely on these terms, even as the expanding, Arnoldian sense of culture begins to appear in his writings. And yet even Burke, whose defense of chivalry attracted such ire from his opponents, is (as we have seen) not much given to invoke civility or politeness. Jane Austen's *Pride and Prejudice* provides clear evidence of the shift in emphasis in the vocabulary describing social and sociable interactions. Civility, occurring seventeen times, is a clearly negative attribute in all but a third of them; meanwhile, civil denotes a hypocritical front rather than a genuinely polite gesture in nine of its eleven uses. In the case of politeness and polite, the balance is reversed. Seven cases of the first are positive (including two neutral but not negative); only one is negative ("cold politeness"). The same goes for polite. Austen thus for the most part hangs on to politeness at the frequent expense of civility.[30] The toing and froing continues among the major exponents of the novel of manners. Thackeray's *Vanity Fair* does not use civility, is mostly neutral in its employment of civil as polite, often ironizes polite/ness and always undercuts refined/refinement. Trollope (on the evidence of four novels) does not make heavy use of civility, but when he does (six times), it is always negative. The same pattern holds for the 'industrial' novels of the mid-nineteenth century. Gaskell's *Mary Barton* accepts civil as polite (five times) but has no use for politeness; Dickens's *Hard Times* makes no use of civility, and its few instances of polite/ness are negative all but once. Meanwhile, George Eliot's *Middlemarch* is given to a positive coding of polite but a largely negative one of politeness, seeming happier with an adjective than with a more portentous, substantive concept.

There are other examples, but enough has been said, I hope, to suggest that the nineteenth-century novel, perhaps the dominant medium for depicting and directing the manners of the reading (and listening) classes, remained as acutely concerned with finding the right words for social interaction as *Pamela* had been. It may not be accidental that many of the novels so highly attuned to the discrimination of civility terms were written by women, whose status had for centuries been deployed as measuring rods for the progress of a male-dominated 'civilization.' There is a visible turn away from civility as a good word for doing the job and a less emphatic but still visible suspicion of politeness.[31] Culture, as we have seen with Arnold, appears in nonfictional prose (in its sense as *Bildung*) as a new shibboleth. Accompanying this is an emphasis on manners, another imprecise word describing both simple habits and the general-systematic practices that govern societies at large (as in the French *moeurs*), at which point it overlaps with the anthropological sense of culture.[32] Burke's *Reflections* makes a great deal of the importance of manners, which for him are more important than laws in governing human behavior and far more efficient in subduing violence. In his anti-Jacobin writings throughout the 1790s, manners figure consistently as a key to social and political consensus, invoked along with "laws, customs . . . and habits of life."[33] They seem to be akin to customs and habits but quite different from the law. They are more important than laws because they operate constantly rather than occasionally, in a "constant, steady, uniform, insensible operation, like that of the air we breathe in." As such they "give their whole form and colour to our lives" (pp. 99–100). Wollstonecraft's *Vindication of the Rights of Woman* invokes manners even more frequently than Burke, but in a more critical sense: the dominance of manners over morals is the cause of all our troubles, and female manners in particular are in need of a revolution: virtuous sincerity must displace politeness, sentiment and sensibility.[34] Her book is indeed introduced as a treatise "on female rights and manners."[35] Richardson, interestingly, had made very little of manners in the first three volumes of *Pamela*; only in the fourth does the word begin to feature commonly, and here mostly in a low-key sense, indicating degrees of polite behavior and only touching occasionally on its more general sense as customs. Manners, for Burke and others, fills the conceptual slot abdicated by civility and politeness, doing the work that the inherited terms appear unable to sustain. But culture's grander ambitions would prove more persuasive in holding the line against the specter of violence. How was the discussion being shaped in the other dominantly anglophone sector of the globe?

Democracy in America: Civility without Literature?

Consulting James Fenimore Cooper's *The American Democrat* (1838) might persuade us that civility is a very important word indeed. "Civility and decency" are the roots of all civilization, "civility and respect" the "sure accompaniments of a high civilization."[36] But civilization is used here in a circumscribed, personal sense; it does not invoke the expanded present-day designation of the progress of a nation or of the human species. The topic that here frames Cooper's discussion is that of "deportment." Deportment comprises both "breeding" and "that which, though less distinguished for finesse and finish, denoting a sense of civility and respect, is usually termed manners" (p. 151). Taking over Burke's vocabulary, Cooper finds that manners above all are "indispensable to civilization," and manners are open to all to achieve, "as easily acquired as reading and writing," while breeding is inevitably more restrictive. Cooper then goes on to make a remarkable claim: civility is "an inherent quality of the American character" (p. 153) and not dependent upon breeding. Inherent civility and acquired manners, it seems, can happily guide the social destiny of the nation.

Can reading and writing help? What does it mean to imagine civility as "inherent" in "character," and a national character at that? It seems not to come *from* reading and writing, even though it is as easily acquired *as* reading and writing. To exercise civility is a "moral obligation," and "common civilities" are basic to all social life (pp. 155–56): Cooper would feel very much at home in our current rhetorical climate. Although America occupies only a "middle place in the scale" of civilization (as measured in manners), that civilization is "more equally diffused" there than it is anywhere else (p. 163). Thus, the "national deportment" is generally good, "without being polished, supplying the deficiency in this last essential by great kindness and civility" (p. 152). Democracy, it seems, does a better job than old-world hierarchy in diffusing the most essential conditions of nonviolent social cohesion. Can this be the same author who published *The Pioneers* (1823), which had no use for the word civility and makes only one ironic mention of politeness? The rapidly growing town of Templeton is populated by wily lawyers and sharp tradesmen among whom manners are often either minimal or part of a strategy of cynical self-advancement. Environmental destruction (fish, birds, timber) follows settlement, which displaces not only the last Indian but the upright backwoodsman who is the hero of the Leatherstocking novels. If kindness and civility are to rule, why are they are in such short supply on the western frontier that Cooper represents in his novel? Natty Bumppo is kind and civil enough, albeit also an efficient killer, but there is no place for him in the new settlement. His tragic irony is to devote his best virtues to enabling the progress of those same destructive energies that will push him further into exile as their pathfinder. The juxtaposition of Cooper's political tract with his findings as a novelist suggests a fundamental schism in his imagining of an American national character: a potentially complacent self-esteem stands beside a raw exposure of the devastating effects of racism and emergent entrepreneurial capitalism. The nonfiction seems fictive, while the fiction represents a world that looks very real.

The same tension can also be seen in the commentaries on American manners that were a lively part of the book trade in the nineteenth century. British travelers especially—Fanny Trollope, Captain Basil Hall, and Charles Dickens famously among them—found much to complain of in the new world: violence, self-interest, surly servants, chewing and spitting tobacco and a far-too-influential and vitriolic newspaper culture, along with the scarcity of any more substantial literature. Although Fanny Trollope actually admired a number of American writers, there was widespread agreement on both sides of the Atlantic until the middle of the century that America had no important literature of its own. The best it could do was to rely on imports from Britain, which brought with them the best thoughts in the best language. The nativist consensus generated around *Pamela* in England could not occur in a place whose literary standards came from abroad, and from a place whose political identity was, moreover, predominantly monarchist. National adaptations could be made—hence Cooper was widely received as the American Walter Scott—but it could never be imagined that American manners would be determined solely by an American literature as long as few actual Americans were reading it.[37] American civility, as Cooper argued, must then be "inherent" to the degree that it does not come from reading novels. Reading was always important to the cultivation of gentility and to what came to be called "mental culture," as Richard Bushman has made clear, and sentimental fiction focusing on the condition of women was its major component; but when *Pamela* was first widely circulated, it was not the product of a foreign country. After 1776, it became so.[38]

Further, as *The Pioneers* demonstrates, an American literature cannot promise to represent an unclouded dissemination of civility throughout the expanding nation. Walt Whitman does indeed articulate the democratic shout, but gothic violence, race hatred and slavery are inescapable in the literature of the evolving republic, as in the world it is compelled to record.[39] In this respect American literature might be deemed more reflective of its larger historical conditions than much of what was being written in Britain, where the events (and often outrages) of empire formation mostly appear marginal to an introspective 'condition of England' mentality.[40] The strained performance of civility governing the interactions between the naïve New England sea captain and the crew of the *San Dominick* in Melville's "Benito Cereno" barely serves to keep at bay the simmering violence immanent in the slave trade. *Moby-Dick*, *The Confidence Man*, *The Scarlet Letter*, and other novels like them, are hardly available to serve as conduct manuals for refined living. Colin Dayan suggests that the violent, gothic fabric of so much American fiction may have to do not only with the appeal of a literary genre but also with the very fabric of American legal culture in its weird mechanics devoted to "making and unmaking persons" and calling for a "resilient acceptance of unreality" in its efforts to contain the bizarre conditions of chattel slavery. Thus, she finds, "specters are very much part of the legal domain."[41]

The tone of Cooper's *The American Democrat* suggests that nonfictional addresses to American civic and political life, implicitly the domain of white former Europeans, might offer a more promising source of self-esteem. Writing about an America that has no distinctive literature of its own could provide permission to ignore the literature it did have, when that literature reflects an unfavorable picture of the national destiny by insisting on representing all of those persons not recognized as citizens: blacks, Native Americans, women. For whatever reason, assessing the consequences of this perceived lack of a national literature became a leitmotif of cultural commentary before the middle of the century. Tocqueville, writing in 1835, confirms the absence of "literary genius" in the United States, attributing it to the nonexistence of any "freedom of mind." The majority lives in a state of complacent self-esteem, projecting a "sort of disfavor" for "literature properly so-called."[42] But this is not a disabling condition. The "Anglo-Americans" were already "civilized" when they crossed the ocean, and it is from hands-on political engagement that Americans learn to live together. Instead of private life informing public life, as it does in Europe, it is public life that comes first: the "great work of society" is a participatory activity where citizens (implicitly white and male) learn the protocols of self-governance (pp. 290–92). The passage from private to public sphere by way of reading and conversation that Habermas proposes as typical of eighteenth-century Britain therefore does not apply to America. This does not mean that nobody read novels or paid attention to conduct books: many historians have made clear that they did. But it does mean, according to Tocqueville, that the essential functions of American democracy do not depend on exemplary fictions or on "speculative studies" (p. 403). Further, religious rigor among the founders was "naturally little favorable to the fine arts" or the "advanced sciences" (pp. 428–29), and the agitation exhibited by citizens of a democracy is not conducive to the "meditation" and "calm necessary to the profound combinations of the intellect" (p. 434). Such a society will always favor the useful over the beautiful (p. 439), thus embodying exactly the historical tendency most feared by Schiller and Arnold. In the absence of a national culture, there circulates a preponderance of English authors who "transport into the midst of a democracy the ideas and literary usages that are current in the aristocratic nation they have taken for a model" (p. 445). They are therefore "rarely popular" and "do not act on mores" (p. 446). The American literature to come will be a more demotic thing—bold, bizarre, rapidly produced, appealing more to passion than to taste (p. 449). For the time being, and perhaps luckily, American civility must remain decoupled from literary reading and pedagogy.

Tocqueville's prognosis is of course no very exact index of a world in which British authors did continue to exercise authority over subcultural elites and in which, in a very few years, an American author would write and publish *Moby-Dick* (though not at first to any popular acclaim). The American language, Tocqueville also speculates, "will abandon little by little the terrain of metaphysics and theology" (p. 454)—another dubious hypothesis, at least in terms of literary language. The topics of poetry, he thinks, will become more grandiose and sublime, owing to the proclivity to envision "the human race as a single whole" (p. 462). And the language of the general population will drift toward greater and greater use of "generic terms and abstract words" because they are more economical but also more vague. Thus, "an abstract word is like a box with a false bottom: one puts in it the ideas one desires and one takes them out without anyone's seeing it." In this way they at once "enlarge and veil a thought" (pp. 456–57). Hobbes had warned long before of the slipperiness of abstract terms and their availability for deceiving and manipulating a public. Civility and politeness, one might think, with their history of antithetical designations (sincerity and hypocrisy, kindness and self-interest), would be in practice popular in the world that Tocqueville here describes.

The written record, however, suggests that they were not deemed fundamental in theory, perhaps because they were all-too-ready resources for the confidence man. As terms of convenience and over-general identification, they could not function convincingly as foundations of positive sociability. Tocqueville does not see language and literature working this way at all; what contributes most critically to the maintenance of democracy is lived experience within conditions of equality. This equality is more important to Americans than freedom itself: they will tolerate "poverty, enslavement, barbarism, but they will not tolerate aristocracy" (p. 482). In America, unusually, equality is equally distributed between civil and political associations, each contributing to the cultivation of the other. Associations in general are the "mother science": "The progress of all the others depends on the progress of that one" (p. 492). America is full of associations. Persons (male citizens) of all kinds "constantly unite" (p. 489), so the division between civil society and the state that marks so many other theories of governance is not here a radical one. What mediates the potential disjunction is *local* politics, where everyone can expect to participate and where the alienating attributes of a representative democracy do not pertain. This underpins Tocqueville's famous endorsement of the New England township, whose "communal and political freedoms" (p. 381) would become the gold standard for so many later political scientists, both as a participatory ideal and as a countertype to the power of federal government.[43]

The township is, needless to say, an exemplary instance of a small-group formation, where issues of inclusion and expression can be pitched at a face-to-face level and adjudicated interpersonally: the round tables that featured in anglophone rhetoric after 1989 served the same purpose. This in turn sponsors a model of peaceful evolution, where the work that civility might otherwise be called upon to perform is already done. Notwithstanding Tocqueville's famous remarks on the irritability, agitation and clamor of American democracy, its restiveness and openness to a possible tyranny of the majority, large sections of his book project a conviction that the United States is characterized by an overarching peace and tranquility. The country, being one large nation, has no fear of war (p. 160), and being an "empty continent" (p. 267) there is room for all to establish themselves on an expanding frontier without violent mutual competition (Tocqueville's working assumption is that the Native American is inevitably disappearing). The model of the township "impresses on society a continual, but at the same time peaceful, movement that agitates it without troubling it" (p. 65). Thus, the necessary energy (agitation) that powers society is contained by "the slow and tranquil action of society on itself" (p. 379).[44] What Tocqueville describes is a perfect Arnoldian paradigm where evolution preempts the appeal of revolution, rendering violence unnecessary. In the United States, this allows for a weak and relatively distant central (federal) government. It is equality, not strong government, that holds persons in check and makes them peaceable: the more equality there is, the less warlike they become (pp. 535, 617).

This is a very different model from the Hobbesian one, which relies upon a strong centralized state possessing the power of violence over its citizens as the guarantor of civic order.[45] It differs also from Arnold's model in needing no recourse to the best that is known and thought in the world. So powerful is the equality condition that it requires little or no assistance from pedagogy or from reading the right kind of literature:

> When ranks are almost equal in a people, all men having nearly the same manner of thinking and feeling, each of them can judge the sensations of all the others in a moment: he casts a rapid glance at himself; that is enough for him. There is therefore no misery he does not conceive without trouble and whose extent a secret instinct does not discover for him. It makes no difference whether it is a question of strangers or of enemies: imagination immediately puts him in their place. (p. 538)

There is nothing here of the strenuous effort at adjusting one's feelings and responses to an acceptable norm, upon which Adam Smith's theory of sociability famously depends. Nothing here either about the value of sentimental novels as an important means for allowing us to imagine the condition of others. Perhaps Tocqueville was too preoccupied with the purported influence of literature and philosophy as primary causes of the French Revolution to want to rely upon them here in his brave new world. Whatever his reasons, he sees imagined equality as itself enough to overcome all the bedeviling effects of divided labor, class and education. Living under assumptions of equality causes us to imagine that there are no critical differences between one person and another. (The United States remains a country wherein multimillionaires can successfully project themselves as ordinary people.) This remains the case whether an actual or more complex equality be fact or fiction. Vast fortunes might be made by some at the expense of others, but as long as basic political equality remains, we are disposed to accept that we have no grounds for complaint.[46] In Tocqueville's model, that same equality—a state of mind rather than of voting rights—solves the problem of civility. Manners are no longer identified as the property of a limited group, so they do not need conscious dissemination or discussion; one mode of behavior works for all. If I offend my neighbor, it is not because I am not his equal, so any misunderstandings that might occur are much less threatening and critical than they are in class-based societies. This is of course an ideal or normative construction, one not infrequently tested in the rough and tumble of actual, historical life.[47] As such it is fenced off from any mention of race (slavery and genocide), which appears in the book only as a quite separate discussion to which we will soon come. For now let us note that it reflects a displacement of both civility and literature as foundational principles of social bonding. Something similar was happening to civility in nineteenth-century Britain, but few British opinion makers were invested in discovering or endorsing full equality, which mostly remained part of the rhetoric of radicalism. There, literature remained important, perhaps all the more important because faith in civility was diminishing and because it could be readily deployed for the fashioning of a bureaucratic and pedagogic elite.

How typical is Tocqueville's relative marginalization of both literature and civility as essential agents of American democracy? A different representative case might be Emerson, certainly not the least bookish of American writers. Throughout his career Emerson maintains that the flowering of American literature is yet to come and that it will come only when the worship of European models is given up. But the lack of a literary tradition is not critical, because, as Emerson argues in "The American Scholar" (1837), even the scholar's mind is influenced first by nature and by "action" and only secondarily by books. Books can in fact even be a threat to the "active soul," given that they "look backward and not forward." (Fanon would agree with this.) And action is as important to the true scholar as it is to any other man.[48] What is most important to manners emerges "spontaneous from the mind's own sense of good and fair," while books are "for the scholar's idle times" (1:73). Emerson's immersion in Goethe, Coleridge and Wordsworth has not led him to privilege any Arnoldian conservation of literatures of the past, although he shares Arnold's faith in the importance of "culture" (*Bildung*) as the "upbuilding of a man" toward "oneness of the mind" (1:86–87). Culture is the necessary corrective to the influence of unfettered wealth and power; books contribute to it, but they are not everything and should not be used as a refuge from the inspirations of ordinary life: "You send your child to the schoolmaster, but 'tis the schoolboys who educate him" (5:114). Culture has some of the qualities of Shaftesbury's inmate controller: it is "the suggestion from certain best thoughts, that a man has a range of affinities, through which he can modulate the violence of any master-tones that have a droning preponderance in his scale, and succor him against himself" (5:109). It is thus a kind of internal civility of the self toward itself, countering tendencies toward violence before they emerge in public. It is founded in the "moral sentiment" and provides a self-reliance and "personal independence which the monarch cannot look down, and to which he must often succumb" (6:159, 168). Emerson's adoption of the German idea of *Bildung* combines the emphasis on introspection and solitary self-cultivation (readily conformable to the one great idea of his Transcendentalist philosophy) with an easeful participation in the rituals of an American everyday life governed by "acts of good-nature, common civility, and Christian charity" (6:153). And both sit beside a powerfully Shelleyan model of the poet as creator and medium of universal and enduring beauty and connectivity whose American incarnation is yet to come.

Emerson's essay "Civilisation" absorbs into its conceptual catchment both culture and civility. Civilization is explained as a "vague, complex name, of many degrees" that implies "the evolution of a highly-organised man, brought to supreme delicacy of sentiment, as in practical power, religion, liberty, sense of honour, and taste" (5:281). Each "nation" has its own civilization, which is made synonymous with both culture and civility, as well as "civil freedom" (5:283, 285, 286). As well as having local-national inflections, "civility" (as civilization) evolves historically, for example, with the passage from hunting to pasturage to agriculture as described by eighteenth-century stadial theory (5:283). The racialized assumptions of much stadial theory persist: hot climates do not favor the "highest civility," which cannot persist without "a deep morality" (5:286–87). Civility is measured by the degree to which the state is committed to work for "the greatest good of the greatest number" (5:293). Emerson here conflates three of the terms (civility, civilization, culture) whose identities and distinctions appear throughout the history of social and political thought, and he gives them their weightiest inflections. All extend well beyond the description of mere polite behavior and direct attention away from individual qualities toward a more extensive notion of *moeurs* as governing the disposition of larger groups and larger issues of the sort we often now refer to as culture in its anthropological sense. There is an overlap, but the relation is never made fully clear. Emerson himself observes that "there is something equivocal in all the words in use to express the excellence of manners and social cultivation, because the quantities are fluxional, and the last effect is assumed by the senses as the cause" (2:403). But one can and should preserve a primary respect for the idea of the gentleman as based on a "personal force" (2:404) that is above and beyond what is recognized by the fashionable world and its tolerance for courtesy as sometimes merely a "means of selfishness" (2:422).

Emerson's analysis of manners thus steers our focus away from how we deport ourselves at fashionable gatherings toward a metaphysical grounding in culture, which is culture of the self, very much in the Arnoldian sense: a quite different model from Tocqueville's reliance upon the rough and tumble of the public sphere. Civility has a positive role insofar as it is just another term for civilization, and culture now includes nature: introspection and openness to nature are more important than any social interactions. Sympathy is assumed, rather as it is in Tocqueville, albeit for different reasons: culture and universal human nature rather than political equality govern Emerson's world. In neither case is there a primary need for literature as countering violence. But there is a need for nature, whose medicinal powers "sober and heal us" (2:442). Nature too participates in the Wordsworthian injunction to up and quit our books and hear the woodland linnet. In Britain, John Stuart Mill takes an Emersonian position in his focus on nature and on self-reliance—which he too calls culture—but remains much more visibly committed to the resources of literature. Starting out with the desire to be a "reformer of the world," Mill famously found himself impaled on the horns of the dilemma so powerfully described by Schiller, that of being forced to choose the intellect at the expense of the feelings.[49] A chance reading of Marmontel opened him to the value of the feelings and did for him what the game of backgammon did for Hume: "I gradually found that the ordinary incidents of life could give me some pleasure; that I could again find enjoyment, not intense, but sufficient for cheerfulness, in sunshine and sky, in books, in conversation, in public affairs" (p. 85). What Marmontel began, a reading of Wordsworth completed, unifying all the disparate elements of Mill's personality—"thought coloured by feeling, under the excitement of beauty" (p. 89)—and bridging the gap between the self and the natural world. And with this comes a new onset of sympathy and sociability, no longer purely abstract ideas but felt experiences operating against the besetting national obsession with self-interest, giving him something of the "frank sociability and amiability" more typical of French than English life (p. 38). But it is *reading* Wordsworth write *about* nature that saves Mill's sanity, not wandering in person over hill and dale.

Mill's order of operations suggests that the proper blend of thinking and feeling first comes from an "internal culture of the individual" (p. 86), and as such it is consonant with an anglicized version of *Bildung* that turned not to the Greeks but to Wordsworth for an experience having "no connection with struggle or imperfection" and discovering "real, permanent happiness in tranquil contemplation" (p. 89). The self, in other words, cultures itself *before* facing the social world, and not by way of it;

culture must precede society if one is to live a happy and fulfilling life. Even nature seems to enter his experience principally by way of a written medium. The experience of literature is preserved free from the violence that affects the social sphere, and it purifies the self of its own depressive or destructive impulses. Violence and conflict are thus not constitutive of subjectivity itself, intrinsic to its self-experience and being in the world, and here Mill is in the mainstream of anglophone philosophy: for a different inflection we turn to Hegel, Nietzsche, Schopenhauer and Freud.[50] Violence for Mill and Arnold, as for Schiller and Shelley before them, came from the outside, from the deforming influences of vested interest and divided labor or from the riotous behavior of political zealots and excitable crowds. Good literature eschews and defends against violence.

This does not work to describe the American literature that was coming into being despite the widespread presumption against its likely emergence. The gothic imaginations of Brockden Brown, Hawthorne and Melville are energized by struggles with the dark forces invoked by the sterner Puritan theologies, and Cooper, the American Walter Scott, is finally unable to mimic the progressive modernization narrative of his distinguished precursor. The American frontier is colonized at the point of a gun rather than by the peaceful persuasions of an expanding commercial economy. *Uncle Tom's Cabin*, the book that Lincoln claimed (or so it is widely held) to have started a war, sustains its Christian sentimentalism without flinching from its indictment of the most cruel and evil manifestation of the national destiny. Tocqueville himself could maintain his theoretical equanimity only by leaving aside, for long tracts of his argument, the actual conditions within which the white American played out his imagined democratic rituals. Only after some three hundred pages does he bring up the questions raised by the coexistence of two other "races" on the same continent, and then only with a note of awkward apology:

> My subject has often led me to speak of the Indians and the Negroes, but I have never had the time to stop in order to show what position these two races occupy in the midst of the democratic people that I was occupied with depicting.[51]

To have done so would definitely have disturbed the depiction. These races are deemed "American without being democratic" and are thus peripheral or residual to the main topic at hand. They have separate destinies, ones that bring out the very worst in the white man's America: "He makes them serve his use, and when he cannot bend them, he destroys them" (p. 303). Blacks are conditioned to servile mimicry, Indians to a stubborn resistance that ends only in death. Indians will thus inevitably perish, as they are already doing; the challenge they present will soon pass away. Blacks, on the other hand, present a problem that will not disappear with the abolition of slavery, should it ever come: the problem of racism. The two races, Tocqueville projects, "will never come to live on a footing of equality" (p. 341). Initially this possibility is preempted by white supremacy and its commitment to mastery; now, things are so bad that, with or without the continuation of slavery itself, there is no foreseeable outcome other than radical violence. If the slaves are refused their freedom, "they will in the end seize it violently themselves; if one grants it to them, they will not be slow to abuse it" (p. 348). Tocqueville himself appears not to be free of the racism he professes to analyze.

So we have here the image of a white democracy—again, a democracy limited to white males—that is engaged in genocide toward Native Americans while desperately trying to hold down the eruptive violence threatened by African Americans. No theorization of civility could be expected to handle such circumstances; the natural civility that white citizens emanate is a racialized attribute that cannot be applied to those outside the democratic umbrella and cannot appeal to those brought across the ocean against their will and consigned to a life of slavery. Nor can literature readily propose itself as a place of refuge where the nurturing of *Bildung* can be carried on. *Uncle Tom's Cabin*, published as a single narrative in 1852, reportedly sold 150,000 copies in America alone in the first six months.[52] Sales figures are notoriously imprecise, and no one knows how many people read each copy. But Stowe's sales were clearly huge: Richard D. Altick lists forty editions within twelve months and proposes a figure of 1.5 million books in the same period, "including colonial sales."[53] What is remarkable here is not just the sales figures, give or take, but the topic of the novel: chattel slavery, which seems to have commanded the attentions of a global anglophone readership. Dickens's most overtly 'activist' novels, *Hard Times* and *Oliver Twist*, sold well but were not his best sellers, nor did the 'condition of England' novel in general achieve anything like Stowe's notoriety. Cooper and Stowe together chronicle the two great emanations of American violence: slavery and the destruction of Native

America. The evolution of empire in the United States is at this time predominantly continental: it is occurring across a land mass continuous with the physical environment of the white settlers, where Indians are assigned to a shrinking frontier and blacks specified as a threat from within.[54] Violence is omnipresent and hard to ignore, and as the energy fueling continental expansion it can hardly be done away with.[55] In Britain, the novel is more habitually concerned with marriage, money and morality in the provincial mode. The shadow of empire impinges, of course, as Edward Said's *Culture and Imperialism* has made clear: in the penumbral plantation economy that sustains Mansfield Park; in the exotic orientalist characters of *Vanity Fair*, *The Moonstone*, *The Sign of Four*; in the Caribbean affiliations of *Belinda* and *Jane Eyre*; in the toing and froing between the homeland and the Australian territories. These moments nag at the edges of the fictional canon rather like the war wound Dr. Watson brought back from the Afghan campaign, mostly dormant and needing attention only from time to time. But Britain has no *Uncle Tom's Cabin*, no established classic of the violence of empire: of the Opium Wars, the Indian Mutiny, the scramble for Africa. City life and country life, farm and factory, form the core of the Victorian novel: the collective national history that is the Waverley Novels is similarly insular. Ireland barely registers. At the end of the century, the constant but seemingly purposeless motion that drives so many of Conrad's protagonists appears as an epic of pure mobility aiming beyond the setting sun. The empire's eventual revenge—*The Beetle*, *Pharos the Egyptian*, *She*—is vivid enough in the gothic manner, but its violence is no match for that of the mother country.

Teaching Literature against Violence

Although the proximity of Ireland did complicate matters, the general remoteness of most of the empire enables British fiction largely to restrict the confrontation with racial violence to the peripheries of the national consciousness. The *Bildungsroman* can thus develop within a largely nativist ethos, more commonly encountering the violence of class consciousness and industrialization than the dynamics of racism itself. More optimism can be attached to a literature that transcribes theoretically resolvable conflicts than to one addressing the implacable divisions that Tocqueville described in America. Sweetness and light can cope more easily with class and educational differences than with an added, intransigent racism.[56] Arnold famously took issue with the pompous self-worship of the 'Anglo-Saxon race' and argued for a cosmopolitanism of both place and time. He ranged more than most beyond the borders of Europe in his enthusiasms and acknowledgments. But the core of his literary canon, though not dominantly anglophone, was principally classical and European. Nonetheless, it has been plausibly argued that the formation of anglophone literary pedagogy as a distinct practice was the result of encounters with both national and global-racial differences in Scotland and India, respectively. Robert Crawford proposes the origins of 'English' literature in provincial sites where it caters to "socio-economic ambition" and compensates for "anti-provincial linguistic prejudice."[57] His major focus is Scotland, where the lectures on rhetoric given by Adam Smith (in Glasgow) and Hugh Blair (in Edinburgh) provide a formalized grammatical and elocutionary asset, mediated through literature, to an aspiring professional class.[58] After the Jacobite rebellions of 1715 and 1745, Scotland undergoes a process of pacification and assimilation that projects large numbers of qualified Scots into the administrative and educational cadres of both Britain and its empire.

The case of India is very different. Here, the sheer numbers of those being governed, the size of the subcontinent and its distance from the motherland, along with the continual physical violence of exploitation and repression, made for much more anxious efforts at developing coping mechanisms for keeping the masses in a peaceably huddled condition. Gauri Viswanathan has given us a detailed account of attempts at managing British India through the teaching of literature. The 1813 Charter Act established British responsibility for educating its subjects, and from 1835 that education stipulated a study of English literature, almost forty years before the British domestic school system (in 1872) took the same step.[59] The Indian sphere raised questions not encountered in Britain: debates between anglicists and orientalists, arguments for and against Christianization and decisions about how to interact with India's own diverse faiths. Macaulay's 1835 "Minute on Indian Education" has become notorious for its dismissal of the value of printing and circulating items of native culture, but there had also been a countervailing, positive estimate of Indian literature and philosophy in the work of Sir William Jones from the 1780s on. Viswanathan suggests that while a good deal of Christian doctrine could be smuggled in along with the teaching of literature without resorting to any formal theology, the full potential of *Bildung*, with its commitment to autonomous self-development, could not be offered to the natives without becoming a source of subversion and discontent. Encouraging Indians to imbibe British culture without offering them tangible rewards was a risk, one further enhanced by the inevitable racism directed by the colonizers at the colonized.[60] Thus, it is argued, India's version of "the Western literary canon evolved out of a position of vulnerability, not of strength" (p. 168).

There are no novels in this canon; poetry, drama, history and belles lettres dominate the curricula, with Romantic writers figuring in the missionary lists, and eighteenth-century writers in those of the government schools.[61] So too the Arnoldian paradigm imagined for domestic use ignores the British novel that had been visibly flourishing for over a hundred years. The novel is apparently imagined more as entertainment for the common reader than as a sophisticated genre requiring learned skills and vocabularies for its appreciation. It is also prone to going beyond the cultivation of a merely contemplative reading subject in its representation of a range of social, educational and economic types. It is thereby more likely to have to register incidences of violence, even when they are finessed. Arnoldian culture (as *Bildung*) was conceived along Schillerian lines as an antidote to violence, which meant that it had to remain very selective about what kinds of literature it could sponsor, as well as staying away from the more disturbing possibilities opened up in the inevitable modern compulsion to "the dialogue of the mind with itself," the possibilities opened up by theory, Romantic irony and (eventually) psychoanalysis.[62] Literature specifically, as long as it is the best, offers to heal or avoid the tendency for religion to lapse into divisiveness and dogma. Not everyone agreed. But even John Henry Newman, who held that literature could never overcome the sinful condition of man or provide the severe and sublime inspiration that religion alone afforded, was willing to sustain a liberal education as the core of a university regime, able to restrain "passion and self-will" and displace "the excitements of sense by . . . those of the intellect."[63] In a fully Arnoldian spirit, Newman cites Copleston on the cultivation of literature as that which "unites the jarring sects and subdivisions into one interest, which supplies common topics, and kindles common feelings, unmixed with those narrow prejudices with which all professions are more or less infected" (p. 128). It is a good thing to be the "gentleman" that liberal education aims to produce and to "have a cultivated intellect, a delicate taste, a candid, equitable, dispassionate mind, a noble and courteous bearing in the conduct of life," but these things are not to be mistaken for conscience, humility or faith. A measure of the long-standing discomfort with politeness and civility appears in Newman's reminder that these attributes may "attach to the man of the world, to the profligate, to the heartless" (p. 91). The product of liberal education is a fine example of Hume's conversable man, but he acquires a skill that can be adapted to dishonest and deceptive ends as he learns "how to accommodate himself to others, how to throw himself into their state of mind, how to bring before them his own, how to influence them" (p. 135). Newman here echoes the worries raised among many readers of Chesterfield's *Letters*. Literature likewise "persuades instead of convincing, it seduces, it carries captive" (p. 178). Literature here is identified with rhetoric rather than *Bildung*: the liberal gentleman is thus never fully distinguishable from the confidence man. But at least the true gentleman "never inflicts pain" and works toward peace, "his great concern being to make every one at their ease and at home" (p. 159). This cannot ever be a full-fledged virtue, but it is an important agent of social stability and cohesion, and literature is part of its technology.

Again, in the later nineteenth century in Britain, and with the notable exception of the Irish question, fears of violence were not generally or inevitably racialized, as they were in India and in the Caribbean. But the dramatic increase in population, which more or less quadrupled between 1800 and 1900, meant that fear of the masses was never far away.[64] And violence began to appear as an object of positive theory rather than just a phobia to be conjured away. Perhaps it is not accidental that the Arnoldian effort to anticipate and manage social violence would take on a more exigent theorization in France, which had experienced more than a century of radical-revolutionary activity since 1789. Georges Sorel, advocating in 1906 for a creative turn to violence, saw a need to direct the working class away from culture and from "that section of the middle classes which concerns itself professionally with matters of the intellect."[65] Sorel, anticipating Fanon, delivers a warning against the worship of literary authors whose output is always a residue of an aristocratic culture modified by the needs of a consolidating middle class. Thus, we must beware of "an aesthetic education of the proletariat under the tutelage of modern artists" (p. 54). In fact, "literary, moral, or sociological considerations have very little effect upon people born outside the ranks of the middle classes" (p. 72). Antagonisms are to be embraced rather than suppressed by dialogic rituals; working-class violence, in the form of riots and strikes, is an effective tool for change and should not be disparaged. Far from being an emanation of barbarism, as the pacifists maintain, it may actually "save the world from barbarism" (p. 98). It can do so because its aim is the complete overthrow of the existing order, "without hatred and without the spirit of revenge" (p. 115), and in a way that makes impossible the reversion to charismatic leadership (of the sort that would in fact occur with European fascism). Revolutionary syndicalism will and must above all avoid the brutal legitimations of the French Revolution that gave violence a bad name (pp. 103, 116, 275), including the literary and academic justifications advanced by the "men of letters, professors of philosophy, and historians of the Revolution" (p. 115). The violence of the proletarian general strike must therefore come as a "catastrophe" that "baffles description," an as-if unpremeditated bolt from the blue, one without any judicial-political rationale, one whose aim is simply the destruction of what has been given (p. 148). As such, it is to be welcomed.

British modernists such as Wyndham Lewis and T. E. Hulme (Sorel's translator), like their expatriate American friends Pound and Eliot, tended toward right-wing affiliations, sometimes including validations of violence. Harder to categorize is Walter Benjamin's "Critique of Violence," written in a divided and chaotic postwar Germany, which commends a role for a "divine violence" that, while owing much to Sorel, offers as one of its leading examples precisely the sphere of education and "letters" that Sorel himself so loudly decried. Divine violence also comes as a lightning bolt, out of nowhere, with no political program or judicial rationale; only thus can it preserve its purity and its immunity from bureaucratic co-optation and entanglement with the law. It is thus essentially nonviolent in its very violence: that is the conundrum it presents for us to decipher. Nonviolent (*gewaltlos*) resolution of human disputes *is* possible, as in the experience of dialogue, conversation and conferencing (*Unterredung*), exchanges based in a "civilized outlook." Benjamin echoes the nineteenth-century spirit of *Bildung* in invoking as the basis of this outlook the "culture of the hearts of men" (*die Kultur des Herzens des Menschen*).[66] The preconditions for this include "courtesy" (*Herzenshöflichkeit*) and "peaceableness" (*Friedensliebe*), the familiar components of civility. Divine violence (*göttliche Gewalt*) as pure violence may on the contrary involve death and extinction but is outside the law, a means without an end. Benjamin's first example of divine violence is familiar: the proletarian general strike as postulated by Sorel, which destroys what is in place without establishing any specific political alternative. His second example, somewhat obscurely, is the "educative power" (*erzieherische Gewalt*) that, in German, hovers between violence and the power of violence (not captured in translation) but is "annihilating" (*vernichtend*) if not of the "soul" of the living, at least "relatively" of the realm of ethical goods and rights and, in some sense, of life itself (*Güter, Recht, Leben*).[67] The echo of Schiller's key word (*erzieherische*) may be contingent or deliberate; but the specification of this function as "outside the law" suggests something either private or within the university, a disinterested, nonutilitarian practice of pedagogy very much in the spirit of Schiller's aesthetic education. The indifference to political ends also conforms to the earlier model. Benjamin's two examples taken together are indeed weighted toward the protocols of the aesthetic, since the proletarian general strike also displays a distance from empirical outcomes. Both avoid the necessity for physical conflict; in this sense they accord much more comfortably with the conventions of literature and civility. They are called (the power of) violence, but they are not conventionally violent.

The difficulty of parsing Benjamin's essay comes in part from trying to serve or perhaps to distinguish two different incarnations of *Gewalt*, one psycho-aesthetic and one distinctly physical and material. It is as if Schiller and Sorel and perhaps Lenin are each given a seat at the table, without our ever being told whether they could agree on what to order. Even Habermas might be imagined as a guest at this particular symposium whose rules include an apparent prohibition on taking the life of another but also a permitted exceptionalism about exactly that. Benjamin conjoins advocacy of a world-changing event he calls divine (power of) violence with an educational program that is at most reformist and a strike that is revolutionary in its "sole task of destroying state power" but that remains, as "pure means . . . nonviolent" (p. 246). Benjamin's text is not for easy comprehension, but one might argue that the idea of a "wholly transformed work" that the general strike aims to achieve without violence is the ultimate incursion of Schillerian aesthetics into politics. Certainly the notion of any goal-directed violence could only have been harder to defend after the events of 1914–18. The revolutionaries of 1789 and 1917 have both been deemed by some historians to have fallen into the trap of ruling by violence; at the same time they have been identified with a moment of pure means that was briefly bloodless before judicial, legislative and military habits and necessities reasserted themselves and ruined everything.[68] That moment, the moment of Benjamin's divine violence, appeals because it effects a radical change in the world without incurring an inevitable reversion to the shedding of blood. That it has not, historically, escaped that reversion nonetheless remains the case.

Benjamin was working on his essay toward the end of 1920, the year that also saw the founding of the League of Nations, whose ambition was nothing less than the avoidance of all future world wars. The Congress of Vienna in 1815 had had no such ambitions, and the commitment to diplomacy over armed conflict expressed by the subsequent Concert of Europe did not survive the Crimean War, nor was it ever much of an inhibition on the imperial violence deployed by Europeans in other parts of the world. The League of Nations fared little better, seeming doomed from the start by the unwillingness of the world powers to give up their sovereignty over other peoples or to build down the military world order. Nationalism, in short, continued to overpower internationalism, free-trade doctrines notwithstanding. Some Futurists and Surrealists weaponized the vocabulary of aesthetic theory in proposing art and literature as explosive and percussive, effective in a radical manner analogous to bombs and bullets. This language remained in place even after the Great War, leaving open the question of whether it was celebrating a literally destructive violence or refiguring it for creative purposes.[69] The somewhat less controversial language of lightning, shudder and shock continued to be acceptable by a generation committed to disturbing the complacency of modern society without seeming to approve the power of a yet more radical violence: art and literature should work to destroy prejudices but not lives. And yet, in the embrace of an aesthetic of explosiveness, some literary practitioners seem to have moved far away from any assimilation of literature with civility, as well as from the serene ideal of Arnoldian culture as a blueprint for individual lives.

How did this inform the college classrooms and tutorials that were taking shape around the time of Sorel's and Benjamin's theories? How, if at all, could they enact the directives of divine violence—identified by Benjamin as a pedagogic event—and what alternatives might they offer to Sorel's general strike? The inculcation of an energized and concerned response to violence, unignorable after the Great War as a destructive component of the 'civilized' nations themselves, was the ambition of a number of anglophone literary critics through the 1920s and beyond. Sometimes, like I. A. Richards, they explicitly referenced global military violence; more commonly and more modestly, the protocols of literary study were devised to address small-group conflict resolution of the sorts that arose from social and doctrinal differences, very much in the spirit of civility culture. Teaching literature took on the individualist project of culture as *Bildung*, with its emphasis on introspection and self-cultivation, and fed it into a more professionalized version of Hume's game of backgammon: the seminar or discussion group assembled around poems, plays and (eventually) novels. Private reading is preparatory to the miniature public sphere made up of educated readers committed to critical dialogue and the construction of consensus around the meaning of a text. F. R. Leavis, who scorned any notion of civility as mere politeness (which indeed he often flouted), nonetheless argued for a "third realm" of interaction, neither private nor fully public, where interpretations could be posited and tested in the protected space of the classroom, from which they might be carried forth into the wider world by those entering the teaching profession. The third realm is situated between private and public spheres, beyond singularity and poised at the point of entrance into a wider world. The meanings thus produced are neither *in* the text, in some essential way, nor the results of random contingencies but the outcome of encounters between pre-given language data, the words on the page and the communal intelligence embodied in the "re-creative response of individual minds."[70] The text thereby provides a place "in which minds can meet . . . in what is in some sense a public world" capable of a collaborative renewal of a "cultural community or consciousness." The past is carried into the present and directed toward the future, and while there is room for disagreement—indeed it is essential to invite "qualifications, reserves, corrections"—the sense of common endeavor and the relative disinterest involved in aesthetic experience make that disagreement finally nonviolent, sublimated into a common good (p. 28).

What is enacted here is very close to the practice of civility as described by Shaftesbury and Hume, a bringing together of differences openly expressed but held back from outright conflict. It is not just tolerance that makes this possible: Leavis is clear that the literary encounter does not simply leave things as they were but puts together a new consensus about what meanings matter and why, in a "living creative response to change in the present" (p. 27). His ambition is Arnoldian, and he shares T. S. Eliot's conviction that the critic's job is to "compose his differences with as many of his fellows as possible, in the common pursuit of true judgment."[71] The origins of this common pursuit are in small-group assemblies—even in a medium-sized lecture hall it is hard for every voice to be heard—but through publication and the training of a pedagogic discipleship in Leavisite protocols it was feasible to project a wider influence on British national culture. This commitment was carried into the schools and universities with a messianic fervor that intensified and formalized the ambitions of civility culture, now clearly dependent upon a qualified elite. In its efforts to circumvent the divisive effects of class and occupational distinctions (which Leavis associated with industrialization, advertising and the disappearance of craft workers), it aspired to a much more energetic effect on national life, far beyond civility's conservative function of limiting and tamping down conflict per se. Because historical shifts and mass culture have created a world in which "there is no Common Reader," it requires "conscious effort" to preserve what is most valuable in the human experience.[72] And this calls for some necessary level of dispute and contestation, the "creative quarreling" that Leavis learned from William Blake: "It is not unanimity that characterizes a real educated public."[73] A measure of incivility, it seems, is no bad thing, providing that it is discursively channeled through the discussion of an aesthetic experience that is far enough from personal needs and desires to be coped with yet close enough to the real world of needs and desires to be worth arguing about.

Leavis's understanding of the critically conflictual core of literary pedagogy socializes what I. A. Richards had largely restricted to the workings of individual minds. In this respect Richards pursues the introspective component of Arnoldian culture (originating with Schiller), wherein the great virtue of aesthetic experience (especially poetry) is its capacity to open the mind to ambiguity and manifoldness by way of its use of pseudo-statements, statements that seem as if they embody or indicate a world while essentially they do not. In reading poetry, in other words, we know we are reading poetry, not acting in a social world. The scientific revolution, Richards argued, had stripped the world of the mythic and magical beliefs necessary to our mental health. Poetry restores those beliefs, but without bringing them into conflict with the rational conduct of everyday life. The consequences of living without it are dire indeed:

> It is very probable that the Hindenburg Line to which the defence of our traditions retired as a result of the onslaughts of the last century will be blown up in the near future. If this should happen a mental chaos such as man has never experienced may be expected. We shall then be thrown back, as Matthew Arnold foresaw, upon poetry. It is capable of saving us; it is a perfectly possible means of overcoming chaos. But whether man is capable of the reorientation required, whether he can loosen in time the entanglement with belief which now takes from poetry half its power and would then take all, is another question.[74]

The chaos that poetry can overcome is in the first instance personal. As Richards makes clear in the rewritten 1935 version of this passage, what we are rescued from is "confusion and frustration."[75] Good poetry is therapeutic in allowing us to "order ourselves."[76] It helps us avoid repression and function more efficiently in the world, reducing "waste and frustration."[77] As such its effects are akin to those of successful psychoanalysis: "reconciliation of impulses" (p. 234) and a state of "disinterestedness" (p. 251). There is little doubt that Richards is here driven to some degree by a liberal-utilitarian incentive toward keeping us all contentedly in line. More generously interpreted, he is aiming at the more widespread cultivation of the aesthetic as a forum for playing out and working through the strains and stresses of modern life without recourse to actual violence. The events of 1914–18 gave ample evidence of the results of choosing "conquest" over "conciliation"; what poetry can at best enable is "a League of Nations for the moral ordering of the impulses," one that begins with individual minds (the emphasis of culture in its nineteenth-century form) but is in theory open to extending throughout a properly educated society.[78] The "greatest possible degree of freedom" (p. 38) experienced by an individual in the proper reading of poetry creates an openness to the claims and identities of other individuals who, thus trained, are far less likely to resort to violence: read more poetry, fight fewer wars.

Richards's writings in the 1920s stand as an exemplary effort to sort through the inheritances of Kant and Schiller in the light of a commitment to British utilitarian priorities. He is adamant that there is no such thing as an "aesthetic state," that artistic perceptions belong in the sphere of the ordinary and that to approach poetry purely for pleasure is an "inadequate attitude."[79] Art does not stand apart from morality, but to make their conjunction work, morality is redescribed as something other than ethical doctrine, a value carried in "the exercise of impulses and the satisfaction of their appetencies" leading to a "fine ordering of responses" (pp. 58, 62). Any invocation of beauty is to be discouraged, but Richards restores the Kantian focus on judgments *about* what is beautiful as properly a part of the human subject's effort to communicate to others (pp. 20–21). He thus goes behind the reifications of nineteenth-century aestheticism to reclaim the power of the aesthetic itself. Schiller is not his primary mentor, but the value of "free direct play" as a way of removing "interference" and "disorganization" pushes Schillerian ideas toward a "successful adjustment" to the world we are given (pp. 202, 231–34, 284).[80] The critique of modern life is still visible: mass communication, the cinema, the radio all undermine psychic integrity and push us to perform stock responses. But it is Coleridge rather than Schiller who stands most solidly behind Richards's argument about the "delicate accommodation or reconciliation of impulses" (p. 234) afforded by the right reading of poetry. In 1934 he published *Coleridge on Imagination*, in which it is argued that a proper assimilation of Coleridge's understanding of the relation between fancy and imagination will bring about a change in "the order of our universes."[81] In *Practical Criticism*, another formative account of Richards's classroom practice, the discipline of poetry is our best means of educating ourselves in "the power of choice," and poetry is up to the task.[82]

It is here worth recalling the language of Coleridge's famous account, drawing upon both Schiller and Schelling, of the imagination as bringing about "the balance or reconciliation of opposite or discordant qualities":[83] balance *or* reconciliation; opposite *or* discordant. Is the *or* inclusive or exclusive? Can one can balance without reconciling or sense the discordant without its being made opposite? Violent appetencies (to use Richards's word) have their place in the mind and are pitched into the mix of things requiring adjudication and appeasement. Pushed further, this would allow for the aesthetic experience of violent drives without their breaching the protective custody afforded by the art form. In other words this would be poetry *with* violence in order finally to act against it, to set it aside. Perhaps this has something to do with Richards's commendation of tragedy as "perhaps the most general, all-accepting, all-ordering experience known."[84] It is tragedy that dares to put extreme violence on the stage and demand that we make some engagement with it. Teaching tragedy (which has remained a key component of the English course that Richards helped bring to life at Cambridge) insists on a confrontation with the questions raised by rendering violence in aesthetic form. Civility is not invoked as a specific code of conduct, but the interpersonal benefits of a successfully organized psyche are clear: "humane, sympathetic and friendly relations between individuals" that are themselves the source of "whole ranges of important values."[85] Shaftesbury would have recognized here the important work of the inmate controller rewritten in the language of utilitarian psychology.

Both Leavis and Richards are committed to the production and maintenance of elite readers whose findings can be disseminated by education and publication: small-group formations doing missionary work in the wider world.[86] Richards's Arnoldian focus on poetry seems to invite only a cadre of specialist readers; Leavis too believes in a trained elite but moves beyond poetry by incorporating the novel into its competences. In the work of Raymond Williams, who spent much of his career working through the implications and possibilities of the idea of culture, the aesthetic function is pointedly democratized; the novel comes to the forefront, along with the modern media that Leavis and Richards had both initially distrusted: cinema, television and popular fiction. Culture is no longer the property of an exemplary individual or small elite but the expression of an entire social-historical moment created and inhabited by all. The "structures of feeling" that Williams identified in (above all) the novel are the written records of key historical shifts in the course of national life that can be identified in literature just before or just as they appear in the fabric of everyday experience: the individual writers who give expression to these structures are already embedded in the social world whose features they delineate. The prime mover for both writers and readers is not the aesthetic response itself, and its recourse to pseudo-statements, but the common urge to communicate, which is the "learned human response to a disturbance of any kind."[87] Williams seeks to open Leavis's seminar room to everyone so that the obligation to "active mutual responsibility" is now community-wide.[88] Nothing less is at stake here than the breaching of class and subgroup interests by a wider dialogic relation, "the conversion of the defensive elements of solidarity into the wider and more positive practice of neighbourhood" (p. 319). Such a general distribution of civil coexistence is imaginable partly because of Williams's faith in the novel and drama as operative beyond the restrictive readerships for poetry and his willingness to entertain (as Richards eventually came to do) creative rather than pernicious outcomes for the media of mass culture.

Richards explicitly associated scientific culture with the disenchantment of the world and the extinction of the magical thinking he regarded as hardwired into human nature and now best met by the reading of poetry. But what of science itself? Schiller had been clear that the progress of the species was unimaginable without modern scientific culture and made no case for impeding it; he thus proposed the aesthetic as from the first a compensatory survival mechanism, and a model for possible futures, rather than a potentially whole or exclusive way of life. In mid-twentieth-century Britain the humanities-science divide that Schiller foreshadowed was hardened in the popular consciousness by the bitter (and often uncivil) debate between Leavis and C. P. Snow. Snow took up one side of Schiller's analysis, declaring that science "has made it possible to remove unnecessary suffering from a billion individual human lives."[89] Humanities scholarship is too often marked by an "anti-social feeling" (p. 8), too much given to elitism, nationalism and even fascism, especially in its ruralist, anti-industrial proclivities. That is Snow's reading of the coterie quality of the literary seminar. Scientific method as Snow describes it also works at modeling and expanding a consensus. Respect for evidence is fundamental to both, but scientific evidence is to be judged independently of class or national origins; science has its own exacting civility codes. In respecting the findings of others and abiding by a willingness to subject one's own work to rigorous critique, the scientist models an ideal of disinterestedness and commitment to bringing together disparate persons within a common cause.[90] It is, one might object, unthinkable to fully do away with the elements of trust and good faith that had, Steven Shapin has argued, lain at the very heart of the experimental method in its earliest days. When it was almost impossible to replicate results with any exactness, owing to the unreliability of primitive equipment, it was very important to know who did the experiment and with what likely degree of competence and responsibility.[91] And of course the application of scientific findings, even when agreed upon as reliable, are always subject to debate, often bitter debate (as in the case of the atom bomb and the World Wide Web).

In one important respect Snow is correct: scientific consensus is relatively immune to the influence of the national languages, while literary pedagogy is almost inseparable from them. Snow looked to scientific work as compassionately cosmopolitan, seeing in its procedures the kinds of moral enrichment that others had claimed for the novel: "One can try to understand the condition of lives, not close to one's own, which one cannot know face to face."[92] Literary pedagogy has sought to compensate for its language-bound predicament by turning to translation and to comparative studies, and one could argue that its unavoidable confrontation with difference bears a potential for a deeper moral education than the one that relies upon an assumption of transparent meanings. And, being less visibly use-oriented than science, literature is often less vulnerable to the demands of national self-interest. In extreme situations, however, as during the Cold War, both have been weaponized. While the Pentagon was trying to build the biggest bombs, the CIA was busy smuggling anti-Soviet literature into the Eastern Bloc. There is no doubt that literary studies have always had to face up to a tendency toward privileging what is written in one's own language. Leavis, writing in 1972, pronounced that it would become harder to focus on "the essential human problem" if Britain were to become (as for a while it did) part of an "integrated

Europe."[93] Richards had taken another route, devoting much of his later life to the campaign for BASIC, an international second language with simple grammar and a small vocabulary based on English but open to being easily learned by anyone engaged in trade and commerce (which like all liberals he regarded as peaceable and peace-making acts), even if it could not be expected to produce high literature. Teaching English literature had long been deployed as a medium for justifying and solidifying the administration of empire, especially in India and Africa. BASIC set out as far as possible to minimize the coercive, top-down history of linguistic hegemony in favor of a more participatory medium, and in so doing it diminished the specific role of literary reading. It is not ambiguity and complexity that are inculcated here but simple communication and practical comprehension. The limited civilities called for by world trading and global politics do not require literary pedagogy, which sets a much too exclusive standard of competence. When Japan invaded China in 1937, Richards was negotiating with the Chinese to establish BASIC in the teaching system of the world's most populous country; after the war, internationalisms of all kinds came under pressure from the constraints of Cold War ideology and of variously violent global decolonization events. The concept of a world literature would be reinvented in the strenuous context of those conditions, and the idea of Europe would transform itself accordingly. Civility, long pushed into the rhetorical background by the precedence of culture, would make a surprising return as a key term in post-Soviet-era self-description.

5

Civility after 1989

Romancing Small Groups

The 'Velvet Revolutions'

The year 1989 was very big for the apologists and spokespersons of the Western democracies. Over much of the communist world, dissident groups demanding what the West appeared already to possess got their chance to come out and say so for the first time without (for the most part) risking immediate and overwhelming punishment. China was the major exception: there opposition activity was punished and suppressed after what has come to be remembered under the name of Tiananmen Square. But a host of Eastern Bloc states broke (and were allowed to break) more or less peacefully away from the Soviet alliance and from an enforced replication of state communism. The Soviet Union itself imploded, the Berlin wall came down, East Germany (the DDR) ceased to exist and radical transformations were set going in Poland, Hungary, Bulgaria, Czechoslovakia and elsewhere. Eager ideologues in the West took this as proof of the end of history as we had known it—the end of a radical divide between liberal democracy and communism, with democracy now immanently established as the way forward for all nations on earth. Some hitherto more or less level-headed intellectuals even felt able to announce that henceforth no one should even bother to study Marx or Marxism or any of the traditionally affiliated socialisms, since these could have no relevance to the brave new world now upon us. Western economists and political scientists had their moment in the sun as consultants to the new about-to-be democracies and market societies. The idea of global culture was suddenly transformed from an ideological crusade to an emergent, self-evident state of affairs: no longer what the Western states projected or imposed but, somehow, simply what everyone wanted and deserved. Boardroom seminars and normative projections managed to sustain their optimism even in the face of the ongoing and violent breakup of Yugoslavia. At the same time 'the West' itself began to disaggregate as tensions developed between the United States and a Europe that was itself internally under strain as it moved to incorporate more and more states within its union.

These historic shifts in the political identities of the old communist bloc were self-generated but also finally encouraged by the traditional party elites who saw something to be gained as well as lost from signing on to the new world order.[1] The transitions (outside the Balkans) were thus largely nonviolent, and ways had to be found to manage change without the usual recourse to tanks and curfews. Who could or should speak for whom in designing the new society? Communist states had not generally encouraged the existence or survival of nongovernmental entities, seeing them as sources of dissent and challenge. Some preexisting organizations were in place (for example, in Poland), but in many cases new forms of representation and interaction had to be made up from scratch. These went by the generic name of civil society, and their voluntarist associational profiles seemed to rely heavily upon the protocols of civility: listening to others, communal decision-making, deferential manners. There was, for example, an epidemic of "round table talks" in which antigovernment and nongovernmental groups sat down with their former rulers to hammer out new rules for living.[2] Round tables are a potent image in political and cultural folklore. King Arthur was supposed to have had one to symbolize the fact that all his knights were equal with him and among themselves (though of course they were not, as most of the legends and their literary reworkings make all too clear). In Britain the Round Table is the name of a nationwide charitable organization, much like the American Rotary Club: both opt for the rhetoric of circles and conjure up images of happy cooperation where no selfish behavior is allowed. Above all, the round table is a figure of uncoercive exchange and small-group interaction. It is a civilized forum, where civil society itself can take form as civility and do its business. Even Miss Manners, in 1995, approvingly noted a "current civility boom."[3]

The high valuation of civil society (as nongovernmental association) that was already in place in Western political thinking thus became turbocharged during and after 1989, once again employing civility as its most important enabler. John Keane, one of the most historically informed of the theorists of civil society, had published two volumes in 1988 that, he later admitted, "were among those lucky books that are held aloft after launch by warm winds of opinion" and thus able to become classics.[4] Keane himself is a man of his times in declaring that state socialism worked to undermine "citizens' confidence in their ability to direct their own lives," but he works hard to prevent his account becoming merely lip service to an "ideological concept" and to the smug consensus that "the Age of Civil Society is nigh."[5] He does not think that civil society can or should replace the state, and he takes issue with the view that it is "the incarnation of social virtue in opposition to political vice," as well as with its adoption by the political right as "a poorly defined synonym for the market."[6] Indeed, many commentators, like Keane himself, regard state and civil society as partners rather than rivals, each necessary to correct the excesses and supplement the deficiencies of the other.[7] But insofar as civil society *has* become a popular ideological concept, and it has, then it calls for a careful critical inspection and not just a celebration. Adam Seligman, for one, responded to the reappearance of a "250-year-old concept long relegated to disuse" by insisting that it simply cannot be resurrected in the modern world.[8]

That celebration reached a high point in the 1990s, insouciantly coincident with the (racialized) massacres and ethnic cleansings in the former Yugoslavia. Keane proposes that the contemporary renewal of interest in civil society began among Japanese political theorists in the 1960s, although this went largely unnoticed in the West.[9] Andrew Arato has argued for the primacy of the 'southern' revolutions (Spain, Portugal, Greece, Argentina, Chile, Brazil) in setting the model for the post-Soviet territories.[10] But whatever its exemplary origins, the civil society paradigm became identified overwhelmingly with the idea of the new Europe. From there it went everywhere, a "quest for panacea in the post-everything age" that soon "acquired the hardening outlines of neomodern myth."[11] In the rapid import-export trade of virtual concepts that constitutes the global cultural economy, stocks in civil society seemed to be at an all-time high. In Britain, the movement represented by Tony Blair's 'Third Way' had clear affiliations with the international civil society movement (though no avowed relation to Leavis's third realm). Blair himself was reported to be a devotee of Hans Küng's Global Ethics Foundation and of Küng's view that "the market economy functions effectively only if it is based on a sound democratic civil society, rooted in basic ethical standards." Along with this there came permission to go ahead with cuts in public spending and "reconstruction" of the welfare state.[12] Blair, significantly, avowed himself an admirer of certain aspects of Margaret Thatcher's agenda, one that was fundamentally wedded to an uncritical view of the virtues of economic privatization and personal self-discipline.

Literature was not visibly engineered as a primary conduit of the new world order, in the way that it had been by the CIA during the Cold War years. Some of the key figures were indeed writers (Václav Havel, Czesław Miłosz), and the Rushdie *fatwa*, beginning in 1989, served to keep the relation between aesthetics and politics very much in the public eye: Thatcher's protection of Rushdie was applauded as a commendable commitment to freedom of expression. Literature and literary theory had, as we will see, a role to play in the articulation and critique of a world now inclining toward acceptance of the terms of the Washington consensus. But for the most part the argument about the positive functions of civility, seeming so nearly synonymous with civil society, was now carried on by political scientists and sociologists. Among the advisers to Blair's New Labour party and its declared 'Third Way' between traditional left and right, Geoff Mulgan was its most assiduous theorist. Mulgan was the director of Demos (1993–98) and a policy adviser to the prime minister. He shares with the theorists of civil society a conviction that "the forms of modern politics are in irreversible decay," that we live with "an unmistakable undercurrent of doubt and fear" and that the massive transfer of government enterprises worldwide to the private sector—worth an estimated $185 billion in the 1980s alone—is both inevitable and largely desirable.[13] He approves of what he calls, taking a metaphor from physics, "flexible, weak power structures" that seek "to mobilize people's commitment and mental powers rather than to exploit them more intensively" (p. 119). Networking and trust must replace control from above: "ethos, self-esteem and peer pressure are emphasized" (p. 121), just as they had been by Chesterfield and Adam Smith. Much of Mulgan's own rhetoric has its origins in the management and business schools that developed new models to account for the commercial and technological success of the information economy: politics too must now have "a new practice and theory around a multiplicity of mutually rewarding and richly communicative relationships." Henceforth, as in so many Woody Allen movies, "the defining questions are all about relationships" (p. 34). Predictably enough this is accompanied by a return to ethics: "Relatively timeless ethics rather than historical ideologies have proven better starting points for politics and progress" (p. 3).[14] Here indeed is the end of history, the inscription of Western democratic man as the measure of a transhistorical set of values and practices: "As ideologies wane, ethical principles again come to the fore, like old rock formations revealed by erosion" (p. 33). So also the end of ideology. The end of both is imaged by heavy investment in the model of interpersonal, small-group interaction: "Only very recently have the potentials of new technologies suggested an evolution back toward dialogic forms and the multiplication of smaller publics" (p. 11). Back, in other words, to the dynamics, and the limits, of civility and conversation.

Mulgan's own rhetorical preferences display a predilection for terms denoting lightness, fluidity and virtuality. As politics increasingly devolve or "evolve back" (as he prefers to say) "to the quality and nature of social relationships," so those relationships come to be best imagined as mutual, consensual and noninvasive, in an endorsement of "what Italo Calvino described . . . as the qualities of the coming era, an ear of swiftness and lightness, exactitude and multiplicity, that may contrast sharply with the slow, heavy, standardizing bluntness of so much government and administration this century."[15] The earlier Modernist fascination with percussive violence is supplanted by this postmodern commitment to mobility and virtuality. Mulgan is bedazzled with the "weightlessness of the economy" and with a world in which "bigness has lost its lustre."[16] Leaders and politicians will still exist, but their job is one of safeguarding instead of ruling: people must "freely choose behaviour patterns that assist in the adaptation and survival of the system of which they are a part" (p. 157). Government and corporate cultures must become less hierarchical and more like clubs: "Clubs are based on members, and share values and mutual commitment. They are, almost by definition, reciprocal" (p. 222). But clubs, of course, are the sites of privileged conversation, interactions between like-minded persons with time on their hands and a disposition to share it with persons like themselves (and to keep out others not deemed like themselves). Mulgan indeed sees the new democracy as becoming "more of a permanent conversation" (p. 16) whose positive evolution depends, like a good deal of contemporary corporate development, on managed disagreement and controlled contention (p. 31). The more face-to-face our interactions become, the more "polite" and "sensitive" we are likely to be (p. 29). The "return to smallness" (p. 99) promises to place us in "a moral republic, with no absolute authorities and no divine rights, but rather a continuous conversation" (p. 126).

This prognosis takes us right back to the eighteenth century, with its appetite for clubs and associations (as described by Peter Clark) and its consistent admission by philosophers and political economists that the best prospects for civility and civil society subsist in those groups that set themselves limits: our loyalties are easier to develop and preserve as long as they are not extended too far from the local and familiar. Same-sex groups are easier to manage than mixed ones; the new liberal world order was still very much a man's world. What has changed, of course, is that the new social media appear to promise an indefinite geographical reach well beyond the parochial space, and even beyond its extension in the form of printed books like *Pamela* and *Robinson Crusoe.* The smallness and lightness that Mulgan celebrates thus has within it the potential for global coverage. Nonetheless, he notes that "social psychology has shown that there is a rough upper limit of four to the ability to take part equally in a conversation." The same research, it seems, suggests that there is a limit of "around a dozen" to our capacity to maintain intimate connections with other people.[17] Questions then arise: How are we to imagine the application of paradigms that properly belong to groups of a dozen or so to the pursuit of national, let alone global political and social relations? How do we have the "national conversation" that Sheldon Hackney, the chairman of the NEH, promised to initiate in the United States in the mid-1990s?[18] George W. Bush, in his speech after the end of the protracted 2000 presidential election process, announced that "together, we will address some of society's deepest problems one person at a time, by encouraging and empowering the good hearts and good works of the American people."[19] It is mind-boggling to imagine how long one might have to wait in line for a turn at having one's particular problem solved in a nation of some three hundred million people. Bush's rhetoric speaks for the personalization and interpersonalization of politics that was at the heart of the new civil society talk. There were many true believers. Faced with the vigorous public protests at the Genoa G8 summit in July 2001, a perplexed but doggedly self-righteous Tony Blair opined that "it would be good to have a dialogue with people on issues like globalization but the problem is these demonstrators do not want a dialogue, they want to storm the building and create an outrage."[20] Such language is patently self-justificatory and seems to have been unaccompanied by any effort by those in power to create the conditions for dialogue with anyone not like themselves. On this same day, Italian police shot and killed one of those demonstrators. Not for the first time, civility culture for some was sustained by violence against others.

The romance of small groups, weightlessly open to imagined globalization by way of the new social media and displacing dogma by dialogic ethics, did not go uncontested. Chantal Mouffe, like Marcuse and others before her, argued that antagonism, and even violence, is an ineradicable element of democratic politics, one that we should not pretend to ignore or repress.[21] To wish away the potential for violence is to wish away any worthwhile democracy that is not a mere apologia for the status quo. Defenses of civility have always been dogged by this concern: that it is not a form of politics but a repression of politics. All through the high romance of the 1990s with civility and civil society, racism and racist violence persisted, and not only on the borders of the new Europe: Rodney King's beating (in 1991) and the acquittal of his assailants (in 1993) are simply some of the headlines. The brief optimism that flickered with the election of a black American president—and one explicitly committed to the value of civility—in 2008 was quieted with the 2016 election. After 2020, matters are still very much to be decided.

Back in the USA: Guardians of Democracy

In the United States in the 1990s, civil society became, in the words of one scholar, "the chicken soup of political theory."[22] Along with it, there came a notable increase in the number of books and articles about civility, both popular and academic. But, during this same decade leading up to the 2000 presidential election and its aftermath, the fetishization of civil society was in almost inverse proportion to the civility index in American life. During Newt Gingrich's leadership of the House, it was felt necessary to set up a bipartisan retreat (held in Hershey, Pennsylvania) where politicians might learn to treat one another with respect: Gingrich had apparently not spoken at all to his opposite number, Dick Gephardt, during the entire then-current session.[23] In 1997 the National League of Cities made "the problem of unruliness at local meetings its top focus"; local authorities felt the need to hand out printed civility codes.[24] Teachers lamented the breakdown of civility in the classroom (exactly as they still do), evidenced by chatting, napping, coming late and leaving early.[25] In December that same year the president of the Modern Language Association felt herself so threatened by the hate mail she was receiving that she hired four armed bodyguards to attend her at the association's annual convention.[26] University of Pennsylvania president Judith Rodin convened a national commission to undertake an extended study of incivility in public life; and at Johns Hopkins two professors, Pier Massimo Forni and Giuila Sissi, founded the Hopkins Civility Project. Everyone seemed to agree that there was a problem to be solved, and we have ever since been frequently reminded that it has not been solved.[27] Meanwhile, George W. Bush made an electioneering promise to restore civility and respect to Washington. After he won, a group of women senators committed themselves to, in the words of Senator Barbara Mikulski, taking off "party hats to work on civility."[28] The Velvet Revolution had apparently not made it across the Atlantic, or perhaps round tables were proving hard to come by.

The chicken soup of civil society was thus clearly not being ingested by enough people; or, to put it better, civility was not being passively accepted as the recipe for the health of that same civil society, which might well, as Ferguson and Kames had reasoned, require more vigorous and aggressive participation than its elites were recommending. Those advocating for the roles of nongovernmental associations in reinvigorating

American political life were not simply asking for peace and quiet: they wanted participation, though admittedly without too many of its rough edges. They believed that if people developed the habit of mingling and talking together, disputes would be solved more amiably and easily. Civil society is not always the preferred term in these publications, although it is cognate with the terms that are used. In the 1980s and early 1990s *community* was the favored word for specifying in the most marketable way the most important quality that America was losing or had lost and ought to be regaining. Some have looked critically at community as a local gratification or limitation that is less important than the achievement of a sophisticated cosmopolitan personality. With the modern dispersal of networks and affiliations, community is one of those things seen to be most under threat: thus it becomes readily available as an object of nostalgia, a longing for a smaller world. Many of the 'how to fix America' books invoke community as the critical building block for a creative and properly democratic future. Amitai Etzioni's much-discussed 1993 book *The Spirit of Community* was among the most visible of these, and it is perfectly frank about the degree to which communal consciousness is a necessary corrective to an otherwise rampant self-interest that cannot be fully restrained without changing the foundational assumptions of capitalism itself. Communitarians, it is said, are not in favor of the complete abolition of regulatory state governance or of entrepreneurial individualism; they seek "a judicious mix of self-interest, self-expression, and commitment to the commons."[29] Jean Bethke Elshtain is more firmly antigovernment, describing the figure of the statist as one who "wants to thin out the ties of civil society and to erode the force of the plural loyalties and diverse imperatives these ties give rise to and sustain."[30] For her, civil society is the absolute core of democratic culture and that which is most threatened (pp. 6–8); its demise is the main reason why "our American democracy is faltering" (p. 1). The so-called culture wars also played their part. For scholars like Elshtain, literary theory was another index of the national decline, its emphasis on irony and self-reflexivity seen as threatening to a commonsense (i.e., dominant elite) version of social solidarity.

Robert D. Putnam's *Bowling Alone* (2000), the book-length extension of a highly influential article published in 1995, transformed its author almost overnight from an ordinary academic to a media star and the companion of presidents.[31] He was showered with support by foundations and trusts, including Pew, Wallace, Macarthur, Rockefeller, Carnegie, Lilly, the Aspen Institute and the Trilateral Commission. Putnam chronicles the eroding of the "long civic generation" (pp. 271–72), evident in the decline in churchgoing, bridge playing, league bowling and charitable giving; the evidence is at once densely documented and polemically summarized. The book was a best seller and provided ample material for jeremiads against the state of modern culture, as well as a clear (though by no means unqualified) case against the disasters of big government. Those societies with a high "social capital index" (which measures trust and sociability) are the healthiest and happiest (pp. 296ff.). Civility also pays: those who share and cooperate make more money than those who don't, largely owing to the operation of social networks (pp. 321–25). The self-interested spirit of Chesterfield's *Letters* is here very much alive. But what Chesterfield saw as an opportunity is here pitched as more of an elegy: America is at risk of losing its way and desperately needs rescuing. The accompanying sentimental celebration by politicians of 'small businesses' continues apace as monopolies get bigger and bigger.

What is striking about these arguments, and they are typical of many others then and since, is that they are offered as indicators of radical crisis at the very moment when the West appears to have won the Cold War once and forever. Mulgan, after all, responded to the new European situation by resorting to the classic Whig idea that "we are born with the traits needed for a healthy social order, including mutual understanding and respect. . . . We are well made to police ourselves."[32] All we need to do, presumably, is to free ourselves up. Francis Fukuyama made international headlines with his simplified rewriting of eighteenth-century stadial theory, contending that there was "a fundamental process at work that dictates a common evolutionary pattern for *all* human societies—in short, something like a Universal History of mankind in the direction of liberal democracy," and that "man's natural state" is not one of Hobbesian competition "but rather a civil society made orderly by the presence of a host of moral rules."[33] The insouciance of these assertions is indicative of the self-confidence of free-market neoliberals after 1989, but it could perhaps also be taken to suggest that if the success of the American way is thus assured by history, then its failures can only be the result of its own internal, willfully perpetrated flaws. Like the major empires of the past, America can be imaged as most vulnerable at the point of its own greatest success, at the point when its citizens slacken in their vigilance and give way to excesses of the sort made possible by world hegemony and economic affluence—in the eighteenth century those of luxury, self-indulgence and declining military efficiency, now augmented by the self-questionings of what had come to be called postmodernism. So, just at the point when "all of the really big questions" have been "settled," we are told to be vigilant and to make sure that our own backyards are in good order: "For democracy to work, citizens need to develop an irrational pride in their own democratic institutions, and must also develop what Tocqueville called the 'art of associating,' which rests on prideful attachment to small communities."[34] At the same time what governs the new world order is in fact global capital, "technologically driven economic growth and the capitalist social relations necessary to produce and sustain it" (p. 126), of the sort that by no means assures the well-being of those small communities that are not themselves at the source and center of the new prosperity.

The flourishing of communitarians and civil society advocates leads Steven Pinker to declare the 1990s a decade given over to a "recivilizing process," or at least to a "civilizing offensive": the military vocabulary is revealing.[35] For him this is a good thing, but it can also be understood as an effort to limit (or ideologically appease) the socially unsettling consequences of self-interest at a time when income inequality is, beginning in the 1970s, radically increasing, as it still is, consistently along racialized lines. Recommending a culture of participation endorses the experience of belonging, of being 'empowered,' of being a 'stakeholder,' but has nothing to do with any redistribution of economic or political power. Fukuyama applauds the fact that "there are enough hierarchies scattered about in modern societies that most people can end up in the middle to upper range of at least one of them," making everyone happy.[36] But if this means that you perfect your bowling averages while I make a fortune by insider trading on Wall Street, then we are talking about very different kinds and degrees of happiness, with very divergent results. Uncritically endorsing "recivilizing" initiatives often looks like an effort to keep less fortunate persons in their place while projecting existing elites as icons of good and gracious feeling. In suggesting that civility is natural to human nature while violent dissent is an anomaly to be disciplined away, we forget that, in John Keane's words, "incivility is a chronic feature of civil societies" because of the "plurality of forms of life" with which they must cope, making them "prone to stress, anxiety, and revenge."[37] The licensed aggression required for the progress of liberal society had been recognized by the eighteenth-century political economists as creating a social turbulence calling for constant management. There is no static point between inertia and destructive violence; the balance must be worked out through ongoing vigilance and understood as paradox. There are always two sides to every statement; all positives can turn negative.

Civil society and the democracy that it sustains are thus by definition always at risk. At times the message is antigovernment, as it was for some in the 1990s. At other times the threat comes from a worship of individualism, of going it alone. Edward Shils's writings from the 1950s about the virtues and threats to civility received new attention in the 1980s and 1990s; one updated essay diagnosed an increase in the "range and intensity" of the pressure groups that had always characterized liberal society.[38] Shils recognized that liberalism required for its operation a "more visible disharmony of interests" (p. 76) than some other kinds of political organization, making a high evaluation of civility (along with the nation-state or national imaginary) indispensable for its peaceful functioning. He also recognized (as did John Stuart Mill) that liberalism should not and could not aspire to an absolutely civil society, which would be "boring, spiritually impoverished, and intellectually infertile" (p. 97). The question, as always, is about where to draw the line, a question that can never be finally solved because the line is always changing and always disputed. It always looks better to have people police themselves than to have police in the streets, but American governments of all kinds, local and federal, have never thus far been reluctant to resort to violence. Shils's offering "civil politics" an alternative to the "ideological politics" typified by fascism and communism is standard Cold War rhetoric (p. 49). At the same time he warned that civility itself must beware of becoming an ideology (p. 59).

Between the far-too-big group represented by government and the far-too-small group of one or two, there floats the ideal of the well-adjusted group, still small but big enough to qualify as social. As early as 1927 John Dewey's *The Public and Its Problems* speaks presciently to the communitarian priorities of the 1980s and 1990s in its claim that the "individualistic philosophy" cannot "meet the needs and direct the factors of the new age."[39] Individualism for Dewey is a category mistake: there is no such thing. But because new associational forms go unrecognized in a world where connections and traditions have been scrambled and rendered invisible, individual agency appears as a desired and possible alternative. The progress of society is at the expense of community, whose erosion brings with it the illusion of freedom from a "mass of old habits, regulations, and institutions" (p. 100) and a heightened sense of voluntary choice. With "the spectacle of a pulverizing of established associations into the desires and intentions of atomic individuals" (p. 101), there is then nothing left of the "inclusive and fraternally associated public" (p. 109) imagined for early America. What emerges is an "inchoate public" made up of lots of little voluntarily created groups unable to see beyond the boundaries of their own immediate circumstances (p. 138). And what has been lost is the supposedly foundational experience of American democracy in "genuine community life, that is, association in local and small centers" (p. 111).

Like many of his later twentieth-century successors, Dewey is on a 'how to fix America' mission. He wants to see the "Great Society" become a "Great Community" by way of "full and moving communication" (p. 184), but he realizes (as had Schiller) that there can be no going back to purely nostalgic forms of local association without some positive "passage through a machine age" (p. 217). Thus, the "Great Community" must function as some sort of generalizing or organizing principle holding together the small-group associations and mediating their relations to a wider world whose importance to modern life cannot be denied:

> In its deepest and richest sense a community must always remain a matter of face-to-face intercourse. This is why the family and neighborhood, with all their deficiencies, have always been the chief agencies of nurture, the means by which dispositions are stably formed and ideas acquired which laid hold on the roots of character. The Great Community, in the sense of free and full communication, is conceivable. But it can never possess all the qualities which mark a local community. It will do its final work in ordering the relations and enriching the experience of local associations. (p. 211)

Once again the positive identity of small groups is affirmed. They will not be like the old ones. The inevitability of the cosmopolitan dimension means that any newly restored "local communal life" will manifest a "fullness, variety and freedom of possession and enjoyment of meanings and goods unknown in the contiguous associations of the past," thanks to the "complex and world-wide scene in which it is enmeshed" (p. 216). Will this new fullness be racially inclusive? How do we integrate the local and the cosmopolitan? Dewey wants a return to "the vitality and depth of close and direct intercourse and attachment" (p. 211), and he explains it by what might now, after Derrida's famous critique of Lévi-Strauss, appear as a romanticized logocentrism:

> The winged words of conversation in immediate intercourse have a vital import lacking in the fixed and frozen words of written speech. . . . The connections of the ear with vital and outgoing thought and emotion are immensely closer and more varied than those of the eye. Vision is a spectator; hearing is a participator. . . . There is no limit to the liberal expansion and confirmation of limited personal intellectual endowment which may proceed from the flow of social intelligence when that circulates by word of mouth from one to another in the communications of the local community. (pp. 218–19)

No limit? Dewey's myth of original integrity, of a moment of "genuine community life" and pioneer spirit carried out in town meetings by "neighborly sociability" (p. 111), proposes that all large groups are but expanding small groups and that no qualitative transformations occur in the passage from one to the other. And what of the local community itself, here imaged as the medium of sincere and constructive communication? Cooper's *The Pioneers* (1823) offered a very different image of the frontier spirit, one riven by class and ethnic rivalries and misunderstandings and kept in constant turmoil by ambitious and sometimes ruthless politicians, lawyers and businessmen.

The respect accorded to word-of-mouth communication is notable here. This is very different from the exhaustive balancing and estimation of appetencies that Richards and Leavis claimed to embody in the literary classroom, where there was always a text to be explained, an inert body of writing given life in the careful adjudication of possible meanings in relation to those bringing their own wishes and desires to the table. Worship of speech over writing was favored by *Mein Kampf* as far more powerful for the purposes of uncritical persuasion. It supplants slow time by urgent time, possibilities by assertions, hesitation by activation. In Richards's terms, it is the medium of stock responses, and Richards had little respect for the radio as the broadcasting of words of mouth. In a similar spirit, Michael Schudson has radically questioned the 'democratic' credentials of early colonial and national politics in suggesting that the much-celebrated New England town meetings were neither well attended nor representative and marked not so much by conversational ease and freedom as by the familiar conventions of hierarchy and deference.[40] Voter turnout in eighteenth-century Massachusetts was no higher than it is today, despite a much more restricted electorate; attendance at meetings was poor even when it was supposedly obligatory, and there was a "normative presumption that open discussion of differences was to be avoided at all costs" (p. 18). The limits of legislators' obligations to their constituencies were vague, and for much of the 1790s, in the wake of the perceived excesses of revolutionary France, the nongovernmental associations that are at the core of our current idea of civil society were positively feared as breeding grounds for radical republicanism.

Schudson's book is an invaluable counterstatement to the more popular pronouncements of Robert Putnam (whom he cogently critiques on pp. 296–301) and others who depend on the myth of a radical fall from grace in the current state of civility and civil society. Various of the set pieces in the national imaginary are debunked or contextualized in ways that are important to a critique of civil society talk: the New England town meeting, the Lincoln-Douglas debate and above all the neoliberal version of Tocqueville.[41] Historical studies like Richard Bushman's *The Refinement of America* and Kenneth Cmiel's *Democratic Eloquence* make clear the degree to which most of the positive models for language or character that have been put forward since colonial times have come burdened with a fearful sense of the ways in which they can be misused or exploited. Polite behavior can mask a rogue, and civility can be used to gain uncivil ends; the popular can become populist, and democracy can slide into demagoguery.[42] This always-imminent slippage from good to bad attributes is true to the antinomic theorization of liberal society itself, whereby our existence as human subjects in place and time is explained in two quite different ways. On the one hand, we are atomic individuals with legal rights and responsibilities that are person-specific. We mostly make critical decisions or stand trial for felony as individuals. On the other hand, we are embedded selves, either persuaded to various forms of association by the conventions of democratic culture (as for Tocqueville), or, as in the more strongly theorized sense of G. H. Mead, we are made into selves in the first place only by "taking the attitude of the social group" to which we belong.[43] Cooperative-associative and individualist opportunities and responsibilities constantly compete, overlap and metamorphose from one to the other, so it is hard to be sure where one is and who one is. There is then something oddly disingenuous in setting out to 'fix' this problem by recourse either to individualism or collectivism or even to a blending of the two, since the processes and consequences of the blending can never be assumed to be the same from one moment to the next. The point of conjunction is not open to prior definition but is instead a deliberately indeterminate space in which various interests and agents are able to compete for attention and effect. Amy Gutmann and Dennis Thompson acknowledge something like this in their willingness to include in a properly "deliberative democracy" the permission for citizens "to take extreme and even offensive stands" and to employ "impassioned and immoderate speech."[44] Teresa Bejan has recently gone back to Roger Williams in search of a paradigm of "low-but-solid" civility that depends on "mutual contempt rather than mutual admiration." Only an "insincere and minimalist understanding of civility" can keep the peace; to ask for more is to incur inevitable disappointment.[45] The attribution of hypocrisy that had so often haunted the defense of civility is now turned to positive effect; a robustly diminished civility can allow for some giving of offense. Civility, in other words, must make space for and tolerate incivility. But extreme and offensive stands are best managed, once again, in small groups, where there is some opportunity for deliberation and less chance of confrontation or radical violence. Failing that, there is violent policing, of which the historical record gives plenty of examples.

Where has American literature stood in relation to the paradoxes about civility and civil society adduced by the political scientists in the late twentieth century? There is of course evidence on all sides. The flourishing of popular romances testifies to the marketability of small-group resolutions to social and historical predicaments: all can be well in the smallest of possible worlds. But the corrosive analysis initiated in *The Pioneers* appears again among the best sellers of the time. *The Color Purple*

(1982) and *Beloved* (1988) achieved something close to mass circulation by confronting the unbearable violence of men against women and white against black. They register nothing at all positive about Putnam's "long civic generation" or Dewey's "genuine community life,"[46] which are at best racialized subcultures maintaining themselves by brute force. Don DeLillo's *Underworld* (1997), which does purport to take on more or less the totality of Cold War America, dismantles almost every one of the reigning pieties about civil society and community. DeLillo had already established himself as the chronicler of terror, mass hysteria, violence, conspiracy theory and ecological disaster (in *Mao II*, *Libra*, *White Noise*). *Underworld* begins with that most sacrosanct of American myths of community and objects of nostalgia: the baseball game. Taking place in the early 1950s, the game is attended by a cross section of the rich and famous, including J. Edgar Hoover, who has just heard about the detonation of the first Russian A-bomb, which happens during the game, and who finds himself preoccupied with a photograph of Bruegel's *The Triumph of Death*, which gives the prologue its title. DeLillo's register of violences spans the global and the trivial, from the bomb to the feral fighting in the stands over picking up the game-winning ball. This is no ordinary game. Played between the Giants and the Dodgers in October 1951, it entered history as a 'shot heard round the world.' Hyperbolic to be sure, but it thus gathered to itself the same language that had been used to describe Lexington and Concord in 1775, and then Sarajevo in 1914, world-changing violent events. Under the umbrella of pure play, all sorts of forces congeal. Indeed, play itself cannot ever be thought by definition innocent. Kipling had written of the 'Great Game' played between Britain and Russia for the control of East Asia. This ludic vocabulary allows Kim (as Edward Said has shown) to inhabit a novel full of boys' own adventures and remain untouched, but it is a game in which many thousands would die.[47] DeLillo's America is no organic community but an assemblage of uncoordinated energies in a state of unpredictable combustibility, not a "migration or a revolution" but an "unseen something" emitting a "territorial roar" wherein "nothing's predictable."[48] The violence of another of the national pastimes, football, had been the subject of *End Zone* (1972). Crowd behavior, robotic and volatile, figured in *Mao II* and *White Noise*. What little there is of coherence and predictability in *Underworld* comes not from civility or local community but from the overarching figment of the Cold War, of the known enemy, the reliable other. For one character the Cold War was "honest" and "dependable"; its ending relocates all the violence of the state into the "personal bloodstream" (p. 170). For another it made power a focused, "tangible thing" that "held the world together." The year 1989 and its aftermath meant that "violence is easier now, it's uprooted, out of control, it has no measure anymore, it has no level of values" (p. 76). The new imaginary is all about money and spectacle, yet in a world where people still believe "everything's connected" (p. 289). There are no town meetings in DeLillo's America. The dystopian image of American civil society that Cooper presented remains a primary literary tradition.

Theory and the Critique of 'Europe'

Ernest Gellner thinks that "civil society" might be a better term for our collective (Western) political ideal than "democracy" itself, since it is so closely "linked to our historical destiny."[49] As such it is especially prone to ideological deployment, in a long process of political self-justification that Dominique Colas has traced back to the Reformation. Noting the "empty universality" of the term and its "present inflationary use," Colas images civil society as somewhat akin to the money system.[50] Just as the free marketeers who became even more influential after 1989 believe in the unrestricted circulation of commerce and wealth, so the civil society that is deemed to sustain these opportunities must remain free of coercive regulations. But until the later nineteenth century, Colas shows, civil society was not conceived as being at odds with the state. Its enduring opposite was fanaticism, and against fanaticism it needed the constraints and protective functions that only the state could provide. It took Marx to break with this tradition; in Hegel's theory it remained intact. The Catholic Church, in its efforts to contest Soviet control of the old Eastern Bloc, saw fit to play up its own commitment to a non-statist model of civil society (p. 87), as did the Western apologists of the free market. But, for Colas, the break from Soviet domination was never about the emergence of a counterstate civil society: it has more to do with "embryonic" states and an "embryonic" civil society seeking to come into being as a representative government under the rule of law (p. 350). That it was marketed as an exclusively civil society phenomenon served the interests of those who ran things in the West. In seeming to set free an ideal civil society from state control, it also put more pressure on informal constraints to do the work of keeping the peace. Civility was chief among them. The less one permits or approves of state regulation, the more reliant one becomes on other forms of discipline to keep us all from a descent into violence. Civility, because it is by definition ambiguous, being partly natural and partly learned and thus immune to absolute legislation while open to persuasive example, is a perfect term for bearing the stresses of this transition.

In Colas's estimation, it failed to do so. By the mid-1990s it was clear to him (as to others at the time) that the former Soviet zone was evolving new forms of fanaticism: ethnic nationalism and overt racism.[51] So too the European Union was reciprocally projecting an "intolerance of otherness" and a desire for closed borders to protect its "internal labor market" (p. xxvii). Since 1997 these tendencies have only become more evident. Civility was failing and has still not succeeded. In the not-so-United States the events of 9/11 inspired an immediate outpouring of what looked like Dewey's "neighborly sociability": giving blood, feeding rescue workers, donating to bereaved families. But above and beyond such acts of personal spontaneity, the attacks were used politically to incite national-patriotic rage and revenge. Civility, for a while, was not even on the rhetorical roster: this was no time to be making nice. But 9/11 gave a huge worldwide boost to attributions of fanaticism—for the designation of the nation's enemies as terrorists and barbarians. Thus, it reinscribed civility and civil society as that which 'we' practice and cherish and 'they' don't. At the same time there appeared a growing conviction that we do not actually demonstrate civility and that civil society can be positively theorized only by ignoring, as Tocqueville did for so much of his narrative, the implacable poison of a besetting racism and xenophobia. If it seems that we have made no progress, it may be because progress is not, despite appearances, that which civility talk is deeply designed to enable. That is one reason why we seem compelled to talk about it over and over again, both in the United States and in Europe.

A lot has happened in Europe since the years immediately following the "fall" of the Soviet Empire in 1989, when a civil society premised on civility culture was projected by so many as the new best hope for a nonviolent future. This paradigm, ever since its exemplary modern formation in the eighteenth century, has relied (implicitly or explicitly) on small-group assemblages, where no one gets too far away from face-to-face interactions. In every phase of its post-1945 evolution, even at its smallest, the European Union (EU) has been too big to reflect any such ideal. According to its detractors, its attempt to move away from statist self-interest produced only an anonymous and unaccountable bureaucracy pursuing neoliberal interests without any responsibility to any electorate. The EU has been getting bigger, absorbing many more entities than ever before. From an original Franco-German economic treaty it had, by the turn of the twenty-first century, become a union that included all of southern and most of eastern Europe—much of the former Soviet Empire. Economic stresses (the inclusion of very different national economies, arguments over the euro and the much-reviled austerity policy), crises around the definition and management of borders and a consistent lack of popular commitment to the European parliamentary elections made even its supporters wonder if things were out of control. The British exit vote and the visible appearance of effectively nondemocratic 'strong man' politicians trading in refurbished nationalisms have put the EU in greater jeopardy than ever before. Meanwhile, potentially divisive decisions about militarization have become critical in the light of the palpable US reluctance to fund NATO at the traditional levels. The postwar transatlantic alliance has been more than usually fragile since the Iraq War of 2003 and is further stressed by US protectionist gestures and by its reaffirmation of support for aggressive right-wing governments in the Middle East.

In his magisterial *Postwar* (2005), Tony Judt speculated that the most powerful force holding together the imaginary thing called Europe was a "compensatory surplus of memory," a model of "restored humanity" based on a collective recognition of the continent's dead Jews. He has radical doubts about the ongoing sufficiency of this condition.[52] In 2011 his estate published a book based on lectures given in 1995, under a title that tells all: *A Grand Illusion?* The lectures are prescient in proposing that the "*strong* idea of 'Europe'" was a Cold-War construction whose time has passed, and that the primacy of separate nation-states that it sought to challenge is far from expiring.[53] Unable to offer a model of hospitable cosmopolitanism to the rest of the world, Judt's Europe is "steadily if somewhat furtively engaged in closing in upon itself" (p. 122) in an effort to head off the challenges of "further in-migration" (p. 125). While such pessimism is not out of line with a good deal that has been going on since the triumphalist moment of 1989, Judt's questions remain open for contestation, as is signaled perhaps most dramatically in Angela Merkel's simultaneous embrace of both economic austerity and (briefly) increased immigration. Anthony Giddens, in 2014, was still calling for a "bottom-up" input into a "European-wide civil society" as a viable way forward.[54] But now the "small circles of people" (p. 6) who have been privileged in conceptions of how civil society operates are the problem rather than the solution: too many are left out, both ordinary citizens and national parliaments.[55] The EU must make more efforts to accommodate and work with states, while at the same time pursuing a "cosmopolitan imperative" based on new cultures of "super-diversity" (p. 122) and "interculturalism" (p. 139)—a condition wherein no one lays claim to one single identity.

At the periphery of mainstream political science, but very much in the flow of literary theory—the same 'theory' that took form with Romanticism as an alternative to analytic certitudes and that produces, for example, a reading of Kant as a philosopher of the aporetic—there has been an important response to the crisis of 'Europe.' Jacques Derrida's 1991 *The Other Heading* (*L'autre cap*) certainly replicates the then-dominant appeal to the 'West' as the bearer of a positive future, but does so by claiming that the message of Europe is that "*what is proper to culture is not to be identical with itself*."[56] The commitment of Europe should thus be to a permanent state of self-reflexivity and an openness to hospitality toward the other. The unity of Europe is to be understood as a constant reckoning with the manifold that can never be 'one'; it is this that must distinguish it from the metaphysics of mainstream nineteenth-century *Bildung* and from the American model. The need for an alternative European construction of the West became much more acute in the wake of 9/11 and the hardening of borders and ideologies and led to a jointly authored declaration by Derrida and Habermas gesturing toward the unprecedented "birth of a European public sphere" in opposition to the "hegemonic unilateralism of the United States."[57] This is possible insofar as Europe never forgets that it has experienced both the acquisition and dispersal of empire, that it has recognized the limitations of the Eurocentrism that Hegel adopted from those political economists who, like Adam Ferguson and Lord Kames, believed that everything progressive and enlightening must emanate from what is now called the West.[58]

Europe, for Derrida, stands for stringent self-critique and for the priority of theory over culture, as it does in Étienne Balibar's essays written in the 1990s and collected together as *We, the People of Europe?* Balibar fears the onset of a peculiarly European apartheid resulting from the indecisive and opportunistic positioning of some regions (e.g., the Balkans) as at once inside and outside, as well as of third-country nationals working in the core states.[59] The exclusion of Russia perpetuates adversarial conceptions of Europe (p. 166), and the whole situation imposes radical stresses on efforts to carry through a "politics of civility" (p. 130), even as the "concrete forms and strategies of civility" (p. 116) must be at the heart of any democratic order that is capable of resisting a decline into violence. In the twenty years since Balibar wrote these words, the migration-refugee crisis has placed and is placing the European consensus under even greater pressure. So what is this politics of civility, for Balibar? Significantly, following Umberto Eco, he affirms that the language of Europe is not and must not be English (p. 177). Europe must not acquiesce in the dissemination of an anglophone world language but must instead commit itself to a "constantly transformed system of crossed usages" best collectively described as *translation* (p. 178). The ethos here is imperfection and incompletion, not mastery and proper meaning. Two social sectors in particular are aware of and living with this condition: the "anonymous migrant workers" and the "writers of uprooting and exile" (Canetti, Heine, Conrad, Joyce are mentioned), including the intellectuals "educated in the liberal arts and sciences" (p. 178). Poets, novelists and intellectuals might here be imagined as playing active and consequential roles in the performance of democracy in the making. For them, Europeanness should be a condition of dispersal, of living in translation.[60] There must be no assumptions of single languages expressive of single cultures, no possession of either an origin or a destiny. This has been the emphasis of much already written by Europeans in the name of theory, most recently and powerfully by Derrida. Rodolph Gasché has demonstrated the roles of Husserl, Heidegger, Patočka and Derrida in laying out the "infinite task" that constitutes the idea of Europe, one whose classical Greek affiliations are not with established core doctrines in politics and aesthetics but with the uncanny, with a freeing oneself of "everything of the order of the native" and with an openness to "the arrival of the unforeseeable" and the "noncalculable."[61] Philosophy thus conceived is that which disturbs "the homeliness of any world" (p. 27) in being "infinitely open . . . to what is other than oneself" (p. 286) with "a responsibility to all others" (p. 340). The names Gasché invokes are those conventionally ignored or sidelined by mainstream anglophone philosophy, which never did accept Derrida into its associational imaginary, and thus represent a 'Europe' whose time is yet to come and whose distinctiveness is all the more urgent in the crises both within and between Europe and the anglosphere. They stand for a theory of discomfort, of living within the aporetic, that makes civility (of reading, teaching, writing) an ideal whose feasibility must be constantly maintained in the orbit of the uncanny, of being not at home when home.

The idea of Europe has always been a figment of the imagination aimed at inscribing the threatening or secondary presence of what is *not* Europe. It has subsisted by defending geographical boundaries (Greeks and barbarians, Western and oriental, north and south, metropole and colony) that are themselves internally divided (Gothic and Mediterranean, classical and modern, Protestant and Catholic), even within entities that call themselves nations. Italy sustains a radical north-south distinction within its own borders, and there are long-standing arguments about who if anyone among Gauls, Franks and Romans is originally 'French.' Chivalry (and hence civility, by one possible route) has been deemed to be of Arabic origin, coming by way of southern Spain, while the progressive Europe identified by Hegel belongs to the northern rather than the Mediterranean regions. Europe works well enough as a yardstick (or cudgel) set up to measure outsiders, and perhaps for outsiders to measure themselves, even as the outsiders are by various measures already insiders.[62] But it is and always has been riven by hierarchies and differently imagined identities. Supremacy, and the anxiety that comes with trying to uphold it, is fundamental to its history. The conflicts with the European Union, which has always been a union with and within limits, are another phase of that history.

It is striking that Balibar's argument resuscitates the term *civility* as having a key role in this culture of dispersal and discomfort and that the role of writers and intellectuals living in translation (conceiving theory also as a mode of literariness in the reflexive tradition of Friedrich Schlegel) is a significant articulation of it. In an essay of 1996–97, written at the height of the debate about civility and civil society, Balibar argued for civility (as distinct from both emancipation and transformation) as a concept that "takes as its 'object' the very violence of identities."[63] In order to make it thinkable with "an autonomy of the multitude" (p. 30), he dissociates civility from the conversational-dialogic model that is traditional to the term, allowing room for those who cannot "present themselves *in person* as political subjects" or "emancipate themselves" (p. 24). Speech and face-to-face presence are here both displaced in favor of a civility from below, "bottom up" (p. 34). This model recognizes (instead of effacing) the immanent violence that is built into social and political life and into the identity fantasies it sustains; it imagines a participatory function for those who cannot speak for themselves and whose presence may appear in nonlinguistic forms such as rioting. But it does not seem to have at its disposal any effective force beyond those of "statements, signs, and roles" (p. 35). It is something other than a direct politics. Hence, one assumes, the importance of writers and intellectuals.

At around the same time, in 1996, Balibar devoted the Wellek lectures, given at the University of California, Irvine, to the topic of violence and civility. These remained unpublished for fifteen years, appearing in French in 2010 and in English (in a shorter version) only in 2015. With an engaging candor the author admits that he had failed to find a "clear conclusion, which I spent years looking for in various directions, none of which proved satisfactory."[64] Eventually, he writes, it became apparent to him that conclusiveness was not possible in this search for the "unprecedented forms of civility" whose integrity could only depend upon new modes of "subjectivation" (p. x) posited in the light of an equally unprecedented omnipresence of violence in the entire order of life and thought. This means that the traditional notion of politics as aiming toward the extinction of violence needs to be completely rethought. (Yugoslavia is very much on his mind.) As alternatives to nonviolence (there is no nonviolence) and counterviolence, Balibar offers the term *antiviolence* (first formulated in a lecture in 1992) as congruent with a reinvented civility (p. 22), one that takes as its task the thinking through of violence as inconvertible, not to be transformed into spiritual or productive outcomes, and he accepts that its role can only be one of mitigation, warding off extremes rather than eradicating cruelty and violence altogether (p. 101). The task is "to introduce the antiviolence that I call civility into the very heart of the violence of a social transformation" (p. 103). Balibar invokes an imagining of Hegelian *Sittlichkeit*, without its assumption of normality, and of Deleuze and Guattari's ideas about becoming minoritarian, as one way to begin constructing a model of the "deconstruction and reconstruction of affiliations" that can bear the project of antiviolence (p. 113). But what is the role of the literary mode in this process—that literary mode that accounted, in *We, the People of Europe?*, for one of two primary groups experiencing the condition of translation? And what is its relation to the other group, the anonymous migrants? Language culture was here the fourth "worksite" for democracy, able to contribute to "turning public space back into civic space."[65] That same language culture had been, since the early modern period, at the core of theorizations of civility and the primary vehicle of its transmission. What might it promise in the twenty-first century? When civility is invoked from the left, as a representation and analysis of violence rather than an ideological fantasy of its displacement, what is the role open to literature?

In *The Art of the Novel*, first published in 1986 and collecting together his essays of the 1980s, Milan Kundera cast the novel as the faithful companion of man in the modern era. As "Europe's creation," it belongs to Europe and speaks for an "imaginative realm where no one owns the truth and everyone has the right to be understood." The novel is, "by definition, the ironic art," incompatible with totalitarianism.[66] Richard Rorty, perhaps the exemplary anglophone liberal philosopher of the decade, cites Kundera in the epigraph to his own collected essays, published in 1989. He too mounts a defense of "ironism" as a way of understanding and ideally preempting the pain and humiliation of others. Literature and literary criticism, and above all the novel, are the natural media of ironism: Nabokov, Proust, Dickens, Orwell and Baudelaire all feature in Rorty's argument for the importance of redescription over the search for foundations in the conduct of intellectual and social life.[67] Martha Nussbaum, who has little enthusiasm for literary theory in the Derridean style, nonetheless makes a passionate case for the novel in disseminating an "ideal of the equality and dignity of all human life."[68] In fact the entire body of Derridean deconstruction is, as is often said, staged in a language that is at once literary and theoretical: a language, indeed, of *literary* theory, and one that fully exploits the complex potential of irony and self-reflexivity, of saying more than one thing at a time, in the cause of advancing a distinct effort at social justice.

To whom are these inspirations available? In what languages and under what regimes? The terse but prophetic remarks in *The Communist Manifesto* that predict the erosion of national boundaries and the formation of a world literature promise an emerging cooperative cosmopolitanism only to the extent that class exploitation diminishes. Otherwise, world literature may be nothing more than world ideology. Nothing suggests that we are reducing our level of economic and racial exploitation, and there is a large body of dystopian fiction that chronicles its mechanisms. One of the most visible genres now current is the migration novel, a response to the massive movement of persons that is driven by wars, revolutions, economic hardships and ecological disaster. Living thus in and under translation is a form of subjectification that poses radical questions about the relation between civility and violence. Sometimes the resolution is tragic (Ghassan Kanafani's *Men in the Sun*, Tahar Ben Jelloun's *Leaving Tangier*); at others, less definitively evaluated. The encounter with the stranger-foreigner is open to various representations along the entire spectrum that separates (and connects) love and hatred, as the integrity of each confronts the challenge of the other: novels can do anything they like. Jenny Erpenbeck's *Go, Went, Gone* (2015) represents the immigration crisis in Germany through the eyes of a retired college professor whose besetting insularity is gradually whittled away by a growing acquaintance with a group of African refugees who are being shuttled around his city while waiting to hear the outcome of their visa applications.[69] Informal German hospitality works to offset bureaucratic indifference as Richard (the retiree) opens his house as a home shelter to some of the men whom he has come to know: a small act of love and loyalty that functions within and aside from the national debate about immigration and hospitality. Speaking for a different and still recent history, W. G. Sebald's novels address the consequences of radical failures of hospitality, of a racism so massively destructive as to be almost beyond imagining, and certainly beyond laying to rest. In *Exit West* (2017) Mohsin Hamid resorts to a measure of magic realism to avoid transcribing the deadly and brutal historical record of sinking boats, freezing families and drowned children that marks the passage to Europe for so many of the world's poor and oppressed. Instead, his characters simply pass through doors, leaving one place and arriving in another with no passing of time or physical transit. Nativist backlash occurs in the host countries, but it is not violent or sustained enough to prevent the growth of migrant communities in the most implausible locations: Kensington-Chelsea and Marin County, for example. It seems that "the whole planet was on the move," resulting in the development of new conurbations of migrants who establish a way of life in new places, perhaps because the locals are finally not cruel enough to kill them all, perhaps because they sense that there are simply too many doors through which people are passing in all directions to allow for any kind of control.[70] Again it is love that holds firm in this constantly evolving global village; love between the main characters, Nadia and Saeed, but also, for example, the love that happens between two old men, strangers who happen to pass through the doors between Rio and Amsterdam (pp. 173–76). Hamid's magical narrative takes the risk of seeming hopelessly utopian or sentimental, but it registers—as does Erpenbeck—a possibility for the novel genre that is not dominantly dystopian, not given over to the task of recording historical violence without offering some positive encouragement for the living of lives of solidarity and love.[71] Many other novels that represent the interaction of dominant and subaltern persons come to less affirmative conclusions and find it more difficult to imagine a world in which the nonviolence of the immigrants could really be a way of "shaming their attackers into civility."[72] But the traditional commitment of the novel to the extrapolation of intense personal relationships remains attentive to the interactions of love and violence, even when the one expresses itself as the other. In writing *Beloved*, Toni Morrison does not choose her title casually.

6

The Reach of Literature

The Return of Civility

As a shorthand for good behavior, civility has had a long career in the common language, even when it was widely deemed (in the nineteenth century and beyond) unable to sustain a weightier conceptual burden. Its revalidation after 1989 under the lexical umbrella of civil society was largely the work of the (neo)liberal apologists of the Washington consensus. So it is striking to find a Marxist philosopher like Balibar admitting to having "borrowed the old concept of *civility*" to supplement and qualify (but not displace) the categories of emancipation and transformation.[1] How is civility working differently from these two more familiarly approved political goals? What is modified or preserved when an old concept is "borrowed"? In what way is its residual apparatus important to us now? Why is it useful to attempt to reinvigorate the long-standing relation between civility and literary pedagogy I have been describing in this book? Civility began its career in close alliance with literature, which is a medium for slowing down and rendering deliberative the changes that emancipation and transformation portend; both are components of the reflective detachment that Elias theorized as critical to modernity. Throughout, civility has been claimed as offering an inhibition on the potential for immediate violence, even as it enacted its own microaggressions in upholding a social peace between small groups that themselves mostly ignored the immanent violence of the whole (for example, in states profiting from chattel slavery). Balibar also appears to endorse civility's effort at distance from violence but insists that violence can never be fully mitigated or displaced. Violence is always present and inconvertible, so civility must be thought out explicitly *with* (not just against) violence to enable and justify its identity as antiviolence. Migrant workers and exiled writers are presented as allies in Balibar's program for a newly imagined Europe. And many writers, exiled or not, themselves often write about migrants. Is literature more generally still also an optimum vehicle for antiviolence, for the dispersal and disassembly of affiliations and identities that antiviolence models?

Such might seem to be the case. Balibar's idea of civility's effort at "a distantiation internal to those identifications without which there can be no human solidarity," bringing about a "retreat from the collective," is close to Rorty's ironism and very much what literary pedagogy has conventionally been about.[2] The construction of national literatures (or even class solidarities) might seem to have done exactly the opposite, binding together precisely those "substantialist images of the political community" that Balibar most wishes to unsettle (p. 145). But what print culture can bring together, it can also push apart. Nationalist consolidations have usually been achieved by negation, by some form of violence, whether by way of the simple agreement to forget that Renan described or by more visible aggressions: book burnings, the banishing or imprisoning of writers, the prohibition of publication or circulation, the forging of simplified canons or the flagrant 'rewriting' that befell, for example, the filming of Leon Feuchtwanger's *Jew Süss* in Nazi Germany.[3] But these substantialist moments are offset by any and every commitment to the slow time of reading, which exits active life, offering a severance of contemplation from application that opens up the prospect not only of inertia and paralysis but also of the unpredictable event. From Schiller to Arnold and beyond, this has been the desideratum of the literary effect in the West. It has been commended by conservative or centrist critics for its capacity to head off explosive violence, first in individuals (through the rituals of *Bildung*) and then in significant groups (through the education system). The accommodationist effect has in turn been the object of critique from the left, as when literature is consigned wholly or dominantly to the domain of ideology. But 'left' aesthetic theory has also consistently worked to secure some sphere of positive potential, analytic or transformative, in the scene of reading, listening or contemplating. Bakhtin, Adorno, Marcuse, Williams and others have taken up the Schillerian 'safe space' of the aesthetic as testing rather than (or as well as) reaffirming the status quo. Hence the apparent contradiction that literature sustains: that poetry makes nothing happen and that "written words are very dangerous things."[4] Balibar's challenge here is significant: if violence is inconvertible, always immanent and fundamental to social and political life, then there can be no expectation that literature (or anything else) could or should remove it or wish it away. Art's function of mitigation, of countering extremes, becomes not a denial or disappearing of violence but an engagement with it, a pointing toward the task of understanding its scope and extent, independent of any contingently activated counterviolence.[5] It becomes, in other words, not a simple negation but a *critique* of violence, a taking of account. The more pervasive violence is seen to be—not just wars and bombings but a phenomenon including long-durational social, political and environmental 'slow' violence (as Rob Nixon calls it)—the less it becomes possible to imagine any literature that can avoid registering its footprints. The capacity of literature to defend an ideology that professes nonviolence is still compelled to present that violence; and, conversely, a literature that appears to be possessed by or even be thought to celebrate violence—Ernst Jünger's *Storm of Steel*, for example—is always, as writing, held at a virtual distance from the unmediated experience of dealing out death. Such immunities do not of course preclude writers being punished for what they write, as Salman Rushdie's career attests, but they do project what they write as eventually (given time) uncontainable by reductive attributions of monolithic meaning: the Hitlerian model of reading. The task of literature is thus to touch constantly and critically on the prevailing forms of violence without ever closing off the inconvertibility (to use Balibar's term) of violence itself. As privileged concepts, both literature and civility are premised on exclusions—the uncivil, the nonliterary—but these relatively minor aggressions are (unless exploited by other interests) framed by a general performance of reflective detachment that inhibits acts of irreversible violence.[6] That violence, Balibar suggests, must still be confronted as potentially beyond transformation.

Accordingly it is no longer possible (if it ever was) to conceive of culture or *Bildung* as outside the orbit of violence, as inhabiting a sequestered place from which one might emerge, inspired and recharged, to confront that violence. Nor can literature be identified with that limited idea of civility (never uncontested, as we have seen) as pure tolerance, urbanity and serenity. The forms and contents of violence are not always predictable, but they are never absent, unless by what Marcuse described as "a leap into a totally other world."[7] The charismatic re-enchantments of magic realism—Carpentier's Caribbean, Marquez's Colombia, Rushdie's India, (Isabel) Allende's Chile—engage with an implacable historical violence that constitutes the occasion for their conjurings. What indeed is magic realism if not the trope by which superficially implausible solutions to or escapes from inconvertible violence are imaged as outwittings of death and destruction? *One Hundred Years of Solitude* begins with a man facing a firing squad. *The Kingdom of This World* creates a political faith out of a death that is not accepted as death, an event that contributes to animating a revolution. The protagonist of Rushdie's *Shalimar the Clown* defies a gravity that is as much historical as physical. Hamid's *Exit West* has doors that open to erase vast spatial distances. Magic realism accords a critical agency to ordinary people that allows for the expression of transformative ideals, making it an appropriate medium for decolonization and national-liberation fictions: hence, perhaps, its relative rarity in mainstream (majoritarian) anglophone fiction, which has tended to employ exemplary small groups as islands of civility. It also allows for the staging of a violence contained (and made bearable) by a second layer of fictionality within what is already fiction.[8] Balibar's "borrowed" and updated civility does not allow for any segregation of virtues: there is no conceptual triumphalism pretending to explain and solve our problems. Again, civility is now *with* violence, even as it differs from it. In staging its own relation to that violence, literature retains a relative distance and capacity for critique, but this offers no absolute guarantees against its capture by violent interests. At the same time, if literature cannot in advance be sure of doing or avoiding harm or being deployed by others either way, it is never, by virtue of its primary commitment to the figurative, *directly* responsible for violence.

This raises an important question about what we mean by 'hate speech,' one of the major current targets of civility culture. If we accept that literature cannot be *directly* responsible for violence, is hate speech then not possible in literature?[9] Can it still *incite* such speech? And, if any writing can arguably be made literary by imposing a certain context, does the same exemption potentially extend to all writing? If I am caught writing 'Kill all the XYZs' on the wall of a building, I am likely to be arrested for a hate crime as well as for defacing property: I am visibly authoring a statement, in real time, in the manner of an act of speech. If I escape detection and the slogan remains without an attributable author, it will still likely be taken as a form of hate speech, even though it is now anonymous. If, however, I put my name to a novel in which this act is described as taking place, even in the first person, I am likely to feel safer: I can invoke the aesthetic alibi. But every one of these examples could be imagined as turning out differently. The very same hateful slogan on a wall might be applauded within a fascist state, while a literary statement on the other side ('Free all the XYZs') could just as readily lead to persecution. The protective assumption about the immunity of literature has been pressured in both theocratic societies (the Rushdie *fatwa*) and liberal-secular ones (the Chatterley and Ulysses trials).[10] All writing is a risk, in other words, however remote that risk might seem. There are no absolute guarantees; immunity and vulnerability are not singular conditions. Neither are violence and nonviolence, or antiviolence.

It is this predicament of inevitable risk (of violence being done *to* authors as well as *by way of* their books) that justifies the appeal for aesthetic immunity, which is never an abstract absolute. Only by defending a position that is *never* a given (the freedom of literature) can a place be made for the possibility of saying anything about everything. That said, there is a strong in-place respect for the claim to aesthetic immunity, both in the positioning of the writer in society (as half out of it) and in the rhetoricity of what is acknowledged as literary writing. Given that, as Derrida puts it, what we call literature is "linked to an authorization to say everything" and that its saying makes sense only in relation to institutions that permit or constrain it, it is always in more than one place with more than one option: a book banned in one place is a cause célèbre in another.[11] Thus, "there is no literature without a *suspended* relation to meaning and reference. *Suspended* means *suspense*, but also *dependence*, condition, conditionality. In its suspended condition, literature can only exceed itself" (p. 48). Literature hangs on (requires) what is around it but pays its debt by creating suspense and suspicion toward those dependencies. Even the most apparently revolting texts generate an interest "from which no intimidation, no dogmatism, no simplification should turn us away" (p. 59). Although the profound meditation on and deconstruction of democracy in Derrida's *Rogues* does not make explicit reference to the literary, its affiliations may be traced in the exposition of the "pure ethics" that is ruined by focusing on the neighbor (thus the small group) at the expense of what is "unrecognizable, beyond all knowledge, all cognition and all recognition."[12] Naomi Tadmor has taught us to be circumspect in our evaluation of neighborliness as made over into English in the King James Bible.[13] As an analogue to the standard literary pedagogy that moves between private reading and the classroom, the image of neighborhood makes sense. But not all pedagogy is thus local (critics write and review books) and literature 'itself' is capable of circulating indefinitely. While the new social media are overwhelmingly used for punctilious, brief and non- or minimally literary communications, one can also read a book on a smartphone. Derrida's "democracy to come" is a literature-like construct, calling for a "militant and interminable political critique," remaining always "aporetic," demanding "the right to self-critique," staying free from "all teleology" and unlimited by "any conditional hospitality on the borders of a policed nation-state."[14] Literature too is always to come, even when it has already been (the text never reads the same twice over). It can pop up who knows where, picked up by who knows whom, left in a waiting room, hiding on a shelf, rescued from the trash. Literature, as deconstruction, is play and pleasure, a virus that does no harm, leaving everything where it is except in our thoughts and imaginations. And those are not predictable. So, again, literature makes nothing happen, but, again, it is a *happening* of nothing, an event, making something exist that was not there before, something soliciting attention. The happening is not violent but is always available for being rendered by someone into something abetting violence.

And yet there continue to be questions about the possible violence of language 'itself.' Judith Butler has recently redirected us to Benjamin's seemingly inexhaustible essay on violence, which makes the gnomic and undeveloped claim that language (*die Sprache*) is "wholly inaccessible" to violence.[15] In an effort to make sense of this notoriously obscure claim, Butler turns to another Benjaminian argument about translation and translatability, both between and within languages. Even this, she concedes, might be a "moment of great idealism" (p. 128). For if we include both written and spoken language under the umbrella of *die Sprache*, then we will run into obvious objections about performative functions like the death sentence, as well as more ordinary instances of hateful speech. These are hard to imagine as "wholly inaccessible" to violence. The written word, arguably, is more intelligible as such. Schiller and others acknowledge that the plastic artist, like the ordinary toolmaker, does not hesitate to do violence (*Gewalt anzutun*) upon his materials, though unlike the artisan he is concerned to efface its traces in the pursuit of a formal beauty.[16] This seems obvious enough in relation to, say, sculpture, where work is done upon a passive medium. (Though it must be said that most of us would not think of chipping into stone as a violence comparable to violating a living body.)[17] But how does it apply to music, or to language, Benjamin's concern in the passage just cited? Language in itself is nothing; it is only in its uses that violence can be imagined. The incidence of hate speech is not a condemnation of speech itself.

A primal violence has nonetheless been associated with *all* instances of designating things by words, as if violence really does reside in language itself:

> What if . . . humans exceed animals in their capacity for violence precisely because they *speak*? . . . Language simplifies the designated thing, reducing it to a single feature. It dismembers the thing, destroying its organic unity, treating its parts and properties as autonomous. It inserts the thing into a field of meaning which is ultimately external to it.[18]

There is something wrong with this. Language does not dismember anything; it represents and incites attention. Žižek's example is the word gold, whose uses and associations for us have nothing to do with its "immediate reality" or "natural texture." But, leaving aside the troubling question of what is real and natural, does gold care or suffer? Is this the same as describing, say, a bear as monstrous or a human as savage? For those born into a language community (all of us), there is no immediacy as soon as there is a word, and there is no language that is not already full of words in use. Heidegger is invoked as the theorist of the originary violence that creates language, gives names and makes possible its subsequent compliance with all forms of ideology and divisiveness. This is indeed a kind of epistemic violence, a limiting of our sense of actual difference by the imposition of conceptual unities: tree, chair, metal. It is an abstract, proleptic violence, a provision of the tools for future application, tools that perhaps condition us *for* violence by encouraging the passing over of fine distinctions. But (unless perhaps to a pantheist) the applications are not equally consequential for precious metals as for, say, racial minorities. Violence can accrue with or after language but not, or not in the same way, *in* it. And language 'itself' comes in various forms. Do conjunctions and prepositions support the same sorts of constrictive functions as nouns, adjectives, verbs and adverbs? Derrida tells us that "according to Levinas, nonviolent language would be a language which would do without the verb *to be*, that is, without predication."[19] This is a profound insight, one that questions not only the urge to specify the other (person or thing) but also the compulsion to identify oneself. Are all of the violences attested to in words the same sorts of violence? If we can indeed posit a primary, metaphysical violence in language 'itself,' is that as important as the violence exercised in place and time by those who make use of it?

Matthew Arnold has something to say about this. By way of a critique of the self-puffery of the "old Anglo-Saxon race," he offers a newspaper account of "a girl named Wragg" who seems to have murdered her illegitimate child and left its body lying on a hillside. The account concludes bluntly with the sentence "Wragg is in custody."[20] Arnold ponders "the natural growth amongst us of such hideous names,—Higginbottom, Stiggins, Bugg! In Ionia and Attica they were luckier in this respect" (p. 22). What may look at first sight like a nasty piece of class condescension bears closer attention. It is certainly a criticism of popular newspaper rhetoric and seems to reinforce the points later made by Richards and Leavis about the dangerous simplifications of everyday language. The further point is that these names are derivations from Anglo-Saxon. They are quite neutral in themselves, but they appear crude and primitive because they subsist in English alongside names with more refined associations (Arnold, for example). Names of Norman-French origin suggest gentility and status because those who are born into them have historically been at the top of the social and economic ladder, writing the articles and owning the newspapers. It is the acceptance of these names as dominant or normal that makes Wragg and Bugg seem ugly or uncouth, and their prevalence in the working class and not elsewhere reflects the social divisions that were put in place after the Norman Conquest and can still be seen in nineteenth-century England. Wragg, in other words, hardly has a chance; her abjection is written into her name, which further signifies the atrocity of her deed.[21] It is the assumption of an already-assumed inhumanity that allows the lopping off of her Christian name. The violence she may have committed is physical and punctilious; the violence to which she is subjected in and by language is both preexisting and lifelong. The ugliness of the person is prescribed long before her act of infanticide. Wragg is easy prey to the editors of the local rag now gone national. There is no invitation to sympathy or concern. A girl *named* Wragg is a girl who could never have named herself. Morrison's *Beloved*—which also works from newspaper reports—will imagine Wragg's deed in a very different way.

Arnold's story is an example not of the violence of language but of the violence that language systems can effectively articulate and preserve. In a world where everyone or no one has a name like Stiggins or Bugg (Ionia or Attica, Arnold claims, would work), no violence would be enacted by way of names. Wragg's name functions as a way to naturalize social difference and to defer or displace the need for its critique. But, in isolating the newspaper phrases as he does, as if it were a poem, Arnold generates the sort of attentiveness associated with literary criticism and restores precisely the social-historical turmoil that Adorno seeks to re-enliven in the experience of high art. The language of critique thus here reactivates and disputes the violence of the statement that is its object. But it is unconvincing to claim that statement and critique offer the same violence, as some property of language 'itself.' To be sure, interpretation is violent to the extent that one reading might fend off or repress another or might lead (others) to violence (say, a class-based revolution in England); yes, we might track a certain ambivalence in Arnold's exposure of the darker side of the Anglo-Saxon imaginary, whereby he cannot fully stand with the Wraggs of this world. But we would be hard put, I think, to discount the utopian element in his anecdote that points toward a world in which no revolution would be needed and where there is much less violence to be imagined than what we currently endure. Any sensed uncertainty in Arnold 'himself' indeed becomes evidence of the power of the literary (critical) experience to fracture unitary subjectivity into a collage of desires and discomforts that is already the signal of an uncontrollable collectivity far exceeding what conventional *Bildung* can contain. While popular outrage at the treatment of Wragg *could* have been generated by Arnold's account and *might* have helped inspire riots or revolution, it could also have encouraged the passage of laws against socially divisive names—very different degrees of violence, or none at all.

To put it simply: the language that allows for the naming of Wragg also allows for a critique of that naming, and there is nothing predetermined about the outcome (or lack of it) when this is revealed. There is violence by way of language, but not *in* language, or in *language*. There is only ever a use of words, not always conscious but never all-determining. One might then describe literature as that which is more resistant than other kinds of language to being deployed in the cause of single or simple messages, a quality it shares with other aesthetic media and with some theory. This is a very traditional and well-tried description: I am saying nothing new here. Irony, ambiguity, paradox, aporia, various kinds of play that may or may not result in a 'result,' are generic terms in the modern concept of literature and of its pedagogic potentials. While the 'making nothing happen' of poetry, like the 'doing nothing' in the way of political action, may be a positive gesture in the face of ambient simplifications, there is no way of avoiding the risk (and the accusation) of evasion, of complicity, of standing by in the presence of atrocity. This is why, as Adorno realized, the scrupulous qualities of critique (and of literature) cannot simply be celebrated. There are no guarantees. The immunities that Kant and Schiller claimed for art and for aesthetic judgment can neither be taken for granted nor confidently dismissed.

Updating Schiller

It is well-known that the insights of what we call Romanticism remain seemingly indispensable in describing our contemporary situation; even as they are regularly exposed and called into question as suspicious and restrictive, we appear to be unable to do without them. The questions then arise: How continuous is this apparent continuity? Are we trapped in mere reproduction, unable to even perceive the needs of a new pedagogical moment, or is there something still unexhausted, still 'to come,' in the paradigms we inherit (or borrow) from Kant and Schiller? Arnold and

Richards, in their deliberate attempt to nourish a liberal subject, had no qualms about adopting the legacy of their predecessors. Our generation—under the pressure of a larger range of unignorable violences—cannot allow itself to be so comfortably indebted, prone as we are to rethinking our own legacy as one of privilege, exclusion, gendered and racial violence. Postromantic writers have been wary of endorsing the play drive as something intact and untouchable by the death drive. But there has yet to emerge any sign of a complete break with the past, one of whose imperatives is indeed that we maintain a constant self-inquiry, consulting with our inmate controllers. We are accordingly impelled to trouble that past, to reread it between the lines, to discover unnoticed possibilities. Derrida is a master of this kind of reading; all of those to whom he has paid close attention now look different (think of Plato, Hegel, Rousseau, Augustine and so many others). The foundational "isms" of philosophy are all rendered unstable and therefore open to rebuilding. The process is intellectually and even emotionally difficult and stressful (for there are various thrones and altars inscribed here), although—as Derrida always insisted—nothing in the world is changed by deconstruction alone. And yet its message is that things could change, and mostly should change, perhaps if the routines of an education could form themselves around the project of deconstruction itself. Critique per se cannot do this work, but it can ask the questions and set the terms through which the work can be undertaken. The play of deconstruction that allowed Derrida to first offer us the glimpse of a grammatology (also to come) was situated in a shift in the dynamics of violence, in the breaking up (which may have been no more than a transformation) of the colonial-imperial order of Euro-America of "an original and powerful ethnocentrism."[22] Thirty some years later Derrida confirms, in *Rogues* and *Specters of Marx*, that the regnant violence is now only more apparent in "the terrible plight of so many millions of human beings."[23] And over the years since those books were written, there has been no radical diminishing of suffering and exploitation. What can a literary pedagogy hope or expect to achieve in the face of this inconvertible violence?

Reckoning with that violence is a palpable compulsion in much of the intellectual work that is being done in the name of theory. Few if any have thought harder and worked harder to address this question than

Gayatri Chakravorty Spivak. She produced the first English translation of *Of Grammatology*; she has served as both formative intelligence and lightning rod for articulating what is called feminist, the postcolonial and the global (leaving none of these terms undisputed); she has throughout her career fronted and advanced critical questions of translation; and, to an uncommon degree, she has traveled up and down and across the pedagogic spectrum with her reflections on disciplinarity in the humanities and in her teaching work both in the high-prestige lecture circuits and seminars of metropolitan 'theory' and in the village primary schools (to use an inadequate shorthand) of rural Bengal. Her collected thoughts on the role of the literary-aesthetic thus command careful attention. And they begin with Schiller or, more precisely, with "sabotaging Schiller."[24] Where Schiller looks to the aesthetic for balance and resolution, working for the formation of an unworldly subject outside the sphere of all violence, Spivak seeks to extricate "an open series of double binds" (p. 19) that still remains within "the aporetic intuition of the German nineteenth century" (p. 20) articulated by both Kant (on one reading) and the irony theorists but then domesticated in Schiller's own reading of Kant. Her road from Kant to Gregory Bateson leads through Paul de Man, whose exposure of an aporetic Romanticism (at odds with the dominant *Bildung* project of harmonious subjectivity) has been widely and rightly acknowledged.[25] But to read Schiller thus is not to abject him or to negate what remains important about the aesthetic alternative: the displacing of "belief onto the terrain of the imagination" and the consequent virtualization of religion and nationalism (p. 10). Spivak's "permission to be figurative" (p. 437) recalls I. A. Richards's work on pseudo-statements (and, perhaps more radically, the fully thought anarchism of Shelley's project), and it is one that only a humanities education has any record or prospect of providing. Her aspiration is that such education should be available to everyone; her sad conjecture is that the corporatization of the global university may make this increasingly unlikely.

With its emphasis on the "slow transformation of the mind" (p. 38) and on making people "ready to listen" as a result of a "long-term and collective method" (p. 66), Spivak's project directly cites those of Schiller, Arnold, Richards and Leavis, although there is no Arnoldian talk of using force to keep down dissent until reform can do its work. Her investment in the "uncoercive rearrangement of desires" (p. 108) has to be staged within an already-violent world, not as a prefatory sideshow or insular refuge. The message is at once hopeful and not so hopeful. At times Spivak seems to feel, like Arnold, that she will die in the wilderness and that the promised land may never appear. Everything short of changing the operations of "capital and data" may be mere "damage control" (p. 1):

> Deep language learning and unconditional ethics are so out of joint with this immensely powerful brave new world-machine that people of our sort make this plea [for aesthetic education] because we cannot do otherwise, because our shared obsession declares that some hope of bringing about the epistemological revolution needed to turn capital around to gendered social justice must still be kept alive against all hope. (p. 26)

Schiller's hoped-for aesthetic state has become a project to be pursued without faith in its success. In a world where there is no consistent commitment to democracy on the part of international civil society (pp. 2, 295), and even less hope from nation-state thinking, what place is there for the aesthetic? Spivak's literary-aesthetic mode echoes Balibar's civility and Derrida's democracy-to-come in its modeling of operations that are non-holistic, fractured, incomplete and inconvertible. Language, closely observed, teaches us that we mostly do not understand each other, whether monolingually or interlingually (p. 518). This "peculiarity" of language comes out most unignorably (as de Man kept saying) in the "singular rhetoricity" of literature (p. 353), in its reminder that "all communicated action, including self-communicated action, is destined for errancy" (p. 28).[26]

This errancy includes not just a wandering offtrack, a getting lost in the forest, but a mistaking, a doing bad, being taken for harm, or the risk thereof. To say, as Spivak does, that "the Euro-U.S. subject must court schizophrenia as a figure" (p. 27) is not a comfortable recommendation even if one accepts the figurative as itself a protective limitation. Insights about the aporetic condition do not preempt action (which is often not possible) as much as make you feel uncomfortable about taking it. So "the typecase of the ethical sentiment is regret, not self-congratulation" (p. 105). The aesthetic demeanor is not particularly (or at all) serene, but this is the ground of any hope we might have for it. An acquiescence in its traditional effort toward depoliticization, or what looks like it, does avoid immediate recourse to the sword but does not bring peace.[27] If it does not seem to embrace the risk of the real, many writers have still been taken to be doing just that and have been punished for it. The profession of pseudo-statement has not protected literary authors from being made to seem dangerous. Literary teaching must work against such judgments, but not by denying a world of violence. The violence must be figured in. What we inherit from Schiller (and should not deny) is not then any credible solution but an exemplary description of the problem that requires him to take himself fully out of the world (of violence) in order to imagine returning to it in a less destructive (and self-destructive) way. Like the moment of midnight, no still point of absolute immunity from living in time, from oscillating between form and sense drives, can ever be held fast, except as an ideal. The *Spieltrieb* (play drive) frees us but cannot, without ceasing to be itself, put us in a new place without putting a stop to its own momentum. The prescription for a life best lived would then be as much time spent with the *Spieltrieb* as possible, but only by accepting that no one can stay there forever or even for long.[28] The experience of beauty is always contingently pressured by the need to return to ordinary life; the best we can do is to dwell with the moment for as long as possible. Education in the aesthetic meanwhile offers a formal opportunity to develop the habits conducive to diminishing any inclination toward violence that comes from failing to question the demands of knowledge or desire, failing to process them as *Schein* (appearance, representation).

Jacques Rancière also begins with Schiller, whom he sees as presenting a challenge: how to align the art of the beautiful with the art of living.[29] Here the disjunction between art and politics is handled somewhat differently: Rancière takes the risk of being accused of aestheticizing politics by proposing a common mechanism shared by art *and* politics even as neither leads to or from the other in any substantive way. The mechanism is *dissensus*, "a conflict between *sense* and *sense* . . . between a sensory presentation and a way of making sense of it." Artworks and politics both function by way of a "dissensual re-configuration of the common experience of the sensible."[30] Neither leads *directly* to any change in the world, but each achieves, in a similar way, "a rupture in the specific configuration that allows us to stay in 'our' assigned places in a given state of things" in a way that "can never be calculated" (p. 143). Art and politics perform incalculable rupture: the "politics of art" and the "poetics of politics" tend toward one another but cannot meet up without "suppressing themselves" (p. 183). Neither should preoccupy itself with converting its disruptive energies into limited events or stable messages; hence Rancière has little time for any turn to ethics. He makes another bold statement. At a time like the present, when a radically disruptive understanding of politics is becoming harder and harder to experience owing to the "shrinking of political space," art becomes more important as a "space of refuge for dissensual practice" (p. 145). Art, it seems, is back in point position. Indeed, "man is a political animal because he is a literary animal who lets himself be diverted from his 'natural' purpose by the power of words."[31]

It is not new to claim that the aesthetic works by incalculable disruption; some version of this has been its avowed function since around 1800 if not before, whether by way of the beautiful or of the sublime (though the disruption of the beautiful is more peaceful and thus more accommodating to the achievement of serenity). What is less familiar is the claim that politics works in the same way, as an activity not to be judged by achieved ends but by its continuance as a disruptive practice "hollowing out" the 'real' and "multiplying it in a polemical way" (p. 149). There is no "real world" except what is offered to us as the "univocal" object of consensus. Dissensus is therefore preferable because it prompts us to refuse what is preordained and to set going the process for ourselves. The art-politics relation is somewhat akin to what Kant theorizes as the relation between the aesthetic and the moral: the one does not produce the other, but they have enough in common that competence in the one can train us *for* the other, albeit without guarantees. Rancière claims a complete parity of process whose integrity is preserved because there is *no* crossover, no linking of the two circuits: politics and art engage separately in an incentive toward the redistribution of the sensible.[32] There is thus no aestheticization *of* politics, against which Walter Benjamin had warned: Rancière's paradigm sponsors no torchlight parades. And yet there is no rule that says we cannot experience both the aesthetic and the political in the course of an hour, a day or a life, as long as neither mistakes itself for the other or sees one as the goal of the other. This part of Rancière's argument looks like a classic anarchist position, which, like Benjamin's divine (power of) violence, insists that only by forswearing all teleology, all tendency toward law (or policing), can the force of pure disruption be affirmed. Any slowing down of the *Spieltrieb*, however locally approvable, is going to betray the energy of constant subversion and to diminish the desire for what Derrida called the democracy to come. Such pure oppositionality must continue to seem appealing in a world where more and more political space is being taken over by repressive agencies. In such a world, the language-based nature of politics is a saving force rather than a restriction. Politics is analogous to the literary arts in that both require an openness to "the power of words" that "introduce lines of fracture and disincorporation into imaginary collective bodies" and produce only "uncertain communities."[33] Words thus deployed can never become commodities because no one can say what they are worth. Art and politics must constantly be set together but just as constantly held apart so as not to collapse into "the indistinctness of ethics."[34]

And what of violence and civility? Rancière's "uncertain communities" accord in their imagined practices with Balibar's notion of civility, and whether they generate explosive energy or mere irritation, their affiliations with what happens in the world are unpredictable and therefore open to persecution or punishment by others in the name of order and security. Aesthetic and political statements are in this sense no safer than hands-on activism. Their power, if they have any, can lie only in their *claim* to autonomy, one that can as readily be denied as acceded to, but one that must be defended as doggedly as possible.[35] That defense must include an avowal of the intellectual-theoretical messiness that comes with denying the holistic construction of the aesthetic, both for what it is (in the sense that can assert, rightly, that there is no such 'thing' as literature) and for how it interacts with whatever is deemed other than aesthetic: the world, the law, the state and so on. Of course, one can make the disruptive and incomplete themselves into a fetish, another icon of pure thinking, thus making virtue of discomfort: Spivak's analogies of the double bind and of schizophrenia work against that impulse. If we are to hold off from rediscovering wholeness, harmony and beauty in the principle of disruption itself, considerable energy must be expended to keep open the awareness of conditioning violence not as the 'other' to art but as immanent in the social medium that produces and disseminates it.

The accusation of making disruption into a new assurance of correct thinking, and thus the end of the story, has become familiar as part of the left critique of post-structuralism, and so it is important that, if the task be one of subsisting *with* violence, any aesthetics of disruption not function as permission to avoid confronting actual violence and discomfort. Spivak's focus on schizophrenia seeks to preclude just this by displacing the curative aspiration of the psychoanalytic movement in favor of its most rebarbative syndrome. To similar ends, much of Terry Eagleton's work has insisted on the connection of the aesthetic to the body, and to a body that suffers or is threatened by suffering. Aesthetic freedom in its modern formation is for him not the result of any pure sensation or intellection but of the dominance of the very commodity form that it claims to oppose. It is the "anonymous freedom of the market place" that releases art from its institutional affiliations (church and state). It is commodity culture, as Marx showed us, that disrupts and reorders the world, melts solids into air, mocking "the obsessive rankings of traditional culture" even as it depends upon them to subsist.[36] Commodity culture is coincident with aesthetic culture, and aesthetics bears within it the contradictions of commodity form as it both reveals and conceals the conditions of its own origins, meeting the ideological needs of bourgeois culture while at the same time threatening to "escalate uncontrollably" and undercut all assurances about what is given: duty, rationality, truth and virtue (p. 103). Aesthetic theory must thus be seen to subsist within a dialectic, inciting *both* pacification *and* subversion. Schiller's paradoxes, for Eagleton, are not the result of some kind of intellectual misconception but "signs of genuine political dilemmas" (p. 113). And these are registered not just in the domain of intellectual work, of theory, but on the "sensuous body," which is the origin and object of play and pleasure, but also of pleasure denied and of outright pain. The aesthetic is thus always an "amphibious concept" subsisting by both creation and uncreation, *both* capitalist ideology *and* its antagonist, an agent of freedom and a servant of repression (p. 9). Most of those writing about it choose one over the other and sidestep the problem of their intimate alliance.[37]

Eagleton thus turns to tragedy, and the debate about it, for evidence of the inevitability of the suffering body and its embeddedness in a higher level of vulnerable passivity than is commonly acknowledged. Critics and theorists have tried to glorify tragedy, rendering it heroic or self-determining, and have thus sidelined the ways in which it is both avoidable and demeaning and not at all "life-affirming."[38] Tragedy is about "finitude and frailty" (p. 288), and to frame it simply in heroic-aristocratic terms is to indulge a nostalgia for what probably never was and to deflect attention from a historical condition in which more abject destructive forces have been dominant: "warfare, butchery, disease, starvation, political murder" (p. 205). Not to recognize this is to misconstrue the nature of violence and the responsibilities of its agents. Eagleton here responds to the challenge set out by Adorno, whose widely circulated thoughts about life after Auschwitz are but the tip of a complex reckoning with the function of the aesthetic in the face (and body) of violence. Much of Eagleton's argument is set out in Adorno: art frees us from reification by registering historical antagonisms as problems (rather than triumphs) of form, but it cannot efface its connection to the fetish or deny its conservative elements: "artworks are, a priori, socially culpable, and each one that deserves its name seeks to expiate this guilt." Art's "objectivation" "implies insensitivity to reality," but we cannot ignore its roots in the utopian aspiration.[39] Being dependent on representation, art is the giver of death but can "heal the wound with the spear that inflicted it." It is "complicitous with ideology in that it feigns the factual existence of reconciliation," but "even in the greatest works of aesthetic unity the echo of social violence is to be heard" by way of the "intransigence" dictated by form (p. 134).

This is not easy to grasp. Form, for Adorno, is what adjudicates the relation between violence and the not-violent in both the aesthetic experience itself (shaping raw materials in the Hegelian mode) and in its historically particular relation to the ambient violence of its world. All art begins in violence, but each artwork models a specifically time-bound instance of other violences. Artworks do "stand for nonviolence"—or, one might say, for not having the power of violence (*Gewaltlosigkeit*). But if the violence of their creation, as form, is already in the past, the activation of this process still takes form as recollection (*Erinnerung*) (pp. 241–42). And that activation is still explosive, coming as something "momentary and sudden," a shudder (*Schauer*) or shock that reproduces (however old the work might be) the "historical antagonism of subject and object" (pp. 79, 84). Adorno calls this, variously, *Schock*, *Explosion*, and *Erschütterung*, adopting in good Modernist style a modified violence in our perception of the aesthetic object as both alternative and allusion (by enactment) to the violence of the world that the passage in and out of representation can be said to mimic.[40] The shock is so brief as to embody "an instant at a standstill," blasting open (*sprengt*), effecting an "incineration of appearances" (*Verbrennen der Erscheinung*) (pp. 84–85). This updating of Schiller's zero moment of time-out-of-time is much more stressful and discomforting than in Schiller's original, perhaps owing to Adorno's enhanced sense of the deadening effects of modern life and ideology, as well as of the weight of recent atrocities. Shock is a "memento of the liquidation of the I" that displaces the distraction offered by the culture industry's perversions of the aesthetic (p. 245) with something more exigent, something not quite uncoercive in its rearrangement of desires, but also something not to be finished with. Something inconvertible, in other words.

Adorno's efforts to embody these insights in the style of writing philosophy are well known: a rebarbative density in the face of the jargon of everyday language. Works of art do have a cognitive content—they are not *mere* representations, pure *Schein*—that is reborn in the shock of the aesthetic encounter, not as a passive 'reader response' but as an intuition of the original and disturbing historical energies informing their coming into being. Living as we do in and through a "damaged" life, art both enacts that damage and, in being made and being seen, read or heard, points to possibilities beyond it. Because the making of representation in an artwork does act upon the material world by changing what is given (good Hegelian doctrine here), that representation, however monstrous, always gives notice that it could have been otherwise, providing an openness in the eye of the listener, reader or beholder that makes a space for art's utopian component. Artworks thus satisfy and fail to satisfy at the same time; the pleasure we might take from them, and the hopes they might project, is offset by a violence in their own creative moment (and our revisiting of it) that, albeit without any power of actual violence, models or echoes the ambient destruction that is endemic in the world. To escape from this, even briefly, is a source of guilt: guilty pleasure. In *Negative Dialectics*, Adorno has this to say, explaining the urge to philosophize:

> The only trouble with self-preservation is that we cannot help suspecting the life to which it attaches us of turning into something that makes us shudder: into a

specter, a piece of the world of ghosts. . . . The guilt of a life which purely as a life will strangle other life, according to statistics that eke out an overwhelming number of killed with a minimal number of rescued . . . this guilt is irreconcilable with living.[41]

Artworks invoke the same responses. They "kill what they objectify by tearing it away from the immediacy of its life," but they work in so doing to "save it from death," making it lifeless to let it live again for an indefinite future. So "the aesthetic image is a protest against nature's fear that it will dissipate into the chaotic." What it achieves is far from "impotent comfort." We may call it "reconciliation" but not in the classical sense: it "feigns" the "factual existence of reconciliation" (and here it is complicit with ideology) but at the same time insists on the "intransigence" of form and "consciousness of the nonidentical."[42] Its enigmatic quality, open to resurrection in every act of contemplation, is carried in its "fracturedness" (*Abgebrochensein*), which is "never transparent to itself in the moment in which it appears" and thus requires interpretation. At this point art and philosophy coincide in their search for "truth content."[43] Adorno is unwilling to endorse the idea of art as without effect; the effect is dependent upon an anxiety of disorigination that makes possible an existence through historical time.

Doing Nothing

The feigning of reconciliation is a clear rewriting of Schiller, for whom feigning (as poesis, *Schein*, representation) was the mechanism of reconciliation itself. It is indeed an inversion of Schiller in the sense that fracturedness is now the mechanism, even the goal of, aesthetic experience and not the condition that the aesthetic must aspire to overcome. The violence that Schiller keeps out is now at the core of the artwork, although the violence is not actual (and may thus be called *gewaltlos*) because, as art, and being already made *as* art, it has no direct social agency. That can only follow, or not, from shock and interpretation. As such it remains compatible with one of Schiller's guiding convictions: the importance of doing nothing, or seeming to. Adorno himself, in the face of the student activism of the late 1960s, (in)famously reproduced Schiller's attitude to the political turmoil of the 1790s in also arguing for doing nothing beyond critical thinking, suspending direct engagement or the avowal of commitment. He warned against the allure of the "pseudo-activity" that can only attempt to "rescue enclaves of immediacy in the midst of a thoroughly mediated and rigidified society" by satisfying itself merely with its own publicity while being driven largely by its own rage.[44] But there is no promise of a protective harmony in aesthetic form or of fashioning an integral subjectivity in the manner of Schiller; and, where Schiller nudges beauty toward morality, Adorno directs it to historical critique and therefore to conflict.[45] The artwork reveals but it does not resolve. Schiller's aesthetic state can be imagined as producing harmony in both individual and society: it would then be civility enacted or a preempting of any need for civility at all.[46] Adorno implies that, in the world we have, invoking civility can only be fantasy and ideology. At the same time his disclaiming of pseudo-activity requires the reactivation of art's latent energy out of a preconditioned inertia that resembles civility in its disinclination for urgent interventionist behavior.

Adorno walks a fine line: the pleasure-giving element of play must never be allowed to disengage itself from its relation to guilt and discomfort, while the acceptance of doing nothing is open to accusations of accommodation with the world as it is, with all its inequities. Often the task seems to be one of demonstrating that doing nothing is in fact doing something, just doing it in a different way. Or it may be just doing nothing after all and thus satisfying the desire to do no further harm while taking the risk that other harms simply build up incrementally while one is standing by. Judith Butler presents nonviolence as a form of action, not inaction, a "physical assertion of the claims of life," even a "way of rerouting aggression for the purposes of affirming ideals of equality and freedom."[47] Meanwhile, the brief moment of clean-handedness that Schiller saw in the aesthetic experience becomes ever more difficult to sustain or defend. We operate, in the words of one critic, in a "theoretical terrain wherein it is all but impossible to think identity or the social bond in the absence of some mechanism of abjection, subjection, possession, or sacrifice, all of which are said to be characterized by violence."[48] Not all responses to this condition have been as exigent and self-lacerating as Adorno's. There has been another and very different effort at rewriting Schiller that sets out to displace or outflank inconvertible violence by exploring versions of what

Roland Barthes called the "neutral": a mode of operation where "meaning must not gel" and where we "live according to nuance" aiming at "the suspension of the conflictual basis of discourse."[49] Suspension, not active engagement. This allies itself with the goals of traditional civility and is again embodied in manners, albeit manners bordering on "the eccentric" (p. 33). It looks also to literature, with its "nonarrogant memory" and its efforts against the "tyranny of the concept" (pp. 157–58). Already in 1976–77, Barthes's lectures were exploring "an ethics (or a physics) of distance between cohabiting subjects," a distance we might call *délicatesse* or tact, warm and affectionate but without the potential for oppression.[50] In the social world this is (once again) best cultivated in "very small groups" where freedom and cohabitation can subsist together (p. 90); the same small groups make up civility's natural environment. Literature, in its virtual life, is a mode of distancing that allows for discretionary intimacy without physically occupying the space of the other, cool and warm at the same time. A theory of coolness emerged much earlier from Weimar Germany, evident, for example, in Helmuth Plessner's advocacy of "tact" as an alternative to the dangers of community and sincerity that would soon arrive packaged as Hitlerism. Better "not coming too close and . . . not being too open," thus "protecting the other for the sake of oneself and protecting oneself for the sake of the other."[51] In a world that can turn violent at any time, indirectness is all, both to avoid doing damage to others and to protect oneself. This blending of an ethical positive and a dubious (or guilt-inducing) ethics goes back to the Romantic ironists, and we have not learned (nor should we) to dispense with taking it seriously. One version appears in the post-Holocaust figuring of art as witnessing, which at once exonerates and accuses the artist: no mere bystander, but incapable of immediate intervention.

The appetite for neutrality or tact, for standing apart or aside, for an involvement that does not spend itself on an irrevocable commitment, looks like a lifestyle implementation of good Schillerian doctrine. It was, as we have seen, identified by David Russell in Hazlitt and Lamb and their nineteenth-century readers as a "democratic practice for uncertain social times."[52] A somewhat different Romantic response to the seemingly unnegotiable gap between aesthetics and what we often call activism has been given impressive exposition in Steven Goldsmith's *Blake's Agitation*.

Goldsmith proposes that William Blake, so long taken as an icon of the writer as radical agent, is actually committed instead to a *literary* affect intended to keep alive "a revolutionary impulse he no longer believed in enacting directly." This must happen by way of the "patient work of close, critical reading and thinking," very much in the manner recommended by Adorno and Derrida (whom he acknowledges, along with Lyotard).[53] Like Kant's "nonparticipant revolutionary spectator," Blake enacts a fusion of the "impassioned work of reading" and "the slow time of waiting" (pp. 35, 316). The syndrome of agitation generates an affective disturbance in the reading subject who feels "engaged in history without having to participate publicly" (p. 72). Agitation's energy is carried in pulsation (poetic rhythm) and in sound (as fracture, noise), which "supplies no authority for violence, but . . . refuses to rule against it" (p. 120). Thought feels like action, but isn't; or, it is a somatic enacting of an action that does not pass directly into the world. It leaves an "affective remainder" (p. 156) that gestures toward a possible future public expression, but it does not go there.

Goldsmith's agitation is a more strenuous experience than Barthes's neutrality, and it locates Blake at the heart of what would become the core protocols of literary pedagogy, from Schiller to Richards and beyond. As we have seen, there are two ways to weight this syndrome: either toward the serene self assurance implicit in the common idea of *Bildung* or toward the more stressful loss of selfhood favored by Adorno, Spivak and others as elemental to critique. The first seeks to minimize any incorporation of violence; the second lives with it all the time. The first accords with a form of civility seen as maintaining an achieved social group or community by living below the radar; the second is a more insecure set of habits of the sort that Balibar specified in his use of the term *civility*, deployed as at best a mitigation (in the form of antiviolence) of an otherwise inconvertible violence. Neither offers any guarantees. Balibar's attempt to relocate civility as describing the second instead of the first of these options plays upon a tension (and a recognition of violence) that was never far from the surface in discussions of that concept but that has never before been so fully exposed as fundamental to its understanding. Nonetheless, tact and neutrality persist, in name and in spirit, as available terminologies for the Schillerian withdrawal from worldly risk and worldly contamination that remains appealing in a world so fraught with inconvertible violence. Steven Connor's case for the value of "turning aside" in the cause of preserving the peace is a model of civility turned inward by way of the "binding force of abstention."[54] Abstention clearly has considerable moral appeal in a world facing species extinction by way of the human agency that has produced catastrophic environmental and social degradation. So too the "weightless, minimally assertive, nonemphatic encounters" that Anne-Lise François writes about in commending a "nonappropriative contentment" that permits "a release from the ethical imperative to *act* upon knowledge."[55] In the manner of Schiller and Barthes, this reticence is a withdrawing from the "modern ideology of improvement" (p. 22) and from the undoubtedly masculinist commitments to "limitless duty, impossible exigency, and heroic responsibility" (p. 8). It can in this sense reasonably claim to be "nonappropriative" (p. 71). In the "lyric of inconsequence" (p. 154), once again, nothing happens, or what does happen barely rises to the noticeable. All of this adds up to a withdrawal from the representation of violence, emanating from a thoroughly commendable effort to model the possibility of a much less violent world than the one we mostly recognize around us.[56] But inevitably, even in the quiet ambience of the unnoticed and unremarkable, violence is remembered, violence resonates and resounds, violence threatens.

Reaching for the Global Novel

John Keane observes that global civil society is "a neologism of the 1990s" and thus an index of that high point of liberalism's faith in the end of conflictual history.[57] He sees that such an ideal requires civility on an almost unimaginable scale, including "respect for others expressed as politeness toward and acceptance of strangers" (p. 12). Needless to say, neither the history of civility theory nor the historical record itself shows this to be a reality, although it remains thinkable as a demand (as in Derrida) within important utopian projects. Thus, civil society can subsist by replicating and strengthening group inequalities, while deliberative democracy finds it hard to imagine itself on anything other than a small scale. Global civil society and global civility remain significant regulative ideals, but it would be a grave mistake to treat them as realities, as credible attributes of a world that seems, notwithstanding the best-intentioned idea of Europe, to have little choice between obedience to the Washington consensus or to nationalist-authoritarian governance or, more often, to a blending of the two. And yet, if political scientist Jens Bartelson is to be believed, the idea of a world community "once constituted the default setting of political thought and action," only to be unseated by the "nationalization of the concept of community" by the French Revolution.[58] The model of a global scholarly community, and of the global university network that grew around it, remains one version of what nationalism displaced; even as the corporatization of the university (itself often a national foundation) proceeds apace, it remains answerable (however nostalgically) to that ideal.[59] Is there any future for a modern version of the global scholarly community that is not based on fiscal-technocratic paradigms or on a restrictively Western political science? Could this still be a viable prospect for (literary) theory, notwithstanding the stringent critique mounted by, for example, Aijaz Ahmad, who warned of the dangers of displacing "an activist culture with a textual culture" and expanding "the centrality of *reading* as the appropriate form of politics"?[60]

It is indeed a faith in reading, and an understanding of how much in our lives depends upon it, that motivates a wide range of theorists who might otherwise seem so different: Arnold and Derrida, for example. Meanwhile, literature is a working category that we still hold apart from reading, theory and pedagogy even as their commonalities are increasingly well publicized. There is an ongoing argument about 'world literature' and an attendant problem about translation. Does world literature have to be published in English in order to qualify as 'world'? What differences matter between works written in English and those translated into it? Is any translation possible without massive redistribution of sense? What about works that go untranslated or that reach significant readerships in languages most English speakers cannot access? These questions come up both descriptively and prescriptively: *Is* there an identifiable global culture, and *should* there be?[61] Can we look, for example, to the global novel as a medium for cosmopolitan dialogue and mutual understanding, or must it tend to conform to hegemonic criteria in order to pass muster for publication and distribution?[62] If it does generate productive critique, is the aesthetic alibi (Martin Jay's phrase) sustainable only as long as it stays in its place as little more than a letting off of steam, creating the facsimile of an alternative world that can be entertained only in fiction, in entertainment itself? These questions cannot be addressed in the abstract; not all novels will obey all the predictions in all times and places. They are singular and subject to singular receptions. They are also viral; most of them circulate harmlessly and do nothing to upset the political order of things, but every so often one of them will get out of control and have a dramatic effect. We still do not know the exact degree to which *Uncle Tom's Cabin* changed the world, but few if any would argue that it did not matter at all. Who is to say exactly how much or how little the massive response to Toni Morrison's *Beloved* in the late 1980s has contributed to what now, as of very recently and thirty years later, seems to be a near-global endorsement of the Black Lives Matter movement? Once again: novels do not change the world directly. Political shifts are not triggered by the mere act of printing. But some books do escape the general acceptance of the aesthetic mode as marginal and inert and provide or assist a creative irritation of the social order.

Much of the burden of hope or expectation for literature, both local and global, has for some time rested on the novel. Edward Said speaks for many in considering the novel as "*the* aesthetic object whose connection to the expanding societies of Britain and France is particularly interesting to study."[63] Wai Chee Dimock offers global literary culture as a "form of civil society" generating a "civility" founded in a "provision for skepticism"; Pheng Cheah argues for the special role of the global south in generating a literature committed to "the endless process of opening itself."[64] The *Bildungsroman*, perhaps the subgenre most visibly conformable with the ideology of bourgeois liberalism, has been specifically proposed by Joseph Slaughter as the fictional analogue of the human rights movement, with which it is "consubstantial and mutually reinforcing."[65] Both deploy a "normative egalitarian imaginary" (p. 5) in which "social outsiders narrate affirmative claims for inclusion in a regime of rights and responsibilities" (p. 27). Unlike the law, literature can resist the "compulsion to decide" (p. 43), rendering it a suitable medium for the exploration of complex and perhaps intransigent motives and impediments that cannot be gathered into narrative resolutions. Both are fundamentally committed to the avoidance of violence, whether the violence of the authoritarian state or of that deemed necessary to displace it; hence they are "cultural alternatives to the eruptive political act of mass revolt" (p. 115). The pacifying career of *Bildung* has been in place since Schiller, and it provides a benchmark of patient inwardness that has always risked identification with the less commendable associations of doing nothing. But it also generated, from the start, alternative transcriptions of conflict and disorder. Adorno and Balibar and others have held on to the core of aesthetic independence and detachment while seeking to activate its capacity to project critical instability and therefore an imagining of change, of alternative worlds. However much the *Bildungsroman* might be focused on an exemplary subject—a David Copperfield or a Wilhelm Meister—it yet remains a novel and is as such committed to registering a social life made up of different and often incompatible needs and interests embodied in its various sociolects. And, as we have seen, it has from the first been understood (by Friedrich Schlegel, for example) as subversive, beyond control. Writing in the 1930s, Lukács regarded the biographical predilection of the novel as a sign of alienation, a mark of the writer's inevitable distance from both the life of the people and any full analysis of the historical moment, both leading to an overestimation of "immediate causation." Thus, "the great driving forces of history are neglected."[66] But, unless the narrative opts for the format of the fairy tale, turbulence and opposition are always latent and often explicit in the story of a life. Diction also tends to the ungovernable. Bakhtin's great treatise on heteroglossia and dialogization remains indispensable for its understanding that, even at the height of critical efforts to impose a unitary language and the political centralization that it claimed to embody, there is in spoken language (and in the novel's transcription of it) an irrepressible centrifugal force pushing out and away from this. As there is no native or national language that is not already shot through with what it seeks to compartmentalize as alien elements, so there is no statement that refers uncontestably to an object; there is only ever a dialogic process of call and response, voice and countervoice. Writers may seek to resist or essentialize the heteroglot by transcribing dominant language registers in major characters (or, according to Bakhtin, by imposing the formal constraints of poetry), but insofar as the novel has any investment in depicting ordinary life, conflict and multiplicity cannot but reappear.[67] For Sartre, the art of prose writing is the only medium sustained by and responsible to a democracy; poetry seeks to give language "the opacity of things" and to locate it beyond all utilization.[68]

Bakhtin's account does not of course guarantee that no novel will ever be deployed in the service of repression, and by no means do all novels consciously attempt the comprehensive representation of heteroglot society that he takes to be normative for the genre: his point is that it happens anyway. The most tersely limited language register—for example, the stream of consciousness narrative of a limited or impaired speaker or, perhaps, the most stringently disciplined lyric poetry—is going to be unable to suppress the already-dialogized element of all language, latent even at the level of the individual word.[69] Bakhtin affirms that interpretability governs both the utterance (or inscription) of words (or a word) and also their reception, their arrival at a destination in reader or hearer. Words subsist in "an actively polyglot world," and the novel comes into being when polyglossia is at its maximum, putting an end to "the period of national languages, coexisting but closed and deaf to each other" (p. 12). Every word hints at other words and at different uses for itself. This undermines efforts at directing literature (and the other arts) toward political messaging, whether in the unabashed manner of authoritarian states (Stalin's Russia, the Rushdie *fatwa*) or the secret promotion of supposedly subversive books (the CIA in the Cold War). Even the most apparently reductive use of language can generate significant complexities: recall William Empson's example of "the increasing vagueness, compactness, and lack of logical distinctions" embodied in the headline: ITALIAN ASSASSIN BOMB PLOT DISASTER.[70] The message can be made sense of in a number of ways; it has all the flexibility of an Imagist poem. Its vagueness is presumably calculated to stimulate curiosity and to sell newspapers, and Empson grants that it is "a very effective piece of writing . . . with a unity like that of metaphor" (p. 237). It is an exercise in building your own sentence, making your own story. It has some of the features of propaganda, but it is self-undermining, recipherable, like some of the slogans in Orwell's *1984* (war is peace, freedom is slavery, ignorance is strength), where the copula that makes metaphor requires us to decide what part of A is identical with what part of B and leaves open a flexibility that calls into question the efficiency of propaganda itself.

So, if all language is marked by dialogism and heteroglossia, then literature, as has often been said, is designated by a permission to call more-than-usual attention to itself in so being. It requires, in order for this to happen, cooperation from its readers, who respond to its signals and conventions by agreeing to read in the literary mode rather than seeing the text as merely neutral or informational. Readers may always refuse or insist on other ways to categorize what they read. Poetry conventionally identifies itself as literature by deploying spatial and syntactic formality, fictional prose by overtly embracing fabulation. Bakhtin may be right to claim that poetry seeks to repress plurivocity more than does prose, but poetry's slow and close focus on words and phrases opens out more obviously and unignorably into conceptual complexity and variable grammaticality (as does Empson's newspaper headline when printed in isolation). It seems fair to say that poetry's density in this respect does support the familiar conviction that more is 'lost' in its translation than is the case for prose, so that prose has greater potential for crossing national language boundaries with more of its core components at least somewhat intact. Add to this the marketing advantage that the novel has over poetry (which is commonly taken to require special reading skills and thus sponsors smaller print runs), and it makes sense that it is the global novel that still embodies our best chances of a transnational literary education and its addresses to violence and civility.[71] Cixun Liu's best-selling sci-fi trilogy negotiates what is for anglophones one of the most challenging of all translations (Chinese to English) to make the case that the threat of interference by an extraterrestrial intelligence ought to impel human beings to explore their deep species commonalities and that the universality of science ought to render sci-fi "the literary genre most accessible to readers of different nations."[72] But when his human protagonists discover a need to protect their communications networks from aliens with much higher technological capacities than their own, it is to literature that they turn: a literature that appears to their literal-functioning Trisolaran overlords "so much like a twisted maze" full of "deformed thoughts."[73] Studying earth's literature convinces the overlords of the dangers of an enemy whose "thoughts are totally opaque" (p. 49), notwithstanding their relative techno-scientific weakness. In the final novel of the trilogy, Yun Tianming creates fairy stories in which to embed and pass on the information vital to species survival. For a long time these stories prove indecipherable to both humans and aliens, because "vagueness and ambiguity are at the heart of literary expression." They have too much meaning to make sense:

"There are too many plausible interpretations, and we can't be certain of any of them," so it is "impossible to tell which one was the message intended by the author."[74] As the possibilities circulate, the stories acquire "a status akin to the Bible," wherein people look for a general reassurance that they are "on the right course" without gaining any specific information (p. 363). Eventually, the riddle is solved, the information received; the relevant modes turn out to be double metaphor and transliteration (pp. 363–74). But there is still a residual motif that cannot be deciphered. And the Trisolarans, who lack the ability to disguise their thoughts at all, remain completely in the dark.

Literary language, then, is here seen as one of the last best refuges of the human and its only successful weapon, its hope for a defense against annihilating violence. What unites the species at this point is not just the possession of a unique kind of communication but the activity of interpreting it, exploring its potential meanings: only art and interpretation can, quite literally in this fiction, save us. Both fabulation and interpretation are required if the species is to be preserved, and for those surviving there is still more meaning to be discovered. Whatever sets of meanings we construct or derive from texts (literary texts especially), we can never exhaust the possibilities for meanings still to come. This may be construed as a gift that keeps on giving or as a threat to thrones and altars, a failure of reverence. Novels that project a high degree of linguistic and narrative ingenuity, Joycean novels, lay down their challenge in unignorable ways. Simon Gikandi (standing for many) puts it very well: one cannot read *The Satanic Verses* "except through its aporetic moments and narrative ellipses."[75] In the realist and documentary modes, the signals are more subtle, but the dynamics of fictionality remain operative in a range of ways from the merely puzzling to the almost unbearable. Take the opening sentences of two novels whose topic is an almost inconceivable violence, both here in translation, from the German and the Russian, respectively:

> The rain stopped at Bazancourt, a small town in Champagne, and we got out.
>
> There was a low mist. You could see the glare of headlamps reflected on the high-voltage cables beside the road.[76]

These are very matter-of-fact statements, scene setters that we are accustomed to hurrying over in order to get on with the story. Passing out of their original languages surely flattens them even further, but they could almost be part of newspaper reports. Or detective stories. They are quite untypical of sentences in Rushdie's novel, but every novel probably uses at least some similar ones. Reading on soon brings us to their topics: the trenches on the Western Front in 1914, the concentration camp in World War II. Most readers, by virtue of choosing to read the book and reading the blurb, will know ahead something about these books that makes the matter-of-factness unstable, even threatening. Bazancourt will not remain the name of just any old town; the high-voltage cables will not prove to be mere attributes of an industrial site, although we do not immediately know whether the camp is run by Germans or Russians or whether the mist is a moral miasma or just a weather event. The situation of these sentences 'as' literature calls up a range of questions, not least the one that foregrounds the integrity or authority of writer-speakers relating to sites whose historical records generate enduring concerns about the ethics of representation itself. Simple words and simple sentences, but they are loaded with innuendo.

Some novels of course set out to avoid, as best they can, engaging with violence at all, even in times when world wars, genocides, decolonization struggles, economic immiseration, global refugee crises and destruction of the environment have dominated the popular consciousness, as they (variously) have for a hundred years or so. The novel is not a fully bounded genre, and some kinds of violence are hard to identify. Rob Nixon has noted the "representational obstacles" that make it hard for literature to register "an attritional violence that is typically not viewed as violence at all" because it does not generate dramatic events, melodrama and spectacle: climate change is an example.[77] We have indeed as of now seen few such novels in comparison with, for example, the slew of fiction that came out after and about 9/11, the ultimate spectacle that provides the absolute opposite of what Nixon diagnoses as a "drama deficit" (p. 52). And yet the novel, given its typical length and commitment to fabulation, and the time it demands of us for its reading, could well prove to be the perfect medium for the recording of slow violence and the complex kinds of connectedness affecting individual lives in contemporary culture, never as local as it may seem. Amitav Ghosh has, like Nixon, also brought attention to "the peculiar forms of resistance that climate change presents to what is now regarded as serious fiction," a resistance embedded in the nineteenth-century conviction that novels need not attend closely to the nonhuman, to barely perceptible time scales or to catastrophic events that are not part of a cycle of a nature that is seen as fundamentally gradualist.[78] But this was only ever one of the available narratives, as Ian Duncan has recently shown, and the interpretive motivations driving our current criticism are (re)discovering more and more of an eighteenth- and nineteenth-century awareness and registration of the catastrophic dynamics of the Anthropocene inscribed not just in the novels of industrial life but also in the features of landscape poetry.[79] Ghosh himself has chronicled the less-written-upon kinds of both environmental and economic violence in many of his own novels, as have a number of the writers discussed by Nixon (among them Saro-Wiwa, Munif, and Ndebele).

In fact, the evidence suggests that the form in which long time scales are becoming perceptible is increasingly going to be that of catastrophic tipping points. If so, then the novelist's problem will be as much one of resisting melodrama as registering deep time. Bushfires, major floods, hurricanes and droughts, for example, are combined 'natural' and man-made crises that are occurring as explosive events rather than slow-moving processes. Increasingly, moments of industrial disaster (Bhopal, Chernobyl, Deepwater Horizon) are becoming embedded in cycles of disasters that occur as man-nature events (Katrina, Sandy, Fukushima). In a case like that of COVID-19, a presumably natural phenomenon is made overwhelmingly more dangerous by human failures of various kinds, from individual behavior to failed-state structures. It is now readily foreseeable that major wildfires and floods will bring about more and more radical dislocations of the lifeworld, making decisions between civility and violence more and more consequential: the extraordinary patience of so many black residents of New Orleans during Katrina, for example, should not be assumed to be the blueprint for any and all future examples of disproportionately racialized suffering. The genius of Kamila Shamsie's *Burnt Shadows* consists not least in its long narrativization of a political-historical time that includes both punctual and long-term violences: the unignorable event of the Nagasaki bomb and the implacable, erosive damage done by small wars, decolonization, racism and neoliberalism. In this novel the potential civility function of multilingual competence as a tool for global understanding and sympathy is here pitted (tragically) against the racialized nationalisms that find their interests threatened by not being in charge of acts of translation. The fragmented subjectivities that have increasingly come to populate the global novel (the novel of globalizing life) can be narrativized as flexible citizenships for the affluent but for the majority are coded as failing lives and vulnerable identities.

The novel genre is a relative latecomer to aesthetic theory. It figures in neither Kant nor Schiller as the object of serious attention, and for Hegel it is at best confined to the sphere of humor, the low end of Romantic art that captures "ordinary daily life" only in its "mutability and finite transitoriness" and never in its "substance."[80] Prose, for Hegel, elides the figurative and concerns itself only with the literal (2:1005), which makes it suitable for philosophic thought but not for art. Friedrich Schlegel, the theorist of irony and the fragmentary, took the novel seriously and recognized *Wilhelm Meister* as one of the distillations of its age, but the mainstream theoretical and academic indifference to the genre lasted throughout much of the nineteenth century.[81] Things had changed by the time that Bakhtin, Lukács, Leavis, Trilling and Raymond Williams paid close attention to prose fiction, but the Kant-Schiller exposition has remained prominent for many aesthetic theorists. Marcuse tries to weld together a Schillerian emphasis on the freedom of the individual and the radical resource that is "aesthetic form," but most of his examples come from drama and poetry.[82] Adorno's closest and most informed focus was on music. And indeed, if the best hope for a radical aesthetics is founded in a preoccupation with form, then the novel presents a problem. How does one apprehend the 'form' of a long story? Certainly not at a glance, as one would a painting or sculpture, in the manner of an aesthetic judgment of taste. One seldom if ever turns to a companion and blurts out spontaneously that X is a beautiful novel, unless by limiting one's remarks to the cover or binding. What is lost in novel reading is the flash of intuition about form and the spontaneous response to it. Holding a copy of *War and Peace* is not like standing in front of *Guernica*. Nor can a novel be open to tact, to touching. The extended more-or-less realist novel that dominates the mainstream tradition is not easily, if at all, apprehended as a form, unless it is that of a calculated formlessness. If shape or structure is discoverable, it is only after patient inspection and analysis, and it may remain unnoticed by many nonspecialist readers. Most novels are stories about the lives of others and evolve in relation to the passage of time. If formal patterns are to be discovered, they are a function of events and their elaborations, the thoughts and virtual consequences they generate through the temporality of reading. Given the tendency of these sorts of stories to generate affect—empathy, sympathy, disgust—they offer prime evidence for those who believe that literature can make us better people or at least expand our imagination to the point of leaving us with a decision about what (if anything) to do with those imaginings. But the reader of a novel is not having the sort of experience that Kant and Schiller theorized as a judgment of taste, a moment of possession demanding communication, or responding to anything either would have admitted as beautiful. What does this mean for an aesthetic theory that places most of its hopes on a novel genre that is not obviously included in the most frequently invoked paradigms of that theory, those devised by Kant and Schiller? Should we be searching for some sort of fit or look instead for a quite different basis for a theory, especially if our priority is a representation of the very violence that Kant, after all, more or less banished from the analytic of the beautiful?

When violence does make an appearance, in the analytic of the sublime, it belongs in nature but not human nature. The violence of the world stays in the natural world; humans must and should respond to it, but they do not generate it. This is perhaps the bargain one strikes to sustain a project of enlightenment: that which causes the feeling of ultimate fear and fragility is not of human making. The Kantian sublime is, strictly speaking, only in thought; there is nothing purposive in nature, no far-off divine event that it contributes to. Nature, as Lyotard puts it, works "only to provide the bad contact that creates the spark."[83] This is an experience of formlessness, a sensing of the dissolution of form itself, one that the subject must recuperate by affirming its own power over the prospect of pain or annihilation. Insofar as this tends toward or is analogous to a moral gesture, it is not shareable and comes with no assumption of communicability, but rather the opposite. Lyotard again: "The sublime feeling is neither moral universality nor aesthetic universalization, but is, rather, the destruction of one by the other in the violence of their differend."[84] A question thus looms about the capacity of Kantian aesthetics to recognize, to subsist with, a human violence that is not to be restricted to a destructive nature, and thus to maintain a civility that must now, I have been arguing, project itself with that violence.[85] Far from admitting to the existence of an inconvertible human violence, the Kantian sublime refuses to recognize such a thing, loading all its agency onto the natural world.

It may well be that Kant is here responding to Burke, for whom, as David Lloyd has made clear, the sublime has more to do with the vulnerable body than with the indomitable mind.[86] Fear and terror can be educed from words on the page as well as from storms and volcanic eruptions, but they register most powerfully on the body, and what dissipates them is not any inclination toward the moral but a recourse to the physical discipline of labor. They can also, as Lloyd stresses, be *caused* by the body, by the sight of the monstrous or appalling that is exemplified, for Burke, in the anecdote of the horrified reaction of a newly seeing (white) person to the sight of a black woman. For Burke, darkness is intrinsically terror inducing; racism thus becomes an ontological given. The deprivation of light, of the ability to see, is a threat that "takes in all mankind" and is "universally terrible."[87] Black "bodies" (a word that handily covers both objects and persons), having less light, are "as so many vacant spaces dispersed among the objects we view" (p. 147). Custom and habit do mitigate the horror, but never completely: "The nature of the original impression still continues" (p. 149). As Lloyd points out, Burke's argument perfectly encapsulates what Fanon will describe as the colonial gaze. But that gaze is not unconditional, not universal, not an attribute of all mankind. And what, we might wonder, of the black child who sees his first white person? Are we to think, with Burke, that such an experience would come about as a joyous recognition of lightness in a dark world or instill its own fear and terror?

The novel, as I have said, is not much susceptible to aesthetic judgments predisposed to share estimates of what is and is not beautiful. There may well still be a plausibly positive component to Kantian judgments of taste, as I suggested in Chapter 1, but it is not easily invoked as a protocol for reading novels.[88] Is the sublime any more useful in explaining its effects? The inheritance of the sublime is essentially bifurcated, drawing us to either Kant's mind-centered or Burke's body-centered theories. We would have either to choose between these options or somehow make sense of their aporetic conjunction. Better perhaps to begin with the monumental work of Georg Lukács, from his early attempt at a theory of the novel launched from within a "permanent despair over the state of the world" and amid a "process of turning from Kant to Hegel," through the many writings on European realism and the effort to imagine a viable response not only to the events of 1848, which, for Lukács, put an end to the core function of the historical novel, but to the presence of fascism in his own immediate world.[89] Such an account is more than I can manage here. But let us at least reflect upon the potential of Lukács's identification of the novel with a "transcendental homelessness" whose elaboration still seems productive for the present moment (p. 41). Notwithstanding the use that can and has been made of the novel toward the assemblage of nationalist movements, or of other forms of group consolidation, there is, as Bakhtin best explains, something almost irresistibly dispersive about extended fabulation, something heteroglossic even at the level of the word.[90] Issues of localization and rootedness, affirmed and undermined, were at the heart of many nineteenth-century novels. They also registered the economic and geographical dislocations that were unsettling any attribution of identity to nature alone, unmodified by human agency. At the same time the ideal incrementalism of the *Bildungsroman*, whereby one makes oneself into someone better or wiser or richer than one was, is always under stress from the unmaking of the self that could be enacted by both historical and aesthetic experiences. When global encounters become the center of fictionized narratives, as they are in novels of empire, decolonization and postcolony, opportunities for extreme self-makings and unmakings become more spectacular, more racialized and more inconvertibly violent. The project of civility is again under radical stress, and it emerges unignorably in the figure of the subaltern.

Confronting the Subaltern

Nancy Armstrong has asked what happens now that novels have "declared the household obsolete as a way of imagining a national community" and notes (in the British novel) the appearance of a "strange and estranging microworld" that disturbs that community to a point beyond rescue.[91] This suggests an instance of the uncanny, of the strange that is familiar, the unhomely that is somehow completely at home, the protected space that is somehow already shared with agencies of an actual or potential violence: an updating and familiarization of the genre that was traditionally recognized as the gothic. The novels of Kazuo Ishiguro are an exemplary instance of the syndrome. They project a desperate compulsion to sympathy and sociability, and thus to a fundamental civility, but embed it within an unbearable suffering and repression. In *The Remains of the Day* (1989) Mr. Stevens's effort at upholding polite formality constantly approaches a breaking point; in *Never Let Me Go* (2005) the children being farmed for organ replacement surgery strive desperately to construct and maintain loving relationships with each other; in *Klara and the Sun* (2021) the 'artificial friend' who is not technically human performs a commitment to the well-being of others that humans can scarcely match, along with a charitable acceptance of the most painful of rejections. Adam Smith's urge for approbation is here exposed as both heroic and desperate, all that we have but not enough to win out over ambient and insidious violence. W. G. Sebald's characters similarly take comfort in the kindness and attention of strangers and casual acquaintances, spinning forth their stories of loss and dispossession in voices that are absolutely compelling but also ghostly, as if already beyond the grave, given life in a traumatic authorship that leaves its readers also haunted and shaken by these recitations of atomic solitude and bereavement. The household is indeed obsolete, quite literally for many of those caught up in the Hitler years. And perhaps its fragility has been before our eyes for a long time. Although it becomes, halfway through *Pamela*, an icon of patriotic localism, the house begins as a carceral space in which a vulnerable young woman is entrapped, as it remains in *Clarissa*. The grandest of Austen's country estates (Sotherton, Rosings, Northanger Abbey, Pemberley) are either dysfunctional or largely showpieces. Dickens's idyllic domestic spaces (Dingley Dell, Wemmick's Castle, Rose Maylie's house, Peggoty's cottage) are theatrically sequestered from an otherwise threatening world. Howards End becomes the possession of Anglo-Germans (and a good thing too). With the consolidation of empire, ethnic diversity becomes more and more unignorable: E. M. Forster's Englishmen in India meet Indians who have spent time in England, but their encounters produce more misunderstandings than solidarities. Adela Quested is baffled by the

Indians and the "echoing walls of their civility."[92] Language floats freely in a social space where neither colonial nor native can stabilize meanings and assumptions: "A pause in the wrong place, an intonation misunderstood, and a whole conversation went awry" (p. 305). The onset of interracial affection only makes things more volatile: when Aziz senses it, he begins to "repeat, exaggerate, contradict" (p. 21). Sometimes "he enjoyed being misunderstood" (p. 56). The confusion encourages predictable racist assumptions on all sides, but most violently so among the British: Forster's own authorial voice occasionally slips into it when it is not protected by the permissions of indirect free style.[93]

Forster, even more thoroughly than Conrad before him, here sets out the format of what we have come to call the predicament of subalternity, a category that David Lloyd has proposed as external to representation itself. The subaltern both suffers violence and embodies the threat of violence for those who cannot figure out its parameters. As the "permanent and inexpungible remainder of the processes of state-formation," the subaltern neither controls representation (as the intellectual seeks to do) nor can be comfortably specified by it.[94] It is neither the adequate object of civility nor its bearer (unless by the deflections of slyness, in Bhabha's terms).[95] It is fundamentally disjunctive, out of line, "recalcitrant to discipline and assimilation" (p. 116). As such it aligns itself, albeit uncomfortably, with one version of that very aesthetic experience whose genesis Lloyd has traced back to a foundational and persistent racism in Kant and his interpreters. The subaltern is "a category unthinkable without the regime of representation that the aesthetic regulated" but nonetheless "spells the limit of the aesthetic's unilateral promise of universality" (p. 158). It holds off from confirming civility, civil society, community, cosmopolitanism, but not from literary reproduction: the novel can thus inscribe subalternity as part of an analysis of "the false promise of aesthetic liberation," as, Lloyd argues, happens in the work of Jean Rhys or Tayeb Salih (p. 11). And if the novel can describe it, then literary pedagogy can teach it. As civility adapts itself to staging a deflection of violence, violence shows through more and unignorably. It was there in the odd moment with which I began, when Crusoe points aside the muzzles of his fowling pieces and plays the gentleman. As the colonizing process evolves, it becomes even more legible and dominant.

Subalternity has the important attribute of being initially deployed to signal something about the process of colonization itself, which is, in its various transformations up to and including decolonization and its aftermath (if we are indeed there yet), a primary component of whatever we might take globality or globalization to involve. It began as a historians' term for reckoning with history from below, specifically with the peasant insurgencies of South Asia.[96] Spivak found in it "a theory of change as the site of the displacement of function between sign-systems," working through the imposition of "cognitive failures" on the archive as "the absolute limit of the place where history is narrativized into logic."[97] Such challenges are not unique to peasant-class figures, even as that class is where the term is first applied. Anyone presenting intractable or recalcitrant qualities and refusing representation in a racialized or classified lifeworld could qualify as subaltern, simply because it is by definition not knowable who or what the person is. The uncanny is a fitting analogue for this suspension of functional knowledge, somewhat in the manner of the "occult instability" that for Fanon describes the place where "the people dwell."[98] Literature too suspends functional knowledge. As Pheng Cheah has remarked, ably summarizing Derrida, literature "is entirely devoid of intentionality and is inaccessible to the subject, it is the privileged locus of the inviolable secret as a figure for the force of otherness that cannot be appropriated by any kind of transcendental, rational, material, or phenomenological subject."[99] Subalternity thus may be implicit in the modern notion of literature itself; nonetheless, it evolves most fully in novel writing as the successor to the supernatural figures of the late nineteenth century and a variant upon the protagonists of magic realism. Its claim to stand as the new 'real' does not deprive it of these residual associations. Indeed, in the case of the bestowing of "civil death" that Colin Dayan describes as at the long-standing disposition of American law, the figures who are made less than human while being recognizably, somehow, like us, incline almost by definition toward the uncanniness of subalternity.[100]

A long view of subalternity indeed suggests that it is not the alternative to but the incremental outcome of the extended historical cycle that Elias describes as the civilizing process. Elias never endorses a straightforward narrative of progress. The monopoly of power by the ruler of the state leads not to absolute control but to its opposite: in order to function, centralization requires more and more delegation to others.[101] Competition for status and advantage among administrators calls up once again the routines of politeness and civility in order that potential turmoil be as far as possible contained. As the modern middle class gains access to some share of the benefits of management, more and more persons become uncertain of who they are and what they are doing: one's mode of conduct becomes an "acute problem." Things that were once taken for granted are no longer self-evident, a process that speeds up as social experience becomes wider and eventually transnational: people learn "to see themselves from a greater distance" (p. 518), leading to the status uncertainty that Tocqueville, for example, found in American democracy. As the middle class embeds itself, it ceases to be a wholly emergent group and becomes more defensive, eager to hold on to what it has in the face of challenges from other groups. The "reflective detachment" (p. 211) of the modern subject is thus even less likely than before to remain serene and satisfied; its experience of *Bildung* becomes anxious and conflicted. Subalternity may be seen as a late stage in this process, adding to distinctions of class and interest those even more exigent differences of race and nationality. Thus, we arrive at the point that Rodolph Gasché specified, as both prognosis and ideal, that marks late twentieth-century Europe: not at home when most at home, open to the unpredictable other and bearing a responsibility to everyone and everything that comes.[102]

If subalternity resists being imagined as universality, it also heads off the ethical pitfalls facing readers who seek to acknowledge their oneness with those whose lives they will never themselves endure: quite simply, one cannot fully identify. Subalternity is a structural category, not an elective lifestyle. Lloyd's characterization (like Bhabha's) suggests that the subaltern persona consists in its refutation of understanding, its refusal of empathic identity, its recalcitrance (to use one of his favorite words). Any turn to the subaltern figure with the gesture of Kantian aesthetic judgment—"look, what a beautiful painting"—would be met with irony, mimicry, anger or silence, a response that no longer confirms the barbarism of the interlocutor but dramatizes the unavoidably disputable assumption of a *sensus communis*. What kind of civility might be imagined here? All civility protocols are founded in the experience of ambiguity, even when they seek to efface them; they are always open to being coded as sincere or hypocritical, shallow or deep, peace making or effectually aggressive. The unstable interaction of subaltern and non-subaltern subjects cannot be constrained by the "mere" civility that Teresa Bejan found embodied in Roger Williams. It is not as self-affirming as Williams's "commitment to mutual contempt rather than mutual admiration," which resolves any confusion by a full embrace of negation, although it does include an incentive to "patience and indifference to offense."[103] It accepts something of the call for "thicker skins and divided selves" but senses that the skin might not be thick enough to escape being vulnerable. The non-subaltern does not hereby see or feel himself or herself *as* subaltern (a false identification) but faces up to the inevitability of a life that includes a figure whose claim can neither be denied nor satisfied, nor even perhaps adequately enunciated. This experience can be hard to hold on to in ordinary life, where such interactions are either too rare or too conflictual, thanks to the ambient racism of our lifeworld, but they are not impossible, and they are readily open to representation in literature, where no one is called upon for immediate response or redress. Reading books can be a practice for praxis. As Wayne Booth has argued, fiction extends a "relatively cost-free offer of trial runs" and efficiently samples more lives "than I can test in a lifetime."[104] Mostly these trials have no consequences. This makes it easier to confront and contemplate the figure of the subaltern, which tells us that we can have an understanding that we do not fully understand and that the image before us cannot rest in a settled form. In the lives not lived through fiction, those in the 'real' world, subaltern encounters can lead to murderous violence, impassioned romantic love and anything in between. They proffer the sort of experience that Spivak denotes as schizophrenia.[105] Experienced through fiction, as representations, they become more readily open to reflective investigation.

But subalternity can never subsist within the Kantian category of the beautiful, nor does it fit the Kantian sublime, which is specified as the place of violence, because violence is not there associated with the human at all but with the forces of nature. The subaltern escapes the Kantian net and thus appears as unshaped, queer, monstrous, something more congruent with the Burkean sublime and its roots in bodily sensations, but not containable within Burke's idea of universal response. Nothing can definitively prevent readers, like their proxies in life, from assimilating such figures as representations of bare life, unworthy even of sacrifice, only minimally human and beneath respectful attention of any kind: this is the deplorable consequence of intransigent racism. But there are in recent fiction so many subaltern figures that they become typical rather than exceptional; they call for a recognition that cannot follow the standard protocols. They refuse abjection or enact it in such theatrical ways as to call attention to its bizarre dynamics. Ishiguro's *Klara and the Sun* suggests that they need not even be figured as conventional 'human' characters, thus forestalling the suspicion that even subalternity might be framed as a final, fragmented nostalgia for a world that was not increasingly populated by artificial intelligence. Bolaño's *2666* devotes hundreds of pages to a police-report-style listing of the names and minimal attributes of some 107 (but I could have miscounted) murdered, tortured and sexually violated women and girls whose bodies are dumped across the landscape of northern Mexico. Whether these details are true or fictional, the effect of the real is near absolute, not least because such events have occurred historically and are still happening. Subalternity cannot here emerge into speech; it is too late already for them. Their record is the result of a writer's witnessing. In contrast, Mohsin Hamid's *The Reluctant Fundamentalist* (2007) is all speech, but one cannot *place* the narrator or resolve the question of which of the two characters holds the decisive power of violence: the American who is a spymaster or mercenary and perhaps an assassin but whose access to habitual power is suspended by his being the only white person in a restaurant in the middle of Lahore, or the Pakistani-American who is at home in the city and may or may not have the ability to threaten his life? Their exchange is a model of unstable civility under the conditions of subalternity, but there is only one speaker, the returned Pakistani, who paraphrases or interpellates all the American's responses, all the way up to the suspended moment of possibly explosive violence that ends the story. Hamid's first sentence is striking: "Excuse me, sir, but may I be of assistance? Ah, I see I have alarmed you. Do not be frightened by my beard: I am a lover of America."[106] We have seen this moment before, almost verbatim, when Robinson Crusoe accosts the kidnapped seamen: "Gentlemen, said I, do not be surprised at me. . . . Can you put a Stranger in the way how to help you, for you seem to me to be in some great Distress?"[107] I would like to think that Hamid intends the echo; being approached by a bearded Pakistani on his native ground in the tense atmosphere after 9/11 might well have seemed to our completely quiet American just as intimidating as the ragged castaway carrying a handful of guns did to Defoe's despondent sailors. But Hamid's narrator is no classic exotic (whatever that is) but one with a hyperarticulate command of the language and of the situation, which completely effaces any clear distinction between predator and prey. His speech is one long example of putting himself in the place of the other, a virtuoso display of the "civility and ambition" that, he says, mark the students he teaches at the local university (p. 181). He constantly anticipates the American's possible feelings in a string of questions to which he himself provides the answers: there is literally no space for the American to talk back. Civility blends with violence in the refusal of dialogue, but its decorous protocols are intact at the literal level. The figure who might be expected to exhibit subalternity (the Friday figure, as it were) fully occupies the novel's space and completely controls the representation of the supposedly dominant other, while remaining himself unrepresentable. But his dominance of the story is still embedded in a world system whose constraints he can never escape, one that is implacably American and doing massive damage far beyond the scope of this brief redistribution of power between two individuals. This is one instance of what the subaltern condition can look like in the contemporary novel. It models a universality that is sustained for the course of the novel's fabular events, thereby opening prospects for a different world: a fairy story in the mode of a complete local realism. It is also a novel full of violence in which there is no physical violence enacted.

The tension generated by Hamid's opaque narrator points us back to an exemplary moment in nineteenth-century literature, Melville's "Benito Cereno." On a morning that dawns with "everything gray"—sky, birds, fog, everything ambiguously between black and white—the American sea captain Amasa Delano also enters a cloud of unknowing in which he cannot distinguish the affiliations of blacks and whites, masters and slaves, cannot see through the screen of elaborate pseudo-civilities that signal to all but him the looming presence of radical violence. Hamid's narrator's performance of civility is hypercompetent, and its excessiveness builds increasing suspense as the story unfolds. The more elaborately deferential he appears, the more it looks like a performance, one organized to an end we cannot be sure of. Hypercompetence also figures in Shamsie's *Burnt Shadows*, another story full of subaltern figures, this time taking form as an extraordinary ability to learn languages that Raza Ashraf shares with and learns from his parents. He thereby pricks the Achilles heel of the anglophone hegemony within which he is entangled by family and fate. That hegemony operates with the assumption that it is the responsibility of the rest of the world to speak English, a condition perhaps even truer now than it was when Matthew Arnold complained about the same thing in the middle of the nineteenth century. Here the Americans are not so quiet, nor are the weapons evenly distributed even for a magic moment. Shamsie too explores the onset after 9/11 of a world shocked into radically rethinking its habits and distributions, especially its distributions of violence. But the utopian project never takes off; the small group of characters embodying a multiracial culture of civility is shattered by the servants of the racialized state. Decency and compassion cannot survive the damage done by racisms large and small. After surviving the Nagasaki bombing and the Indian partition only to end up in a New York transformed by 9/11 into an equally hostile environment for all persons of color, Shamsie's heroine Hiroko never loses her moral compass, her claim to sympathetic organization of the *Bildungsroman* that relates her life. The body of the woman is the exemplary figure of the damage done by her acculturation into life in the West, but all persons who are not white suffer or are at risk. Learning and loving languages and ignoring the color line prove not to be necessary or even possible for those who decide the way of the world. The subaltern's challenge to representation is met by violence, like the response to a speaking that is not understood.

And yet *Burnt Shadows* is also an unashamed homage to love, as is Hamid's own *Exit West*, a love that in no sense conquers or displaces the violence it must confront but somehow subsists along with it, and in despite of it. The romance component that was there in troubled form in, for example, Conrad's fiction, remains alive in the modern global novel. In Nadine Gordimer's *The Pick-Up*, it is erotic love that leads to an unpredicted and rewarding immersion in the culture of the other; in Jenny Erpenbeck's *Go, Went, Gone*, love develops platonically between an old man and those he at first does not even notice and then cannot live without. We are rightly attuned to suspect romantic racism in such portrayals, but the incidence of biracial relationships calls for and deserves a less dismissive accounting: it too is a condition of modern life. Marlow's bifurcated response to the "wild and gorgeous apparition of a woman . . . savage and superb, wild-eyed and magnificent," lays down the standard terms for the white colonial male's response to the subaltern female who threatens to overturn the racial hierarchy and thus incites either fatal violence or helpless infatuation.[108] There can be no peace in this encounter. Marlow finds release in his demonization of tropical nature and its inhabitants, even while admitting, famously, the darkness of metropolitan Europe as something that has by no means been dispelled by the workings of stadial history.[109] In Conrad's first novel, *Almayer's Folly* (1895), a Dutch East Indian longs to 'return' to a Europe he has never seen, is driven by greed to marry a native woman whom he comes to despise and proves completely unable to handle the task of raising a biracial child, "deceived by the emotional estimate of his motives, unable to see the crookedness of his ways, the unreality of his aims, the futility of his regrets."[110] Almayer exemplifies a colonialist personality riven by the pull of romanticism against racism held together only by self-interest, one that leads straight to David Lurie, the protagonist of Coetzee's *Disgrace*, where the complex violence of interracial romance is completely palpable, along with its enduring utopian prospect of a better and more just world to come. In *Age of Iron* (1990), race and class overlap and interact as another aging, indeed dying protagonist becomes close to an impenetrable vagrant man—"because I cannot trust Verceuil I must trust him"—who shelters outside her house, while at the same time living in a "state of shame" and trying to make sense of her entanglement with and obligations to her black housekeeper and her friends and family.[111] Interpersonal encounters with subalternity always remain weird but also locate characters beyond the category of bare life, soliciting engagement of some sort, engagement with what cannot be fully known or represented. Love, if that is what it is, does not take the form of a reconstituted family unit in which young women and men hold hands and look forward to happy parenthood. But there is always a potential for personalization, for an imagining of a world in which love as well as suffering and confusion might be possible. The trials of subalternity cannot erase all traces of social hope, even when the romance plot is confounded and violence seems to rule. Sometimes things go the other way: in Ghosh's

Ibis trilogy, the biracial American seaman Zachary Reid who begins with an affiliation with the dispossessed ends up as a predatory capitalist crook. The emergence of this stark moral contrast is mirrored in the winnowing out of the remarkable linguistic variety that opens the trilogy in *Sea of Poppies*, where it suggests an irrepressible diversity of interests and identities now lost to the banal global English that describes getting, spending and killing. The historical record does not indeed offer much evidence of hope rewarded on the grander scale of events. But in the novel there is hope projected and imagined, for example, when *The Reluctant Fundamentalist* virtually restructures, at least for the time of the book, the global power dynamic, as if one really could imagine a level playing field.[112] The representation of love in the novel can certainly invite and encourage affective absorption, the energy that fuels many readers of romance. It can provide what Martha Nussbaum has called the "cataleptic impression," the sense of certainty in the time of reading that things are absolutely this way and not that way.[113] But the adding up of such impressions and others that come along produces much more of uncertainty, a sense of what Nussbaum eloquently calls "the ethical relevance of uncontrolled happenings" (p. 43). How and whether an ethics devolves from uncontrolled happenings is always to be discussed if not determined. Picking up a book is a civic act and a prospective project of civility but also a commitment to the unknown. The love that is in play here is ultimately the act of making connections, of engaging with metaphor, which is all about imagining and proposing what things might or might not have in common: an effort to bring together things sensed as apart, but one always under stress.[114] The subaltern encounter is a form of disclosing emergency, more manageable when represented in literature than when experienced directly. It is especially appropriate for a description of the 'Western' subject experiencing its own dissolution (or violent reaffirmation) in the face of the racialized other, but it can also impinge upon any normal-seeming experience involving, as in the Hegelian scene, the construction of selfhood through recognition of and by an other. To describe either of these encounters, one apparently habitual and the other apparently exceptional, by using such terms as cosmopolitanism, civility, sympathy, tact, neutrality or conviviality is to impose a latent ideal of easeful interaction that does not do justice to the strenuousness of the relationship. These words come forward, promising a less difficult life, because there do not seem to be others obviously available, so they are under stress, inflected in awkward ways, as if under erasure.[115] Bejan's "mere" civility is an attempt to reclaim the word from any residual aura of benign politeness, but it must always rub up against the common uses already in place. The same condition governs Balibar's use of civility to negotiate sociability in the experience of violence: it reaches for a range of incommensurable attributes that the common use of the word cannot contain. Both want civility to disclose rather than pretend to erase violence but to hold back overt or uninhibited aggression, extreme violence.

The avowed imprecision and incompleteness of Balibar's civility, a "hypothetical name" offering "no a priori strategy," seeking as it does to resist extreme violence (which destroys the possibility of politics) without discounting the emancipatory violence of the "liberating insurgency," makes it an apt articulation of the condition of subalternity.[116] It introduces antiviolence "into the very heart of the violence of a social transformation" (p. 103), without which there can only be an accrual of more and more extreme violence. In subjective experience such civility is marked by "a movement of identification and disidentification" (p. 144) that is continuous with (while more strenuous than) the operations of Shaftesbury's "inmate controller" and Smith's "man within the breast," continuous also, then, with the conventions of literary reading that these operations described. Subalternity, civility and literature all align themselves in engaging with a violence that cannot be effaced or sublimated into modeling a progressive individual *Bildung* or collectively improving civilization. They register the continuance of an inconvertible violence. Literature and civility have both been celebrated and disavowed for deflecting attention away from violence, but in neither case has the effort been successful, and it is even less so in a world like the one we now inhabit, where forms of violence are seen to have proliferated as both idiosyncratic symptoms and grand narratives.

I mentioned at the beginning of this book the irony whereby the popular call for a rejuvenated civility has failed to acknowledge civility's long-standing alliance with the very literary pedagogy whose lack of utility or outcomes has often been deployed to justify withdrawing resources from humanities education. The possible solution, in other words, is being turned into the problem. It is possible that the ways in which the humanities are useful is too threatening to the efficiency and positive self-images of the loyal servants of the state and its corporate embodiments. Schiller, Shelley and Arnold all believed this to be so, not only in their faith in the power of an uncontrollable pleasure and joy but also in their proclivity for sponsoring a critique that is at once rigorous and unassertive, insistent but resistant to instrumentalized summation. Or it is possible to imagine a less absolute but still disabling explanation affirming that for all our efforts over many decades, too many people are still unable or unwilling to take the time and expend the effort required, in the particular case of literary reading, for the better understanding of words and the consequences of failing to do so. So it is that, after all is said and done, civility is still debatable and still "not to be passed on," to cite Toni Morrison's famously ambiguous line from *Beloved*. We are still in want both of civility 'itself,' in some of its preferred forms, and of a sure way of talking about what we mean by using the word at all. Like love, like literature. Instead of assuming that these words work well enough, we can learn a great deal that is useful from understanding why and when they don't and how much that is violent lives by way of their dysfunctions. But we must use the words we have when we cannot make new ones. And we must insist on the most rigorous possible account of who uses them and for what ends. Richards argued that the word "does nothing except what we do with it. Its trickiness derives from our own lack of competence and candor in certain situations."[117] Competence and candor: simple words, immensely difficult to bring to life. The freedom of the aesthetic alibi might be better imagined as an obligation or incentive to reinvent or reimagine what has been given. Schiller (and the Romantic legacy for which he stands) has been variously upended, sabotaged, upstaged and updated but seldom ignored or found irrelevant. We can neither simply go back to Schiller nor apparently get anywhere without him.

This study began with Auden and to Auden go some of its last words. "We must love one another or die" sounds like a pretty desperate injunction in "September 1, 1939," a poem written on the occasion of the outbreak of World War II. Against all the odds, Auden goes on to invoke "ironic points of light" wherever "the Just / Exchange their messages." They are still to be found "dotted everywhere," making up an "affirming flame" to which he aspires to contribute.[118] What is the irony governing these points of light? Partly it derives from the incapacity of literature, love and civility to predictably dispel or overcome forms of violence enacted on such a grand scale as to be seemingly beyond all interpersonal influence. And partly, perhaps, the irony is that there are any such points of light at all, let alone everywhere. Almost a hundred years ago Forster ended *A Passage to India* with the following judgment on the friendship of Fielding and Aziz: "No, not yet . . . No, not there." His novel, like so many since, is the keeping open of an imagining of something better, something that will need either new words or, just as likely, old ones better deployed and understood. Auden's injunction to "love one another or die" is a one-liner, like his comment that "poetry makes nothing happen." Yeats too was a great provider of one-liners about terrible beauty, the best lacking all conviction, the slouching toward Bethlehem, the center cannot hold and so on. Shakespeare, of course, has offered us numerous one-liners, which I need not here enumerate. What can we make of one-liners? Most commonly they are rhetorical flourishes produced to impress people, sway or amuse a meeting or put an end to a conversation. Some of them, for Matthew Arnold, were touchstones, icons of truth and seriousness embodied in diction and movement by which we could measure the worth of all other lines.[119] Arnold mentions very few one-liners that are worthy of being passed down as touchstones: two in Homer and Shakespeare, three in Dante and Milton. Chaucer can manage one despite ultimately falling short in "high seriousness" (p. 23). But they are there, although rare.

I have long pondered the implications of Arnold's touchstones. I admire him for citing Greek and Italian as well as English, keeping alive a point of contact with other languages and setting a challenge to his readers. I also wonder if this miniaturized comparative literature pedagogy is the best he feels he can hope for in a world where (to invoke two of his own one-liners) ignorant armies clash by night and where the best of our kind will likely perish in the wilderness. Already, before the massive efforts of so many critics like Richards, Leavis and Williams to devise and circulate a literary-pedagogical response to modern culture that could provide what Williams called "resources of hope," Arnold hints that it may be too late.[120] So, again, what of Auden's "we must love one another or die"? Touchstone or desperate platitude? Arnold thought that good literature would never be extinguished because it emanates from "the instinct of self-preservation in humanity" (p. 39). Is that instinct still plausibly intact, in the light of so many obviously autodestructive compulsions evident in today's world? Does it all fall upon the shoulders of the young instructor who leads a class on Jane Austen in which it is accepted that certain words cannot be explored at all, and where it is sometimes legal for students and their teacher to show up maskless in a life-threatening pandemic and carrying a loaded gun? In the dark days of 1940, not long after Auden was writing his poem, Richards began a lecture at Yale with the following questions:

> Do literary and linguistic studies or discussions of education have any effects commensurate with the needs of the world? Are we fiddling in the burning city? Could our fiddling make any future city less inflammable?[121]

Many if not most of those writing or teaching literature have been asking themselves these questions for a very long time. We have spent our time spreading as much joy and pleasure as we can in the pursuit of deeper and better thinking and proper attention through slow time to the operations of language (all language), working for a world with more civility and less violence, seeking what Spivak called the "uncoercive rearrangement of desires." For the present moment, as I see it, Richards is again prescient. In the same lecture I have just cited, he goes on to insist that "the kind of attention to language I have in mind can be described as systematic study of *the inherent and necessary opportunities for misunderstanding* which language offers" (p. 74). Language does not just offer misunderstanding: it insists on it. It cannot work without words meaning lots of different things to different people. There *must* be misunderstanding. Instead of classing this attribute of words as a fault, Richards prefers to call it "resourcefulness." Our task is to work with and understand the misunderstandings.

Literature, civility, violence: resourceful words read singly, multiply more so when set together. Richards felt that the "power of minds to influence other minds" by modern mass communication had helped bring about two world wars. Auden wondered what "huge imago made / A psychopathic god."[122] We have followed some exemplary moments (by no means an entire history) in the interactions of three words and concepts that both reinforce and baffle each other. Most broadly we have seen the endurance, under some stress, of the compact between literature, literary pedagogy and civility arrayed against the onset of violence. We have also confronted the incidence of an inconvertible violence that cannot be conjured away by the blandishments of aesthetic experience or aesthetic theory, that must subsist with and within the aesthetic itself. The subaltern syndrome is one instance of the resourcefulness of this formation, one where civility is broken and partial and violence endemic but never unchallenged. It is one example of how literature, if not guaranteed to save us, can continue to be an indispensable agent and helpmate in the making of a world that might appeal to the better instincts that remain and offer them time and space to develop. If it is not too late.

Notes

CHAPTER I

1. Richard Hofstadter and Michael Wallace, eds., *American Violence: A Documentary History* (New York: Alfred A. Knopf, 1970), p. 3.

2. *The Uses of Disorder: Personal Identity and City Life* (New York: Random House, 1970), pp. 147, 184.

3. *Crises of the Republic* (San Diego, CA: Harcourt Brace, 1972), p. 210.

4. "The Problem of Violence and the Radical Opposition," in Douglas Kellner, ed., *The New Left and the 1960s: Collected Papers of Herbert Marcuse* (London: Routledge, 2005), 3:57–75; see p. 63.

5. *These Truths: A History of the United States* (New York: W. W. Norton, 2018), pp. xiv, 785.

6. See the recent citations and discussion in David Bromwich, *How Words Make Things Happen* (Oxford: Oxford University Press, 2019), pp. 70–72.

7. *The Theory of Moral Sentiments*, ed. D. D. Raphael and A. L. Macfie (Oxford: Clarendon Press, 1976), p. 32.

8. I borrow this phrase from Martin Jay, *Cultural Semantics: Keywords of Our Time* (London: Athlone Press, 1998), pp. 109–19.

9. *Heart of Darkness* (Harmondsworth, UK: Penguin, 1977), p. 72.

10. See David Attwell, "Writing after the 'Poor Little Bomb': Fictionality and Sabotage in Nadine Gordimer's *The Late Bourgeois World*," *ELH* 87.1 (2020): 273–91. A full account of this history is Peter D. McDonald, *The Literature Police: Apartheid Censorship and Its Cultural Consequences* (Oxford: Oxford University Press, 2009). See also J. M. Coetzee, *Giving Offense: Essays on Censorship* (Chicago: University of Chicago Press, 1996).

11. The classic account of American historians facing this issue is Peter Novick, *That Noble Dream: The "Objectivity Question" and the American Historical Profession* (Cambridge: Cambridge University Press, 1998). See also Sarah Maza, *Thinking about History* (Chicago: University of Chicago Press, 2017), pp. 199–234. Maza asserts the "essential hybridity" of history writing.

12. *The Collected Poems of W. B. Yeats* (London: Macmillan, 1969), pp. 202–3. Consider also the claim in "Under Ben Bulben" that "some sort of violence" occurs when a "man" confronts fate (p. 398).

13. *The English Auden: Poems, Essays and Dramatic Writings, 1927–1939*, ed. Edward Mendelson (New York: Random House, 1977), p. 212.

14. *The English Auden*, pp. 245–46.

15. Rob Nixon, *Slow Violence and the Environmentalism of the Poor* (Cambridge, MA: Harvard University Press, 2011).

16. *Northanger Abbey*, ed, Marilyn Gaull (New York: Pearson-Longman, 2005), p. 91.

17. *Clarissa,* 4 vols. (London: Dent and Dutton, 1967), 4:553.

18. For example, at 1:118, 235, 281 and thereafter.

19. *Through Other Continents: American Literature across Deep Time* (Princeton, NJ: Princeton University Press, 2006), p. 8. Henry Sussman argues that linguistic activity itself affords the conditions for "individuation and freedom," with artworks specifically sustaining "a certain uneasy balance between the public discourse and individual idiosyncratic usage." See *The Aesthetic Contract: Statutes of Art and Intellectual Work in Modernity* (Stanford, CA: Stanford University Press, 1997), pp. 38, 166.

20. *Spectral Nationality: Passages of Freedom from Kant to Postcolonial Literatures of Liberation* (New York: Columbia University Press, 2003), pp. 8, 76.

21. *What Is a World? On Postcolonial Literature as World Literature* (Durham, NC: Duke University Press, 2016), pp. 5, 11, 126.

22. *Necropolitics*, trans. Steven Corcoran (Durham, NC: Duke University Press, 2019), pp. 22, 107.

23. *Perpetual War: Cosmopolitanism from the Viewpoint of Violence* (Durham, NC: Duke University Press, 2012), p. 5.

24. See Susan Stewart, *Crimes of Writing: Problems in the Containment of Representation* (Durham, NC: Duke University Press, 1994), pp. 11–22.

25. *What Is Literature?*, trans. Bernard Frechtman (New York: Washington Square Press, 1966), p. 29.

26. *The Singularity of Literature* (London: Routledge, 2004), pp. 3, 63–64. This book, in the spirit of Shelley and Derrida, makes a strong and clear case for the importance of reading and writing in the name of literature. David Bromwich also endorses the idea that words make things happen "uncontrollably, unspecifiably" (*How Words Make Things Happen*, p. 82). On singularity, see also Bill Readings, *The University in Ruins* (Cambridge, MA: Harvard University Press, 1996), pp. 115–16. Readings intends the term to indicate "that there is no longer a subject-position available to function as the site of the conscious synthesis of sense-impressions."

27. *What Is Literature?*, pp. 174, 185–86.

28. *The University in Ruins*, pp. 158, 187.

29. Rawls proposes a "natural duty of civility not to invoke the faults of social arrangements as a too-ready excuse for not complying with them" as part of a "due acceptance of defects." The problem is how and when to decide that "certain bounds of injustice" call for the suspension of this duty. See *Political Justice* (Cambridge, MA: Belknap Press, Harvard University Press, 1995), pp. 354–55. The expanded discussion of the duty of civility in *Political Liberalism: Expanded Edition* (New York: Columbia University Press, 2005) is pitched more affirmatively as a "willingness to listen" (p. 217) and an appeal to public reason (p. 226). It describes how to manage consensus without knowing the whole truth and how to tolerate contingent disagreements.

30. Brian O'Connell, *Civil Society: The Underpinnings of American Democracy* (Hanover, NH: University Press of New England, 1999), pp. 25, 122. Robert B. Pippin, *The Persistence of Subjectivity: On the Kantian Aftermath* (Cambridge: Cambridge University Press, 2005), finds civility to be "ethical or normative" (p. 227) and an "indispensable human good" (p. 238).

31. Good examples of each case are, respectively, Stephen L. Carter's *Civility: Manners, Morals, and the Etiquette of Democracy* (New York: Harper, 1999), which chastises people who wear baggy pants; and Mark Caldwell's *A Short History of Rudeness: Manners, Morals and Misbehavior in Modern America* (New York: Picador, 1999). On the constraints devolving from "friendship orthodoxy," see Benjamin DeMott, *The Trouble with Friendship: Why Americans Can't Think Straight about Race* (New Haven, CT: Yale University Press, 1998).

32. *Violence and Civility: The Limits of Political Philosophy*, trans. G. M. Goshgarian (New York: Columbia University Press, 2016).

33. See also Timothy J. Huzar and Clare Woodford, eds., *Toward a Feminist Ethic of Nonviolence* (New York: Fordham University Press, 2021), which frames the work of Adriana Cavarero, Judith Butler and Bonnie Honig around the question of an inescapable violence.

34. *Mere Civility: Disagreement and the Limits of Toleration* (Cambridge, MA: Harvard University Press, 2017). Bejan finds a model in Williams for what Sennett advocated in 1970: more space for the rough and tumble elements of social life.

35. *Cold War Criticism and the Politics of Skepticism* (New York: Oxford University Press, 1993), p. 47.

36. "The Quiet Resistance inside the Trump Administration," *New York Times*, September 6, 2018, p. A21.

37. See Timothy Fitzgerald, *Discourse on Civility and Barbarity: A Critical History of Religion and Related Categories* (New York: Oxford University Press, 2007), for a good account of how every socially binding term depends on a host of others to affirm itself as persuasive.

38. See Jacques Derrida, *Dissemination,* trans. Barbara Johnson (Chicago: University of Chicago Press); and Raymond Williams, *Keywords: A Vocabulary of Culture and Society,* rev. ed. (New York: Oxford University Press, 1983).

39. Adolf Hitler, *Mein Kampf* (New York: Reynal and Hitchcock, 1940), pp. xv, 136. Ten editors and translators oversaw this publication, in English, as a matter of some urgency.

40. Friedrich Nietzsche, *Daybreak: Thoughts on the Prejudices of Morality,* trans. R. J. Hollingdale (Cambridge: Cambridge University Press, 1982), p. 5.

41. "Philosophy and *Weltliteratur,*" trans. Maire and Edward Said, *Centennial Review* 13.1 (1969): 1–17; p. 15.

42. *Crises of the Republic,* p. 142.

43. The same reservations apply to Adriana Cavarero's *Horrorism: Naming Contemporary Violence,* trans. William McCuaig (New York: Columbia University Press, 2009), which asserts a clear distinction between terror and horror, even as the history of usages shows a steady confusion and overlapping of the two. The clear thinking we respect as a good thing for philosophy works as a corrective for language use but not as a description of its history. For a salient account and critique of the tradition, see Jeffrey Masten, *Queer Philologies: Sex, Language and Affect in Shakespeare's Time* (Philadelphia: University of Pennsylvania Press, 2016), pp. 16–24.

44. *How to Read a Page: A Course in Efficient Reading with an Introduction to a Hundred Great Words* (New York: W. W. Norton, 1942), pp. 129, 131. The range and variety of Richards's contributions to various 'disciplines' has arguably obscured the importance of each of them. John Paul Russo, *I. A. Richards: His Life and Work* (Baltimore: Johns Hopkins University Press, 1989), is an invaluable guide to revisiting his writings.

45. *Keywords for Today: A 21st Century Vocabulary,* ed. Colin MacCabe and Holly Yanacek (New York: Oxford University Press, 2018), pp. 41–44. Neither Williams nor his successors make more than a minimal mention of civility.

46. "Civilité, Politesse, Affabilité," https://artflsrv03.uchicago.edu/philologoic4/encyclopedie0521/navigate/3/2201/. See Peter France, *Politeness and Its Discontents: Problems in French Classical Culture* (Cambridge: Cambridge University Press, 1992), pp. 55–64; and Roger Chartier, *Lectures et lecteurs dans la France dans l'ancien régime* (Paris: Seuil, 1987). There is a good account of the French tradition in Benet Davetian, *Civility: A Cultural History* (Toronto: University of Toronto Press, 2009), pp. 98–140.

47. See *De Officiis,* trans. Walter Miller (Cambridge, MA: Harvard University Press, 2005), I:xxv; II:xv. Cicero is already aware of the duplicitous and hypocritical potential of polite rhetoric: see Jon Hall, *Politeness and Politics in Cicero's Letters* (Oxford: Oxford University Press, 2009), esp. pp. 78–106, 169–95.

48. The Freudian text that English speakers know as *Civilization and Its Discontents* is in fact *Das Unbehagen in der Kultur.* See Norbert Elias, *The Civilizing Process,* trans. Edmund Jephcott (Oxford: Blackwell, 1994), pp. 3–28. Elias argues also for a class distinction between middle-class German and courtly French, one that Jaucourt clearly supports. See also Jörg Fisch, "Zivilisation, Kultur," in Otto Brunner, Werner Conze and Reinhart Koselleck, eds., *Geschichtliche Grundbegriffe: Historisches Lexicon zur politisch-sozialen Sprache in Deutschland* (Stuttgart: Klett-Cotta, 1992), 7:679–774. For a good overview, especially of the Italian *vita civile,* see Marvin B. Becker, *Civility and Society in Western Europe, 1300–1600* (Bloomington: Indiana University Press, 1988). A thorough and recent survey of the terminology can be found in Keith Thomas, *In Pursuit of Civility: Manners and Civilization in Early Modern England* (Waltham, MA: Brandeis University Press, 2018), pp. 11–48.

49. See Britta Baumgarten, Dieter Gosewinker and Dieter Rucht, "Civility: Introductory Notes on the History and Systematic Analysis of a Concept," *European Review of History: Revue européenne d'histoire* 18.3 (2011): 293–94. The second citation is of Dieter Rucht, "Civil Society and Civility in Twentieth-Century Theorising," *European Review of History,* pp. 399–400. In the 1990s civility was seen as merely a part of the whole that was civil society.

50. *Leviathan,* ed. Michael Oakeshott (Oxford: Basil Blackwell, 1955), p. 21.

51. *The Civilizing Process,* pp. 211, 504. Markku Peltonen, *The Duel in Early Modern England: Civility, Politeness and Honour* (Cambridge: Cambridge University Press, 2003), argues that the process was always incomplete. Dueling, for example, was readily incorporated into a culture of politeness. Davetian, *Civility,* esp. pp. 346ff., gives a critical summary of the Elias thesis.

52. Joshua Clover, *Riot. Strike. Riot: The New Era of Uprisings* (London: Verso, 2016), distinguishes the riot from the strike in terms that can be affiliated with a civil-uncivil binary.

53. For just one example, see the account of the Chicago police in 2012 offered in W. J. T. Mitchell, Bernard E. Harcourt and Michael Taussig, *Occupy: Three Inquiries in Disobedience* (Chicago: University of Chicago Press, 2013), pp. 78–81.

54. Thus, Astead W. Herndon wonders whether Obama might reflect "a bygone era of civil political rhetoric": "Obama Uplifted Them: Now They Want to Fight," *New York Times,* November 1, 2018, pp. A1, 19.

55. *The Better Angels of Our Nature: Why Violence Has Declined* (New York: Penguin Group, 2012).

56. See, for example, pp. xxv–xxvi, 172–83, 477–79. Lynn Hunt, in *Inventing Human Rights: A History* (New York: W. W. Norton, 2008), gives prominence to the eighteenth-century popularity of the epistolary novel as foundational for inculcating the concept of human rights.

57. *The Civilizing Process,* p. 211.

58. *Civility and Society*, p. 123. See also Peter Burke, *The Art of Conversation* (Ithaca, NY: Cornell University Press, 1993), pp. 89–122.

59. See Peter Burke, *The Fortunes of the Courtier: The European Reception of Castiglione's "Cortegiano"* (University Park: Pennsylvania State University Press, 1996), pp. 99–116. But Burke finds one period in the seventeenth century when the book was deemed not cynical *enough* to satisfy the spirit of the times (p. 124).

60. See the essays by Kenneth Borris, Frank Whigham and Daniel Javitch in *The Spenser Encyclopedia*, ed. A. C. Hamilton (London: Routledge and University of Toronto Press, 1999), pp. 194–99.

61. *The Faerie Queene: Book Six and the Mutabilitie Cantos*, ed. Andrew Hadfield and Abraham Stoll (Indianapolis, IN: Hackett, 2007), p. 223.

62. Spenser's identification of courtesy and civility, with courtesy as elsewhere the "roote of civil conversation" (p. 6), comes from Stefano Guazzo, whose work was translated twice into English as *The Civile Conversation* (1581, 1586). Guazzo specifically indexes the transition from Latin *civilis* to modern notions of civil as "not having relation to the citie, but consideration to the maners and condition which make it civile." Guazzo is cited by Javitch, *The Spenser Encyclopedia*, p. 198.

63. See *Clarissa*, 2:22, 223, 425.

64. Thus we ask Abby, not Adam: Judith Martin (as Miss Manners) is a well-known authority on how to behave.

65. *Critique and Crisis: Enlightenment and the Pathogenesis of Modern Society* (Cambridge, MA: MIT Press, 1988).

66. See Jonathan Arac, "The Media of Sublimity: Johnson and Lamb on King Lear," *Studies in Romanticism* 26 (1987): 209–20. Distance from violence is the topic of Mary A. Favret's important study *War at a Distance: Romanticism and the Making of Modern Wartime* (Princeton, NJ: Princeton University Press, 2010). While Britain remained in many ways a violent place, Favret notes that, after 1745, most large-scale military violence occurred overseas. Assessments of such violence were thereby mediated, largely by print. Along with the newspapers, literature played a significant role for many in engaging this violence.

67. On the Romantic turn to a "poetics of slowness," see Jonathan Sachs, *The Poetics of Decline in British Romanticism* (Cambridge: Cambridge University Press, 2018), esp. chapters 5 and 6.

68. Two recent major books are Davetian, *Civility*, and Thomas, *In Pursuit of Civility*. Both understand civility as a contested category in need of urgent attention in the present. Thomas is particularly attentive to historical relations between civility and violence: see esp. pp. 104–10, 159–82. So too Balibar, *Violence and Civility*.

69. An exemplary analysis of the race-gender complex at work in the early nineteenth century is John Barrell, *The Infection of Thomas De Quincey: A Psychopathology of Imperialism* (New Haven, CT: Yale University Press, 1991).

70. For an important account of the pervasive and incremental recourse to fatal violence throughout the 'long war' years of 1914–45, see Timothy Snyder, *Bloodlands: Europe between Hitler and Stalin* (New York: Basic Books, 2010).

71. *What Is Literature?*, pp. 150, 200.

72. *The Wretched of the Earth*, trans. Constance Farrington (New York: Grove Press, 1968), pp. 77, 132. On Fanon's "duty to violence," see Achille Mbembe, *Critique of Black Reason*, trans. Laurent Dubois (Durham, NC: Duke University Press, 2017), pp. 162–70.

73. *Art and Revolution*, trans. Rose Strunsky (Ann Arbor: University of Michigan Press, 1960), pp. 19, 236.

74. *Under Representation: The Racial Regime of Aesthetics* (New York: Fordham University Press, 2019), p. 3.

75. *Critique of the Power of Judgment*, ed. Paul Guyer (Cambridge: Cambridge University Press, 2000), pp. 177, 250 (sections 41 and 67). Gayatri Chakravorty Spivak has discussed the founding abjection of the aboriginal in *A Critique of Postcolonial Reason: A History of the Vanishing Present* (Cambridge, MA: Harvard University Press, 1999), pp. 21–37.

76. *Art of Judgement* (Oxford: Blackwell, 1989), pp. 2–3, 323–24.

77. *The Fate of Art: Aesthetic Alienation from Kant to Derrida and Adorno* (University Park: Pennsylvania State University Press, 1992), p. 13. Recall Cheah's idea of literature as a "force of making-possible" (*What Is a World?*, p. 126).

78. *Consequences of Enlightenment* (Cambridge: Cambridge University Press, 1999). See especially chapters 2 and 4. See also Robert Kaufman, "Red Kant, or the Persistence of the Third *Critique* in Adorno and Jameson," *Critical Inquiry* 26 (2010): 682–724; and Rebecca Comay, *Mourning Sickness: Hegel and the French Revolution* (Stanford, CA: Stanford University Press, 2011), p. 34, on judgment's role in inventing politics. Hannah Arendt's lectures on Kant have sponsored a good deal of interest in the political potential of the aesthetic: see Jim Josefson, *Hannah Arendt's Aesthetic Politics: Freedom and the Beautiful* (Cham, Switzerland: Palgrave Macmillan-Springer, 2019). So too Lyotard's writings on the sublime.

79. "The Affirmative Character of Culture," reprinted in *Negations: Essays in Critical Theory*, trans. Jeremy J. Shapiro (Boston: Beacon Press, 1969), pp. 88–133; p. 99.

80. See, for example, pp. 7–8, 12, 14–15, 68, 109–10. I speak only here of *The Critique of the Power of Judgment*. In other writings Kant is much more straightforwardly critical of violence and militarization.

81. *Slavery and the Culture of Taste* (Princeton, NJ: Princeton University Press, 2011), e.g., pp. xiii, xv, 8. The same point is made in his earlier *Maps of Englishness: Writing Identity in the Culture of Colonialism* (New York: Columbia University Press, 1996), e.g., pp. 32–33, 121, 125.

82. *The Location of Culture* (London: Routledge, 1994), e.g., pp. 32, 91, 108, 121.

83. See Philippe Lacoue-Labarthe and Jean-Luc Nancy, *The Literary Absolute: The Theory of Literature in German Romanticism*, trans. Philip Barnard and Cheryl Lester (Albany: SUNY Press, 1988).

84. An impressive analysis of this formation can be found in Marc Redfield, *The Politics of Aesthetics: Nationalism, Gender, Romanticism* (Stanford, CA: Stanford University Press, 2003), as well as in the first chapter of his *Phantom Formations: Aesthetic Ideology and the Bildungsroman* (Ithaca, NY: Cornell University Press, 1996).

85. Rawls's phrase is presumably intended as a rebuke of Sartre and Fanon's duty to violence.

86. Cited in Alexandra Popoff, *Vasily Grossman and the Soviet Century* (New Haven, CT: Yale University Press, 2019), p. 275. The manuscript of this novel was "arrested" in 1961 (p. 257).

87. There is of course always the other side: McDonald, in *The Literature Police*, p. 75, cites the South African censor J. C. W. van Rooyen's claim that books could be "useful safety valves for pent-up feelings in a milieu where they would be understood not as a call to political violence but as a literary experience."

88. *The Emigrants*, trans. Michael Hulse (New York: New Directions, 1997), pp. 46, 193.

89. *Shelley's Poetry and Prose*, ed. Donald H. Reiman and Sharon B. Powers (New York: W. W. Norton, 1977), p. 487. Cf. p. 486: "a single word even may be a spark of inextinguishable thought."

90. The force of Elaine Scarry's *The Body in Pain: The Making and Unmaking of the World* (New York: Oxford University Press, 1985) is that it juxtaposes the celebration of aesthetic creativity with the "deconstruction of creation" (p. 22) that obtains in acts of cruelty and violence, maintaining a consistent attention to the play of making and unmaking, wounding and creating. But in its thesis about the morality of imagination as governing the entire range of poesis, from coats to poems, it arguably goes even beyond Schiller. Crusoe, significantly, is deemed to produce his surfeit of objects for living out of "sheer pleasure" rather than, say, anxiety or compulsion (p. 320). In *On Beauty and Being Just* (Princeton, NJ: Princeton University Press, 1999), the relation between the beautiful and the moral is proposed as going beyond analogy (where it resided for Kant) because the sense of beauty is primary.

91. The creators of monuments might seem to be bound to facts, but they often bring those facts into unstable and critical light: thus the Vietnam Memorial, the Berlin Monument to the Murdered Jews and so on. And the claims made for why someone deserves a monument are for the most part highly selective about the facts.

92. *The Reawakening*, trans. Stuart Woolf (New York: Simon and Schuster, 1995), p. 26. Levi is clear that witnessing is not the same as writing history: it is limited to "the things which I myself endured and saw" (p. 222). It makes no judgment but commits to "preparing the ground for the judge" (p. 210): its readers.

93. Robert Harvey, *Witnesses: Beckett, Dante, Levi and the Foundations of Responsibility* (New York: Continuum, 2010), finds witnessing to be "an antidote to despair" and a "spur to moral action" (pp. ix, xi). I am not sure that we can count on what he calls "a universally shared propensity for fellow-feeling and moral action" (p. viii), but this is surely one of the incentives, never to be guaranteed, that literature can extend. There is a huge literature on the ethics of Holocaust representation. For Georges Didi-Huberman, "Auschwitz is only imaginable. . . . We are restricted to the image and must therefore attempt an internal critique so as to deal with this restriction." See *Images in Spite of All: Four Photographs from Auschwitz*, trans. Shane B. Lillis (Chicago: University of Chicago Press, 2003), p. 45.

CHAPTER 2

1. Ian Watt, *Myths of Modern Individualism: Faust, Don Quixote, Don Juan and Robinson Crusoe* (Cambridge: Cambridge University Press, 1996).

2. *Robinson Crusoe*, ed. Michael Shinagel (New York: W. W. Norton, 1975), p. 155. See also Shinagel's *Daniel Defoe and Middle-Class Gentility* (Cambridge, MA: Harvard University Press, 1968).

3. The text of Woodes Rogers's narrative of the Selkirk rescue is printed in *Robinson Crusoe*, ed. Angus Ross (Harmondsworth, UK: Penguin, 1985), p. 306.

4. My source here is the widely available *Eighteenth-Century Catalogue Online* (ECCO); here and for other novels I have consulted the first London edition.

5. *The Works of Daniel Defoe*, ed. G. H. Maynardier, 16 vols. (New York: Jenson Society, 1905), 2:38.

6. In the *Serious Reflections during the Life and Surprising Adventures of Robinson Crusoe* (1720), the third book in the series, the word civil appears more often (ten times), mostly as describing the state-equivalent administration and sometimes in implicit contrast with the religious mandate. Only twice is civil synonymous with polite or decent.

7. *Works*, 2:122–23.

8. *The Works of Aphra Behn*, ed. Janet Todd (London: William Pickering, 1995), 3:62.

9. Daniel Defoe, *Memoirs of a Cavalier*, ed. James T. Boulton (London: Oxford University Press, 1972), pp. 12, 32.

10. Edward Hyde, First Earl of Clarendon, *The History of the Rebellion and Civil Wars in England, Begun in the Year 1641,* ed. W. Dunn Macray, 6 vols. (Oxford: Clarendon Press, 1888), 1:xxii, xxvi. Clarendon died in 1674; his book was published in 1702–4.

11. Paula R. Backscheider, *Daniel Defoe: His Life* (Baltimore: Johns Hopkins University Press, 1989), pp. 102, 104.

12. *Works,* 3:32.

13. Erin Mackie, *Market à la Mode: Fashion, Commodity and Gender in "The Tatler" and "The Spectator"* (Baltimore: Johns Hopkins University Press, 1989), pp. xv, 21. See also John Brewer, *The Pleasures of the Imagination: English Culture in the Eighteenth Century* (New York: Farrar, Straus and Giroux, 1997), pp. 87–122.

14. *Robinson Crusoe,* p. 52.

15. In playful homage to this moment, Wilkie Collins's *The Moonstone* (1868) shows Gabriel Betteredge to be in the habit of opening his copy of *Crusoe* when in need of similar guidance.

16. *The British Essayists; with Prefaces Biographical, Historical and Critical,* ed. Rev. Lionel Thomas Berguer, 45 vols. (London: T. and J. Allman, 1823), 1:xiv, xxxvi.

17. But note that the happy valley of *Rasselas* contains no books.

18. The major account of this strand of political theory is J. G. A. Pocock, *The Machiavellian Moment: Florentine Political Thought and the Atlantic Republican Tradition* (Princeton, NJ: Princeton University Press, 1975).

19. *British Essayists,* 20:240, 242.

20. See Dena Goodman, *The Republic of Letters: A Cultural History of the French Enlightenment* (Ithaca, NY: Cornell University Press, 1994), esp. chapter 3.

21. *Pamela,* 2 vols. (London: Dent and Dutton, 1914), 1:18. On Pamela's career as an icon of civility, see Jenny Davidson, *Hypocrisy and the Politics of Politeness: Manners and Morals from Locke to Austen* (Cambridge: Cambridge University Press, 2004), pp. 108–45; Carey McIntosh, *The Evolution of English Prose, 1700–1800: Style, Politeness, and Print Culture* (Cambridge: Cambridge University Press, 1998), esp. pp. 207–11; Philip Carter, *Men and the Emergence of Polite Society, 1660–1800* (Harlow, UK: Longman, 2001); Moyra Haslett, *Pope to Burney, 1714–1779: Scriblerians to Bluestockings* (Basingstoke, UK: Palgrave Macmillan, 2003), pp. 209–25.

22. *Pamela,* 1:5.

23. Jürgen Habermas, *The Structural Transformation of the Public Sphere: An Inquiry into a Category of Bourgeois Society,* trans. Thomas Burger (Cambridge, MA: MIT Press, 1989).

24. See William B. Warner, *Licensing Entertainment: The Elevation of Novel Reading in Britain, 1684–1750* (Berkeley: University of California Press, 1998), p. 179.

25. *Pamela*, 1:55–56.

26. Peter Clark, *British Clubs and Societies, 1580–1800: The Origins of an Associational World* (Oxford: Oxford University Press, 2000), offers a graphic analysis: see pp. 128, 132. The Society for the Propagation of Christian Knowledge, obviously congruent with Pamela's mission, was founded in 1699 (p. 65).

27. Habermas, in *The Structural Transformation of the Public Sphere*, proposes that the bourgeois public was, from the late seventeenth century, a reading public (p. 23) developed first in "the conjugal family's intimate domain" (p. 28).

28. For a bibliography, see Warner, *Licensing Entertainment*, pp. 296–97. Thomas Keymer gives evidence that Richardson was well able to manage responses by way of the most modern media culture: see *Pamela*, ed. Thomas Keymer and Alice Wakely (Oxford: Oxford University Press, 2001), pp. xxii–xxvii.

29. *The Spread of Novels: Translation and Prose Fiction in the Eighteenth Century* (Princeton, NJ: Princeton University Press, 2010), pp. 115–22. While *Pamela* preached a feisty and contended patriotism, *Clarissa* marketed a universalism of feeling that came to be positively identified with Englishness itself (pp. 122–29).

30. "Britain, 1750–1830," in Franco Moretti, ed., *The Novel*, vol. 1, *History, Geography and Culture* (Princeton, NJ: Princeton University Press, 2006), pp. 429–54. Moretti's *Atlas of the European Novel, 1800–1900* (London: Verso, 1998), is foundational for the analysis of the (uneven) globalization of fiction.

31. *Enlightenment Orientalism: Resisting the Rise of the Novel* (Chicago: University of Chicago Press, 2012), p. 24.

32. *Capital: Volume One*, trans. Ben Fowkes (New York: Random House, 1977), pp. 914–26.

33. *Clarissa*, 4:503.

34. *Licensing Entertainment*, p. 226.

35. *From Courtesy to Civility: Changing Codes of Conduct in Early Modern England* (Oxford: Clarendon Press, 1998), pp. 193–275.

36. See Burke, *The Fortunes of the Courtier*, p. 130.

37. For a sense of the field, see Sydney L. Gulick Jr., *A Chesterfield Bibliography to 1800*, Papers of the Bibliographical Society of America, vol. 29 (Chicago: University of Chicago Press, 1935).

38. See *A Chesterfield Bibliography*, pp. 14–16.

39. *Letters Written by the Late Right Honorable Philip Dormer Stanhope, Earl of Chesterfield, to His Son, Philip Stanhope, Esq. Together with Several Other Pieces on Various Subjects. Published by Mrs. Eugenia Stanhope.* 6th ed., 4 vols. (London: J. Dodsley, 1775), 1:xiv, xv. The sixth substantially reprints the second edition; even exact reprints were commonly described as new editions at the time. According to Richard L. Bushman, *The Refinement of America: Persons, Houses, Cities* (New York: Random House, 1993), p. 36, there were eighteen American versions of Chesterfield before 1800. See also Roger Coxon, *Chesterfield and His Critics*

(London: Routledge, 1925); and Charles Pullen, "Lord Chesterfield and Eighteenth-Century Appearance and Reality," *SEL* 8 (1968): 501–15. See also Philip Carter, *Men and the Emergence of Polite Society*, pp. 76–80; and Davidson, *Hypocrisy*, pp. 56–75.

40. Who exactly belonged to the middle class was of course quite unclear: see Paul Langford, *A Polite and Commercial People: England, 1727–1783* (Oxford: Clarendon Press, 1998), pp. 59–121; and Sara Maza, *The Myth of the French Bourgeoisie: An Essay on the Social Imaginary, 1750–1850* (Cambridge, MA: Harvard University Press, 2009).

41. *Civility*: "civility is a moral issue, not just a matter of habit or convention: it is morally better to be civil than uncivil" (p. xii). Carter's diagnosis of an "incivility crisis" (p. 5) in the 1990s has many echoes in the present.

42. *Sermons by Hugh Blair, D.D.* (London: T. Allman, 1832), p. 58. Critiques of Chesterfield are commonplace. The *Mirror* finds in him "a studied system of frivolity, meanness, flattery and dissimulation"; *Olla Podrida* upbraids his praise for "a hypocritical show of feelings we do not possess"; the *Microcosm* deplores the use of politeness for "mercenary" purposes (*British Essayists*, 34:175, 41:133, 45:123). See also Mary Hamilton's 1788 novel *Munster Village*, ed. Sarah Bayliss (London: Pandora Press, 1987), which comments on his hostility to women (p. 136) and on his commending "barbarity" (p. 138).

43. See John Guillory, *Cultural Capital: The Problem of Literary Canon Formation* (Chicago: University of Chicago Press, 1993), pp. 85–133, for an account of Gray, Wordsworth and the eighteenth-century production of a "vernacular literacy."

44. *The Prose Works of Jonathan Swift, D.D.*, ed. Temple Scott, 12 vols. (London: George Bell, 1907), 11:204. In 1713 the *Guardian* had advised against looking like an "empty formal man who speaks in proverbs, and decides all controversies with a short sentence" (*British Essayists*, 16:117).

45. See Gulick, *A Chesterfield Bibliography*, pp. 62–64.

46. *Letters*, 2:130.

47. *British Essayists*, 34:193. Chesterfield's essay in the *World* elaborately discriminates between civility and good breeding very much in the manner of Jaucourt's *Encyclopédie* article: see *British Essayists*, 28:218–22.

CHAPTER 3

1. Anthony Ashley Cooper, Third Earl of Shaftesbury, *Characteristics of Men, Manners, Opinions, Times*, ed. John M. Robertson, 2 vols in 1 (Indianapolis: Bobbs-Merrill, 1964), 1:46. The more recent edition by Lawrence E. Klein (Cambridge: Cambridge University Press, 2001) is more extensively modernized in spelling and format.

2. This is also an endorsement of the morality of civil society as independent of the state: an anticipation of the spirit of 1989. See Caygill, *Art of Judgement*, pp. 42–53. Mandeville's critique meanwhile insists on the necessity of violence to maintain order.

3. See David Simpson, "Hume's Intimate Voices and the Method of Dialogue," *Texas Studies in Language and Literature* 21 (1979): 68–92. For the model of dialogue as synthesizing philosophy and literature, see Michael Prince, *Philosophical Dialogue in the British Enlightenment: Theology, Aesthetics and the Novel* (Cambridge: Cambridge University Press, 1996).

4. Lawrence E. Klein, *Shaftesbury and the Culture of Politeness: Moral Discourse and Cultural Politics in Early Eighteenth-Century England* (Cambridge: Cambridge University Press, 1994), pp. 81–90, argues that this commitment to interior self-monitoring was a personal discipline as well as a political ethic. Klein's book is essential reading on the "new public and gentlemanly culture of criticism" (p. 8) in relation to "the expansion and elaboration of human interiority" (p. 83).

5. See David Simpson, *Romanticism, Nationalism, and the Revolt against Theory* (Chicago: University of Chicago Press, 1993).

6. It is more often the subject of a ruthless satire, as in *The Tatler* no. 216; but see *The Rambler* nos. 82–83 for a more balanced view.

7. Compare Addison's 1710 animadversions, in *The Tatler* no. 216, against those who spend their lives trying to "discover the sex of a cockle" while scarcely knowing "a horse from an ox" (*British Essayists*, 5:26–27).

8. This is the thesis of Steven Shapin's *A Social History of Truth: Civility and Science in Seventeenth-Century England* (Chicago: University of Chicago Press, 1994). Shapin shows that the informal mechanisms of social bonding (trust, politeness) were crucial in papering over the as-yet inexact routines of the empirical method.

9. Anon (Vicesimus Knox), *Personal Nobility; or, Letters to a Young Nobleman on the Conduct of His Studies and the Dignity of the Peerage* (London: Charles Dilly, 1793), pp. 179, 237.

10. *The Educational Writings of John Locke*, ed. James L. Axtell (Cambridge: Cambridge University Press, 1968), pp. 200–201.

11. *Personal Nobility*, pp. 25, 27.

12. *The Compleat English Gentleman*, ed. Karl D. Bülbring (Folcroft, PA: Folcroft Library Editions, 1972), p. 201.

13. *British Essayists*, 12:124.

14. *British Essayists*, 16:117.

15. *British Essayists*, 22:68.

16. But see Harriet Guest, *Small Change: Women, Learning, Patriotism, 1750–1810* (Chicago: University of Chicago Press, 2000); and Goodman, *The Republic of Letters*, for more complex accounts of the learned woman.

17. See *Women, Writing and the Public Sphere, 1700–1830*, ed. Elizabeth Eger, Charlotte Grant, Clíona Ó Gallchior and Penny Warburton (Cambridge: Cambridge University Press, 2001); Paula McDowell, *The Women of Grub Street: Press, Politics and Gender in the London Literary Marketplace, 1678–1730* (Oxford: Clarendon Press, 1998); Elizabeth Eger, *Bluestockings: Women of Reason from the Enlightenment to Romanticism* (Basingstoke, UK: Palgrave Macmillan, 2010).

18. *British Essayists*, 27:220.

19. David Hume, *A Treatise of Human Nature*, ed. L. A. Selby-Bigge (Oxford: Clarendon Press, 1973), pp. xv, xvi.

20. David Hume, *Essays Moral, Political, and Literary*, ed. Eugene F. Miller (Indianapolis: Liberty Classics, 1985), p. xi. On Hume and the culture of politeness, see Davidson, *Hypocrisy*, pp. 50–55.

21. Thomas Reid, *An Inquiry into the Human Mind*, ed. Thomas Duggan (Chicago: University of Chicago Press, 1970), pp. 13, 15.

22. *Essays*, p. xxxviii; Ernest Campbell Mossner, *The Life of David Hume*, 2nd ed. (Oxford: Clarendon Press, 1980), pp. 117, 139.

23. *Essays*, p. 534.

24. David Hume, *Enquiries concerning Human Understanding and concerning the Principles of Morals*, ed. L. A. Selby-Bigge, 3rd ed. rev. P. H. Nidditch (Oxford: Clarendon Press, 1975), p. x.

25. John Mullan, *Sentiment and Sociability: The Language of Feeling in the Eighteenth Century* (Oxford: Clarendon Press, 2002). Mullan argues (pp. 18–56) that Hume moves away from reliance upon the passions as determining sociability.

26. Mossner, *The Life of David Hume*, p. 138.

27. Robin Valenza and John Bender, "Hume's Learned and Conversible Worlds," in Jonathan Culler and Kevin Lamb, eds., *Just Being Difficult? Academic Writing in the Public Arena* (Stanford, CA: Stanford University Pess, 2003), p. 36. This is a fine essay on Hume's deceptively simple style.

28. Jerome Christensen, *Practicing Enlightenment: Hume and the Formation of a Literary Career* (Madison: University of Wisconsin Press, 1987), p. 29.

29. See Rosalie Colie, "The Essayist in His *Essay*," in John W. Yolton, ed., *John Locke: Problems and Perspectives* (Cambridge: Cambridge University Press, 1969), pp. 234–60; and Christensen, *Practicing Enlightenment*, pp. 130–32. Isaac Watts's *Logick* complained of the rejection of "systematic Learning" evident in the popularity of the essay form: see Mossner, *Life of Hume*, p. 140.

30. Hence, perhaps his recourse to the dialogue form when addressing religion: see Simpson, "Hume's Intimate Voices."

31. This was the century that saw a dramatic efflorescence of time words. See Reinhart Koselleck, "*Neuzeit*: Remarks on the Semantics of Modern Concepts of Movement," in *Futures Past: On the Semantics of Historical Time*, trans. Keith Tribe (New York: Columbia University Press, 2004), pp. 222–54.

32. *Essays*, p. 124.

33. See John Sekora, *Luxury: The Concept in Western Thought, Eden to Smollett* (Baltimore: Johns Hopkins University Press, 1977); Pocock, *The Machiavellian Moment*; Simpson, *Wordsworth and the Figurings of the Real* (London: Macmillan, 1982), pp. 122–69.

34. See Mossner, *Life of Hume*, pp. 301–18.

35. *Enquiries*, p. 223.

36. *The History of England, from the Invasion of Julius Caesar to the Revolution in 1688*, 8 vols. (London: T. Cadell, 1789), 1:1.

37. On civility in relation to stadial theory, see Thomas, *In Pursuit of Civility*, pp. 134–58.

38. *The Fable of the Bees; or, Private Vices, Publick Benefits*, ed. Philip Harth (London: Penguin, 1989), pp. 57, 105. See, again, Davidson, *Hypocrisy*.

39. *Discourse on the Arts and Sciences*, ed. Roger D. Masters and Christopher Kelly (Hanover, NH: University Press of New England, 1992), p. 6.

40. *An Essay on the History of Civil Society, 1767*, ed. Duncan Forbes (Edinburgh: Edinburgh University Press, 1966), pp. 1, 16.

41. On Ferguson's effort to oppose Hume and the theorists of politeness by affirming a classic republican ethos of active political participation recognizing the necessity of strife, see Fania Oz-Salzberger, "Civil Society in the Scottish Enlightenment," in Sudipta Kaviraj and Sunil Khilnani, eds., *Civil Society: History and Possibilities* (Cambridge: Cambridge University Press, 2001), pp. 58–83.

42. Henry Home, Lord Kames, *Sketches of the History of Man*, 4 vols. (Edinburgh: Strahan and Cadell, 1788), 1:30.

43. Smith, *The Theory of Moral Sentiments*, pp. 9–10.

44. Henry Home, Lord Kames, *Elements of Criticism*, 11th ed. (London: Thomas Tegg, 1840), p. v. On Kames, see Caygill, *Art of Judgement*, pp. 62–69.

45. *Sketches*, 2:2–3, 38–41.

46. *The Works of Mary Wollstonecraft*, ed. Janet Todd and Marilyn Butler, 6 vols. (New York: New York University Press, 1989), 5:7, 60.

47. *Works*, 5:123, 127, 167. Jenny Davidson, *Hypocrisy*, considers Wollstonecraft as offering "the most compelling eighteenth-century challenge to the authority of civility" (p. 12); see also pp. 76–107. Even Kames concedes that modern women are best valued as "faithful friends and agreeable companions" who should be judged by "merit, improved by virtuous and refined education"; see *Sketches*, 2:41, 91.

48. My samples are drawn from the searchable text of the first edition reproduced in the *Eighteenth Century Catalogue Online* (ECCO). Although inevitable omissions and small errors populate all such resources, the balance of the evidence is overwhelming. In more than sixty instances of *civil*, all are clearly used in the classical sense. *Civil society* appears thirteen times; the conjunctive contrast

with military ("civil and military") nine times, and so on. Civil war, violence, confusion and disturbance are also popular.

CHAPTER 4

1. *Culture and Anarchy*, ed. J. Dover Wilson (Cambridge: Cambridge University Press, 1978), p. 83.

2. Arnold means an expansion of ideas rather than of empire, but global expansion was of course also happening.

3. *Essays in Criticism: Second Series* (London: Macmillan, 1935), p. 1.

4. Thomas Carlyle, *Critical and Miscellaneous Essays*, 5 vols. (London: Chapman and Hall, 1905), 1:204, 208.

5. *Critical and Miscellaneous Essays*, 1:304, 423, 465.

6. *Essays*, 2:130–31.

7. *Essays*, 2:165.

8. *Essays*, 2:369–70. Elsewhere, Carlyle commends Fichte's idea that "Literary Men" are the appointed ministers of the "Divine Idea" (1:58).

9. *Keywords for Today*, pp. 81–87. Williams's pathbreaking *Culture and Society* was first published in 1958; he wrote another book, *Culture*, in 1981. The word was never far from his mind or his attention.

10. On the anthropological sense of culture, see Christopher Herbert, *Culture and Anomie: Ethnographic Imagination in the Nineteenth Century* (Chicago: University of Chicago Press, 1991).

11. *Keywords for Today*, p. 85.

12. I draw here upon the article by Michel Espagne in Barbara Cassin, ed., *Dictionary of Untranslatables: A Philosophical Lexicon*, ed. and trans. Emily Apter, Jacques Lezra and Michael Wood (Princeton, NJ: Princeton University Press, 2004), pp. 111–20. See also Koselleck, "The Anthropological and Semantic Structure of *Bildung*," in *The Practice of Conceptual History: Timing History, Spacing Concepts*, trans. Todd Samuel Presner and others (Stanford, CA: Stanford University Press, 2002), pp. 170–207. Norbert Elias, *The Civilizing Process*, pp. 3–28, gives an account of the competition between *Kultur* and *Zivilisation*, one very much driven by the urge to distinguish French from German traditions and the middle from the upper class. As always, Brunner, Conze and Koselleck's *Geschichtliche Grundbegriffe* is indispensable: see "Zivilisation/Kultur," 7:679–774. The standard account in English is W. H. Bruford, *The German Tradition of Self-Cultivation: "Bildung" from Humboldt to Thomas Mann* (Cambridge: Cambridge University Press, 1975). There is a useful discussion by the editor in Wilhelm von Humboldt, *The Limits of State Action*, ed. J. W. Burrow (Indianapolis, IN: Liberty Fund, 1993), pp. xvii–lxii.

13. Thus, for Schiller, *Kultur* is responsible for an increase in the division of labor, which must work against the wholeness of being required by *Bildung.* See Friedrich Schiller, *On the Aesthetic Education of Man, in a Series of Letters*, trans. Elizabeth M. Wilkinson and L. A. Willoughby (Oxford: Clarendon Press, 1967), p. 32.

14. Whether the *Bildungsroman* really is a genre or just a retrospective construction is one of the topics of Marc Redfield's *Phantom Formations: Aesthetic Ideology and the "Bildungsroman"* (Ithaca, NY: Cornell University Press, 1996).

15. "The Function of Criticism at the Present Time," in *Essays in Criticism*, 2nd ed. (London: Macmillan, 1869), p. 17.

16. Lacoue-Labarthe and Nancy, *The Literary Absolute*, pp. xxii, 5.

17. See Marc Redfield, *The Politics of Aesthetics: Nationalism, Gender, Romanticism* (Stanford, CA: Stanford University Press, 2003), for an incisive and comprehensive analysis of the modern literary absolute.

18. I owe this citation to Redfield, *The Politics of Aesthetics*, p. 88. Schlegel further describes *Bildung* as an "antithetical synthesis" that is "fulfilled to the point of irony." See Ernst Behler, ed., *Philosophische Lehrjahre, 1796–1828*, Erster Teil (Munich: Verlag Schöningh, 1963), pp. 82–83. Koselleck, *Practice of Conceptual History*, p. 195, claims that *Bildung* was identified as politically progressive before 1848 and increasingly 'bourgeois' thereafter. But Franco Moretti, *The Way of the World: The* Bildungsroman *in European Culture*, new ed., trans. Albert Sbragia (London: Verso, 2000), finds the genre to be more typically representing failure and contradiction than happy resolution. And Lukács, viewing the novel as an incarnation of transcendental homelessness in a world without God, finds "irony" to be its "normative mentality." See *The Theory of the Novel: A Historico-Philosophical Essay on the Forms of Great Epic Literature*, trans. Anna Bostock (Cambridge, MA: MIT Press, 1971), p. 84. In other words, the *Bildungsroman* was always more than just a transcription of the liberal-idealist construction of *Bildung.*

19. *Aesthetic Education*, p. 215.

20. Schiller's importance to Arnold and beyond is central to the argument made by David Lloyd and Paul Thomas, *Culture and the State* (New York: Routledge, 1998). A fuller consideration of the topic than I can aspire to here would call attention to the relative status of the aesthetic mode in, for example, Hegel (whose eventual displacement of art by philosophy represents one version of the priority of theory) and Schelling (whose case for the immanent truth of art inclines more toward the privileging of culture). Humboldt's *Bildung* is aggressively antistatist; beyond protecting us from violence, the state should leave us alone to fashion our own selves.

21. *Aesthetic Education*, pp. 47, 59, 215.

22. *Aesthetic Education*, p. 195.

23. *Essays in Criticism, Second Series*, p. 12; *Essays in Criticism*, pp. 92, 97.

24. *Essays in Criticism, Second Series*, p. 14. The eighteenth-century understanding of aesthetic experience as a physiological and dialectical mind-body event is the topic of Kevis Goodman's *Pathologies of Motion: Historical Thinking in Medicine, Aesthetics, Politics* (New Haven, CT: Yale University Press, 2022). Notably, Schiller's early medical career is here invoked to redescribe his theory of imagination as including a distinct somatic component.

25. An earlier sense, now seemingly lost, refers to beating musical time by using the hand. On the connection between tact and taste, see Caygill, *Art of Judgement*, pp. 38, 185–86.

26. Davidson, *Hypocrisy*, pp. 8, 80, 105–6.

27. Theodor Adorno, *Minima Moralia: Reflections from Damaged Life*, trans. E. F. N. Jephcott (London: Verso, 1985), pp. 35–37.

28. David Russell's *Tact: Aesthetic Liberalism and the Essay Form in Nineteenth-Century Britain* (Princeton, NJ: Princeton University Press, 2017) offers a comprehensive account of its subject that is at once a historical survey and an advocacy of tact as "a democratic social practice for uncertain times" (p. 6) exercised within a "creatively neutral or virtual space" (p. 4). It is thus a form of sociability that does not risk doing harm, a superseding of solitude without an insistence on consensus: between culture and theory.

29. William Godwin, *The Enquirer: Reflections on Education, Manners, and Literature* (London, 1797), pp. 335, 338, 347.

30. My source here, and for other nineteenth-century novels, is the online *Literature Network*. Reservations apply, especially given the use of reprocessed texts (not first-edition facsimiles) and the complexities of indirect free style. But the balance of evidence supports my argument.

31. Christopher Lane, *Hatred and Civility: The Antisocial Life in Victorian England* (New York: Columbia University Press, 2004), proposes that a preoccupation with "antisocial dynamics" (p. xiv) is at the heart of the nineteenth-century novel and that in Charlotte Bronte's fiction, for example, "hatred underwrites citizenship" (p. 85). Before him, D. W. Harding's reading of Jane Austen argued that fear and hatred are central to Austen's social analysis; see Monica Lawler, ed., *Regulated Hatred and Other Essays on Jane Austen* (London: Athlone Press, 1998).

32. The confusion is not a thing of the past: Lionel Trilling, in "Manners, Morals and the Novel," *Kenyon Review* 10.1 (1948): 11–27, begins his essay by puzzling over the precision of this "nearly indefinable subject."

33. *Two Letters Addressed to a Member of the Present Parliament on the Proposals for Peace with the Regicide Directory of France* (London: F. and C. Rivington,

1796), p. 109. Compare Trilling's idea of manners as "half-uttered or unuttered or unutterable expressions of value," the *je ne sais quoi* incarnate ("Manners, Morals," p. 12).

34. On Wollstonecraft and manners, see G. J. Barker-Benfield, *The Culture of Sensibility: Sex and Society in Eighteenth-Century Britain* (Chicago: University of Chicago Press, 1992), esp. pp. 37–103. Interestingly, Burke does not inflect manners as dominantly a gendered attribute, though the tendency of the times was to do exactly that. See, among others, Leonore Davidoff and Catherine Hall, *Family Fortunes: Men and Women of the English Middle Class, 1780–1850* (Chicago: University of Chicago Press, 1991, esp. pp. 397–415.

35. *Works*, 5:73.

36. James Fenimore Cooper, *The American Democrat; or, Hints on the Social and Civic Relations of the United States of America* (Cooperstown, NY: H. and E. Phinney, 1838), pp. 154, 156.

37. Jay Fliegelman, *Prodigals and Pilgrims: The American Revolution against Patriarchal Authority, 1750–1800* (Cambridge: Cambridge University Press, 1984), pp. 83–89, points out that Richardson was reprinted in the United States only in radically abridged (and thus reordered) texts.

38. Bushman, *The Refinement of America*, pp. 280–312. Bushman also makes clear that the conduct books popular in America were mostly translations and adaptations from France, Italy and England (pp. 31–60). On civility in nineteenth-century America, see Davetian, *Civility*, pp. 211–65.

39. This case was powerfully made by Leslie Fiedler in *Love and Death in the American Novel* (New York: Stein and Day, 1966), which argued for terror, horror and violence as the core attributes of the national fiction. The mainstream critical tradition was commonly expressed as genteel, albeit waning as such: see George Santayana's 1913 essay "The Genteel Tradition in American Philosophy," in Richard Colton Lyon, ed., *Santayana on America: Essays, Notes and Letters on American Life, Literature, and Philosophy* (New York: Harcourt, Brace and World, 1968), pp. 36–56. Philip Rahv opted for a dichotomy in his "Paleface and Redskin," *Kenyon Review* 1.3 (1939): 251–56, placing Whitman on one side of the divide and Henry James on the other.

40. Christopher Herbert, *War of No Pity: The Indian Mutiny and Victorian Trauma* (Princeton, NJ: Princeton University Press, 2008), however, offers a powerful case for the displaced figurations of colonial violence in the sensation novel of the 1860s. Since Ronald T. Takaki's important *Iron Cages: Race and Culture in Nineteenth-Century America* (Seattle: University of Washington Press, 1979), there has been a significant body of work on the racialized imagination in the United States.

41. *The Law Is a White Dog: How Legal Rituals Make and Unmake Persons* (Princeton, NJ: Princeton University Press, 2011), pp. xii, 6, 12.

42. Alexis de Tocqueville, *Democracy in America*, ed. and trans. Harvey C. Mansfield and Delba Winthrop (Chicago: University of Chicago Press, 2000), pp. 245, 288. The second volume was published in 1840. Tocqueville wrote in French; the first English version, by Henry Reeve, often renders a slightly different turn of phrase, as do other translations following Reeve (Bowen, Bradley). Mansfield and Winthrop are generally closer to the French original.

43. For more on this topic, see Chapter 5. It is important to be aware that Tocqueville's work supports different arguments and perhaps demonstrates a logic of paradox or antinomy: see F. A. Ankersmit, *Aesthetic Politics: Political Philosophy beyond Fact and Value* (Stanford, CA: Stanford University Press, 1996), pp. 294–343, who argues that Tocqueville intends to show democracy as too manifold for summary or full theorization.

44. Mansfield and Winthrop's translation is closer to the original "mouvement . . . qui s'agite sans le troubler" than Reeve's "animates without disturbing." Agitation has made an interesting comeback as the principle of William Blake's deferred and displaced politics in Steven Goldsmith's *Blake's Agitation: Criticism and the Emotions* (Baltimore: Johns Hopkins University Press, 2013).

45. This is also the core of the civilizing process as theorized by Norbert Elias and adapted by Steven Pinker.

46. Hannah Arendt would endorse the wisdom of the American Revolution over the French to the exact degree that it did not promise economic as well as political equality.

47. See, for example, Richard Bushman's account of the Log Cabin Campaign of 1840, where class consciousness clearly played a part: see *The Refinement of America*, pp. 420ff.

48. *The Works of Ralph Waldo Emerson*, 6 vols. (London: Macmillan, 1883), 1:72, 77.

49. John Stuart Mill, *Autobiography*, ed. Jack Stillinger (Boston: Houghton Mifflin, 1969), p. 80.

50. For further discussion, see Simpson, *States of Terror: History, Theory, Literature* (Chicago: University of Chicago Press, 2019), pp. 205–25.

51. *Democracy in America*, p. 303. Another major distraction is finessed by Tocqueville's minimal and paradoxical discussion of the condition of women (pp. 563–76), whom he deems much freer in girlhood than their European counterparts, and more able to cultivate reason and independence, but much more constrained once they enter the married state. For one who professes to believe that "women make mores" (p. 563), this is an oddly curtailed analysis.

52. Ann Douglas, ed., *Uncle Tom's Cabin; or, Life among the Lowly* (Harmondsworth, UK: Penguin, 1986), p. 9.

53. *The English Common Reader: A Social History of the Mass Reading Public, 1800–1900*, 2nd ed. (Columbus: Ohio State University Press, 1998), p. 384.

54. See Wai-chee Dimock, *Empire for Liberty: Melville and the Poetics of Individualism* (Princeton, NJ: Princeton University Press, 1989).

55. See Gail Bederman, *Manliness and Civilization: A Cultural History of Race and Gender in the United States, 1880–1917* (Chicago: University of Chicago Press, 1996). Bederman analyzes the late onset of the same concerns that animated stadial theorists in the eighteenth century about controlled violence as a corrective to the feminization of society.

56. Hence, those novels dealing with British India were not best sellers, nor did they figure in the evolving pedagogic canon. The Hastings trial was the most public engagement with colonial violence. See Betty Joseph, *Reading the East India Company, 1720–1840* (Chicago: University of Chicago Press, 2004), pp. 61–91.

57. *Devolving English Literature* (Oxford: Clarendon Press, 1992), p. 43. See also Peter Jones, "The Scottish Professoriate and the Polite Academy, 1720–46," in Istvan Hont and Michael Ignatieff, eds., *Wealth and Virtue: The Shaping of Political Economy in the Scottish Enlightenment* (Cambridge: Cambridge University Press, 1983), pp. 89–117.

58. A case has been made by Franklin E. Court, "Adam Smith and the Teaching of English Literature," *History of Education Quarterly* 25.3 (1985): 325–40, that Smith's lectures were the first to privilege literature in English as the core of a modern literary-critical pedagogy, one with the novel at its core. While Smith does indeed discuss the merits of various writers in English and models sympathy as a literary affect, his focus remains on rhetoric and style, and the novel per se is marginal.

59. Gauri Viswanathan, *Masks of Conquest: Literary Study and British Rule in India* (New York: Columbia University Press, 1989), pp. 23, 45, 158. By 1987 not much had changed, but at least the novel had by then made an appearance in the curriculum. See Nivedita Majumdar, *The World in a Grain of Sand: Postcolonial Literature and Radical Universalism* (London: Verso, 2021), p. 1.

60. *Masks of Conquest*, pp. 38, 108, 143. Andrew Sartori, *Bengal in Global Concept History: Culturalism in the Age of Capital* (Chicago: University of Chicago Press, 2008), offers a complex account of the adaptation of what he conceives to have been a "truly global concept" (p. 4)—culture—to a Bengali lifeworld compelled to adjudicate local vocabularies and predicaments alongside protonational and international determinations.

61. *Masks of Conquest*, p. 54.

62. Arnold's phrase comes from the 1853 preface to his poems. See Matthew Arnold, *Selected Prose*, ed. P. J. Keating (Harmondsworth, UK: Penguin, 1970), p. 41.

63. *The Idea of a University*, ed. Martin J. Svaglic (Notre Dame, IN: Notre Dame University Press, 1986), p. 141.

64. Dramatic as this is, Britain's forty million people, in 1900, was barely one-tenth of the population of the British Raj.

65. *Reflections on Violence*, trans. T. E. Hulme and J. Roth (London: Collier-Macmillan, 1970), p. 53.

66. "Critique of Violence," in Marcus Bullock and Michael W. Jennings, eds., *Selected Writings*, vol. 1, *1913–26* (Cambridge, MA: Belknap Press, Harvard University Press, 1996), pp. 235–52; p. 244. The German text is taken from *Walter Benjamin Kairos: Schriften zur Philosophie*, ed. Ralf Konersmann (Frankfurt: Suhrkamp, 2007), pp. 87–109; p. 98. I have given an extended account of this essay in *States of Terror*, pp. 101–17, and will not repeat it here.

67. *Selected Writings*, 1:250; *Walter Benjamin Kairos*, p. 106.

68. Thus, Jonathan Schell, *The Unconquerable World: Power, Nonviolence and the Will of the People* (New York: Henry Holt, 2003), pp. 167–83, argues that even the Bolshevik revolution was initially, like the French, almost bloodless and became inescapably violent only when it found itself without popular support.

69. See Jana Howlett and Rod Mengham, eds., *The Violent Muse: Violence and the Artistic Imagination in Europe, 1910–1939* (Manchester, UK: Manchester University Press, 1994).

70. F. R. Leavis, *Two Cultures? The Significance of C. P. Snow* (London: Chatto and Windus, 1962), p. 28. Leavis's third realm has not had much serious attention from critics and historians: one exception is Gary Day, *Re-reading Leavis: Culture and Literary Criticism* (Basingstoke, UK: Macmillan, 1996). For an important account of the Cambridge critics and their Arnoldian heritage, see Chris Baldick, *The Social Mission of English Criticism, 1832–1932* (Oxford: Clarendon Press, 1987).

71. *Selected Prose of T.S. Eliot*, ed. Frank Kermode (London: Faber and Faber, 1975), p. 69. The citation is from Eliot's 1923 essay "The Function of Criticism."

72. F. R. Leavis, *Education and the University: A Sketch for an "English School,"* new ed. (London: Chatto and Windus, 1948), p. 107.

73. *Nor Shall My Sword: Discourses on Pluralism, Compassion and Social Hope* (London: Chatto and Windus, 1972), p. 205.

74. I. A. Richards, *Science and Poetry* (London: Kegan Paul, Trench and Trubner, 1926), pp. 82–83.

75. *Poetries and Sciences: A Reissue of Science and Poetry (1926, 1935), with Commentary* (New York: W. W. Norton, 1970), p. 78.

76. Richards, *Practical Criticism: A Study of Literary Judgment* (New York: Harcourt, Brace, 1929), p. 351.

77. Richards, *Principles of Literary Criticism* (London : Kegan Paul, Trench and Trubner), p. 59.

78. *Poetries and Sciences*, pp. 39, 40.

79. *Principles of Literary Criticism*, pp. 11–18, 97.

80. And yet . . . while Schiller is oddly disavowed by Richards and his coauthors in 1922 as at once insufficiently known and incorrect, their ideas about synaesthesis and equilibrium are almost pure Schiller. See I. A. Richards, C. K. Ogden and James Wood, *The Foundations of Aesthetics*, 2nd ed. (New York: Lear, 1925), pp. 72–91. The anomaly is discussed in Russo, *I. A. Richards*, pp. 106–8.

81. *Coleridge on Imagination*, 2nd ed. (London: Routledge and Kegan Paul, 1950), p. 72.

82. *Practical Criticism*, pp. 350–51.

83. James Engell and W. Jackson Bate, eds., *Biographia Literaria*, 2 vols. (London: Routledge and Kegan Paul, 1983), 2:16. Richards takes up this formulation in *Principles of Literary Criticism*, p. 251.

84. *Principles of Literary Criticism*, p. 247.

85. *Principles of Literary Criticism*, p. 53.

86. It should be acknowledged that Richards's and Ogden's effort to disseminate BASIC aimed at a much wider franchise. British American Scientific International Commercial (BASIC) was the preoccupation of much of Richards's career from the 1930s. For a brief account, see David Simpson, "Prospects for Global English: Back to BASIC?," *Yale Journal of Criticism* 11.1 (1998): 301–7; and Russo, *I. A. Richards*, pp. 397–429. The BASIC project depends, like Richards's poetics, on what he calls the "extreme versatility and ambiguity of words" (*How to Read a Page*, p. 129).

87. Raymond Williams, *The Long Revolution* (Harmondsworth, UK: Penguin, 1965), p. 43. Accounting for communication was indeed one pillar of Richards's theory: see *Principles of Literary Criticism*, p. 25.

88. *Culture and Society, 1780–1950* (Harmondsworth, UK: Penguin, 1963), p. 316.

89. *The Two Cultures*, ed. Stefan Collini (Cambridge: Cambridge University Press, 2006), p. 78.

90. That this was a far-from-untroubled process is the topic of some of Snow's own fiction, for example, *The New Men* and *The Affair*.

91. Steven Shapin, *A Social History of Truth*.

92. *The Two Cultures*, p. 77.

93. *Nor Shall My Sword*, p. 36.

CHAPTER 5

1. For a comprehensive account, see Tony Judt, *Postwar: A History of Europe since 1945* (London: Penguin, 2006). Judt is clear that 1989 "was Mr. Gorbachev's revolution" (p. 633).

2. See Jon Elster, ed., *The Roundtable Talks and the Breakdown of Communism* (Chicago: University of Chicago Press, 1996).

3. Martin, *Citizen's Guide to Civility*, p. ix.

4. *Civil Society: Old Images, New Visions* (Stanford, CA: Stanford University Press, 1998), p. 12. The earlier books were *Democracy and Civil Society* (London: Verso, 1988), and (as editor) *Civil Society and the State* (London: Verso, 1988).

5. *Democracy and Civil Society*, p. 4; *Civil Society*, p. 65.

6. *Civil Society*, pp. 26, 75; *Civil Society and the State*, p. 13.

7. Thus, John Dunn, "The Contemporary Political Significance of John Locke's Conception of Civil Society," in Kaviraj and Khilnani, *Civil Society*, pp. 39–57, finds it an "absurd assumption" (p. 53) that state and civil society can be fully separate, suggesting instead that civil society be understood as "the state liked: the non-pathological state" (p. 55). See also the compelling and comprehensive overviews by the two editors, pp. 11–32, 287–323. Joseph A. Buttigieg argues that civil society reinforces hegemony rather than contests it. Civil society is only a version of the state, one colonized in the United States by the political right. See "The Contemporary Discourse on Civil Society: A Gramscian Critique," *boundary 2* 2.1 (2005): 33–52.

8. *The Idea of Civil Society* (New York: Free Press, 1992), pp. 4, 133. Among other arguments, Seligman disputes the adequacy of small-group, face-to-face paradigms for encompassing modern politics.

9. Keane, *Civil Society*, pp. 12–31.

10. *Civil Society, Constitution, and Legitimacy* (Lanham, MD: Rowman and Littlefield, 2000), pp. 21–30.

11. John L. Comaroff and Jean Comaroff, eds., *Civil Society and the Political Imagination in Africa: Critical Perspectives* (Chicago: University of Chicago Press, 1999), pp. vii, 4. The introduction to this volume gives an important account of the phenomenon and its problems.

12. Paul Vallely, "Profile: Hans Küng," *Independent on Sunday*, July 2, 2000, p. 27.

13. G. J. Mulgan, *Politics in an Anti-political Age* (Oxford: Blackwell–Polity Press, 1994), pp. 8, 69, 157.

14. On the return to ethics, see Simpson, *Situatedness, or Why We Keep Saying Where We're Coming From* (Durham, NC: Duke University Press, 2002), pp. 218–30. On the culture of conversation, see Simpson, *The Academic Postmodern: A Report on Half-Knowledge* (Chicago: University of Chicago Press, 1995), pp. 41–71.

15. Geoff Mulgan, ed., *Life after Politics: New Thinking for the Twenty-First Century* (London: HarperCollins, 1997), pp. xii, xvii.

16. *Connexity: How to Live in a Connected World* (Boston: Harvard Business School Press, 1998), pp. 201, 214.

17. *Connexity*, p. 96. Some years later this question would be aired again in anthropologist Robin Dunbar's widely discussed work on correlating brain size

with social behavior. The popular understanding of the 'Dunbar numbers' is that humans tend to sustain networks of around 150 other people, with close support groups of around 5.

18. This was the ambition of the Report of the National Endowment for the Humanities in 1995, which aimed to replace "historical objects" with "historical actors."

19. "Text of Bush's Remarks on End of Race," *New York Times*, December 14, 2000, p. A 18.

20. "The City Burns, a Young Man Lies Dead and the Battle Rages On," *Guardian*, July 21, 2001, p. 1.

21. "Which Ethics for Democracy?," in Marjorie Garber, Beatrice Hanssen and Rebecca L. Walkowitz, eds., *The Turn to Ethics* (New York: Routledge, 2000), pp. 85–94.

22. Nancy L. Rosenblum, cited in D. W. Miller, "Perhaps We Bowl Alone, but Does It Really Matter?," *Chronicle of Higher Education*, July 16, 1999, p. A 16.

23. I owe this to Congressman David Skaggs, speaking at a meeting of the Boulder County Healthy Communities Initiative, Boulder, Colorado, June 14, 1997. The meeting was chaired by Mark Gerzon, the consultant who had organized the congressional retreat.

24. Dirk Johnson, "Civility in Politics: Going, Going, Gone," *New York Times*, December 10, 1997, p. A 14.

25. Alison Schneider, "Insubordination and Intimidation Signal the End of Decorum in Many Classrooms," *Chronicle of Higher Education*, March 27, 1998, pp. A 12–14.

26. Elaine Showalter, "Taming the Rampant Incivility in Academe," *Chronicle of Higher Education*, January 15, 1999, pp. B 4–5.

27. In 2011 the University of Arizona saw a need to found another institute, the National Institute for Civil Discourse. In 2018 Dave Isay, who had founded StoryCorps in 2003, set up a project called One Small Step in which persons of differing views are paired for one-on-one conversation in hopes of mitigating the culture of hatred and contempt Isay sees as increasingly typical of the current situation. Not only is this the ultimate small-group paradigm; participants must apply, are paired up by staff members, and are not allowed to discuss politics. This would seem to be a telling incidence of civility working best when least tested.

28. Lizette Alvarez, "Feminine Mystique Grows in Senate," *New York Times*, December 7, 2000, p. A 22.

29. Amitai Etzioni, *The Spirit of Community: Rights, Responsibilities, and the Communitarian Agenda* (New York: Crown Books, 1993), p. 26.

30. *Democracy on Trial* (New York: HarperCollins, 1995), pp. 18–19.

31. *Bowling Alone: The Collapse and Revival of American Community* (New York: Simon and Schuster, 2000), p. 506.

32. *Connexity*, p. 84.

33. *The End of History and the Last Man* (New York: Avon Books, 1992), p. 48; *The Great Disruption: Human Nature and the Reconstitution of Social Order* (New York: Free Press, 1999), p. 6.

34. *The End of History*, pp. xii, xix. Compare Edward Shils, *The Virtue of Civility: Selected Essays on Liberalism, Tradition, and Civil Society* (Indianapolis, IN: Liberty Fund, 1997), p. 341: "Civility works like a governor of civil society. It limits the intensity of conflict. It reduces the distance between conflicting demands; it is a curb on centrifugal tendencies." The confidence of Fukuyama's appeal to the irrational is striking, and disturbing.

35. *The Better Angels*, pp. 125, 127.

36. *The Great Disruption*, p. 227.

37. Keane, *Civil Society*, pp. 135, 147.

38. *The Virtue of Civility*, p. 19.

39. *The Public and Its Problems* (Athens: Ohio University Press, 1991), p. 96.

40. *The Good Citizen: A History of American Civic Life* (New York: Free Press, 1998), pp. 16–24.

41. *The Good Citizen*, pp. 98–104, 135–43.

42. See Bushman, *The Refinement of America*; and Kenneth Cmiel, *Democratic Eloquence: The Fight over Popular Speech in Nineteenth-Century America* (New York: William Morrow, 1990).

43. George Herbert Mead, *On Social Psychology: Selected Papers*, rev. ed. Anselm Strauss (Chicago: University of Chicago Press, 1964), p. 18.

44. *Democracy and Disagreement* (Cambridge, MA: Belknap Press, Harvard University Press, 1996), pp. 2, 90, 135.

45. Bejan, *Mere Civility*, pp. 14, 80.

46. *Bowling Alone*, p. 271; *The Public and Its Problems*, p. 111.

47. See *Culture and Imperialism* (New York: Random House, 1993), pp. 132–62. Cixin Liu suggests, in *Supernova Era*, trans. Joel Martinsen (New York: Tom Doherty Associates, 2020), that violence is hardwired. Preadolescent children inherit a planet without adults and manage to have fun conducting a game of mutual mass destruction. War is fun, and fun has a high tolerance for death.

48. *Underworld* (New York: Simon and Schuster, 1997), pp. 11, 15, 37.

49. *Conditions of Liberty: Civil Society and Its Rivals* (London: Allen Lane, 1994), pp. 211, 213.

50. *Civil Society and Fanaticism: Conjoined Histories*, trans. Amy Jacobs (Stanford, CA: Stanford University Press, 1997), pp. 31, 39.

51. See Michael Hardt, "The Withering of Civil Society," *Social Text* 45 (1995): 27–44.

52. *Postwar*, pp. 804, 829.

53. Tony Judt, *A Grand Illusion? An Essay on Europe* (New York: New York University Press, 2011), pp. 121, 128.

54. *Turbulent and Mighty Continent: What Future for Europe?* (Cambridge: Polity Press, 2014), p. 43.

55. For a scathing, comprehensive overview of how the EU dispenses its powers, see Perry Anderson, "The Breakaway," *London Review of Books* 43.2 (2021): 3–10.

56. *The Other Heading: Reflections on Today's Europe*, trans. Michael Naas (Bloomington: Indiana University Press, 1992), p. 9.

57. Jürgen Habermas and Jacques Derrida, "February 15, or What Binds Europeans Together," in Lasse Thomassen, ed., *The Derrida-Habermas Reader* (Chicago: University of Chicago Press, 2006), pp. 270–77; pp. 271, 273.

58. This discussion needs to remain ongoing: it impinges, for example, on the European conceptual history project inspired by Koselleck's work.

59. Étienne Balibar, *We, the People of Europe? Reflections on Transnational Citizenship*, trans. James Swenson (Princeton, NJ: Princeton University Press, 2004), pp. 43–44.

60. The important project on the untranslatable, now translated into English, is an indispensable prototype for this dispersal and an effort to contest "the imperium of English thought." See Cassin, *Dictionary of Untranslatables*, p. xiv.

61. *Europe, or the Infinite Task: A Study of a Philosophical Concept* (Stanford, CA: Stanford University Press, 2009), pp. 322–23.

62. See Roberto M. Dainotto, *Europe (in Theory)* (Durham, NC: Duke University Press, 2007), for an account of the function and status of "Europe's own subaltern areas" (p. 5) in its (and their) constructions of identity. Dipesh Chakrabarty, *Provincializing Europe: Postcolonial Thought and Historical Difference* (Princeton, NJ: Princeton University Press, 2000), discusses the effects of Europe being accepted as "the scene of the birth of the modern" (p. 28) by both Europeans themselves and those outside its borders.

63. Étienne Balibar, *Politics and the Other Scene*, trans. Christine Jones, James Swenson and Chris Turner (London: Verso, 2011), p. 23. Civility appeals because it brings together an idea of citizenship (the old sense of the word) with the invocation of habits: see p. 39n36.

64. *Violence and Civility*, p. viii.

65. *We, the People of Europe?*, p. 178.

66. Kundera, *The Art of the Novel*, trans. Linda Asher (New York: Grove Press, 1988), pp. 5, 6, 14, 134, 164.

67. *Contingency, Irony, and Solidarity* (Cambridge: Cambridge University Press, 1989), pp. xv, 45, 73–95.

68. *Poetic Justice: The Literary Imagination in Public Life* (Boston: Beacon Press, 1995), p. 46.

69. *Go, Went, Gone*, trans. Susan Bernofsky (New York: New Directions, 2017).

70. Hamid, *Exit West* (New York: Riverhead Books, 2017), pp. 166, 169.

71. In *Love's Knowledge: Essays on Philosophy and Literature* (New York: Oxford University Press, 1990), Martha Nussbaum presents a sustained argument for the companionate function of the novel in developing our moral and emotional personalities.

72. *Exit West*, p. 154.

CHAPTER 6

1. *Politics and the Other Scene*, p. viii.

2. *Violence and Civility*, p. 144.

3. Ernest Renan, "What Is a Nation?," trans. Martin Thom, in Homi Bhabha, ed., *Nation and Narration* (London: Routledge, 1990), pp. 8–22. Renan's essay has been foundational in the study of nationalism.

4. Richards, *How to Read a Page*, p. 10.

5. Again, this is consistent with the literary task as Rorty sees it: the exploration of pain and humiliation.

6. When civility is understood as synonymous with civilization, as it once was, the risks of inciting or affirming violence are higher; so too with the neutral sense of *civilis* as indicating simple membership of the polis, which can underwrite accepted rituals of violence: torture, execution, warmaking.

7. *Negations*, p. 99.

8. Eleni Coundouriotis, *The People's Right to the Novel: War Fiction in the Postcolony* (New York: Fordham University Press, 2014), has made a case for the war novel as the new form of naturalism appropriate to the African postcolonial experience. The English novel, I would suggest, has been more comfortable reliving the violence of World War II over and over again: for Britain, the last 'good' war.

9. *Mein Kampf* transcribes hate speech while specifically negating any literary reading.

10. Purely liberal-secular states are probably imaginary: the Joyce and Lawrence trials were certainly not conducted without input from religious doctrines and habits.

11. *Acts of Literature*, ed. Derek Attridge (New York: Routledge, 1992), p. 37. And indeed, as Peter McDonald shows in *The Literature Police*, the same book can be banned and unbanned in different times and circumstances.

12. *Rogues: Two Essays on Reason*, trans. Pascale-Anne Brault and Michael Naas (Stanford, CA: Stanford University Press, 2005), p. 60.

13. *The Social Universe of the English Bible: Scripture, Society, and Culture in Early Modern England* (Cambridge: Cambridge University Press, 2010), pp. 23–49. Tadmor addresses the large range of biblical words that are compressed by the King James translation team into the one word *neighbor*.

14. *Rogues*, pp. 86–87.

15. *The Force of Nonviolence: An Ethico-Political Bind* (London: Verso, 2020), p. 126.

16. Schiller, *Aesthetic Education*, p. 19.

17. And yet . . . a thoughtful and extended case for the relationship between tools and weapons (and work and warfare) is part of Elaine Scarry's analysis of the continuum between destruction-pain and creative imagination, making and unmaking, in *The Body in Pain*, pp. 161–80. She suggests that while pain and imagination are in one sense exact opposites, their symmetries can also be disturbing, no least owing to the "conceptual infancy" (p. 280) of our knowledge about creativity. Liu's *Supernova Era* addresses the symmetries.

18. Slavoj Žižek, *Violence: Six Sideways Reflections* (New York: Picador, 2008), p. 61. Key to this discussion is Derrida's essay "Violence and Metaphysics," in *Writing and Difference*, trans. Alan Bass (Chicago: University of Chicago Press, 1978), pp. 79–153: "There is war only after the opening of discourse, and war dies out only at the end of discourse" (p. 117). Hent de Vries, "Violence and Testimony: On Sacrificing Sacrifice," in Hent de Vries and Samuel Weber, eds., *Violence, Identity, and Self-Determination* (Stanford, CA: Stanford University Press, 1997), pp. 14–43, offers a sustained commentary on Derrida and the language-violence conjunction.

19. *Writing and Difference*, p. 147.

20. "The Function of Criticism," in *Essays in Criticism*, pp. 22–23.

21. For a fine analysis of the work of (gendered) abjection in this section of Arnold's essay, see Redfield, *Politics of Aesthetics*, pp. 88–92. Wragg is there read as being "brought into the text in order to bear away the sins of language."

22. *Of Grammatology*, trans. Gayatri Chakravorty Spivak (Baltimore: Johns Hopkins University Press, 1976), p. 3.

23. *Rogues*, p. 86.

24. *An Aesthetic Education in the Era of Globalization* (Cambridge, MA: Harvard University Press, 2012), p. 2. *Sabotage* is a handy word: to destroy, or to render inoperable while keeping in place?

25. See, again, Redfield, *Politics of Aesthetics*.

26. Spivak here references Derrida's critique of Habermas.

27. See Spivak, *Death of a Discipline* (New York: Columbia University Press, 2003), p. 4: "What I am proposing is not a politization of the discipline. We are *in* politics. I am proposing an attempt to depoliticize in an attempt to move away from a politics of hostility, fear and half-solutions." Again, from *Other Asias*

(Oxford: Blackwell, 2008), p. 4: "To read literature as evidence of the author's political inclinations is to undo the special gift of the literary."

28. See *Aesthetic Education*, pp. 111–21, 139–41.

29. *Dissensus: On Politics and Aesthetics*, ed. and trans. Steven Corcoran (London: Bloomsbury, 2014), pp. 115–17. In *The Politics of Aesthetics: The Distribution of the Sensible*, trans. Gabriel Rockhill (London: Continuum, 2006), p. 24, Rancière acknowledges Schiller's work as "in a sense, unsurpassable."

30. *Dissensus*, pp. 139–40.

31. *Politics of Aesthetics*, p. 39. This is also one of the arguments in Cheah's *Spectral Nationality*.

32. Compare Ankersmit, *Aesthetic Politics*, which also argues for politics as a matter of representation and therefore of "brokenness" (p. xiv). Ankersmit's politics-as-aesthetics is governed by irony, aphorism, variation and fragmentation: all literary motifs identifiable in Romantic irony. Its civility-aligned belief in "withdrawal" and "avoidance" (pp. 113–14) signals its purpose as conflict avoidance rather than conflict confrontation. The Shaftesburyan "standing in a relationship to oneself" is often a peaceable gesture. But at the same time "deceitful visions of unity and harmony" (p. 347) are eschewed.

33. *Politics of Aesthetics*, pp. 39–40.

34. *Dissensus*, p. 193. Ankersmit, in *Aesthetic Politics*, pp. 10, 349, shares the distrust of ethics.

35. Thus, Martin Jay, "The Aesthetic Alibi," in *Cultural Semantics*, argues for the aesthetic as "a vital future-oriented function that transcends its status as mere capital in the cultural economy of our day" (p. 119).

36. *The Ideology of the Aesthetic* (Oxford: Blackwell, 1990), pp. 368, 374.

37. Again Scarry, *The Body in Pain*, is a notable exception in offering a sustained account of the relation between destructive and creative instincts. Pain and imagination are both opposites and apposites, suggesting the "conceptual infancy" of our knowledge of creativity (p. 280).

38. *Sweet Violence: The Idea of the Tragic* (Oxford: Blackwell, 2003), p. 132.

39. Theodor W. Adorno, *Aesthetic Theory*, ed. and trans. Robert Hullot-Kentor (Minneapolis: University of Minnesota Press, 1997), p. 234.

40. The same idea animates Santiago Zabala's case for art as addressing our "lack of a sense of emergency" by disclosing disruptions; see *Why Only Art Can Save Us: Aesthetics and the Absence of Emergency* (New York: Columbia University Press, 2019), p. 5.

41. *Negative Dialectics*, trans. E. B. Ashton (New York: Continuum, 1973), p. 364.

42. *Aesthetic Theory*, pp. 133–34.

43. *Aesthetic Theory*, pp. 125–31.

44. "Resignation," in *Critical Models: Interventions and Catchwords*, trans. Henry Pickford (New York: Columbia University Press, 1998), pp. 289–93. This

question has been taken up again by Slavoj Žižek, for example, in *Violence: Six Sideways Reflections* (New York: Picador, 2008), pp. 7–8, 216.

45. So too, according to Jakob Norberg, he turns the popular genre of the conduct book on its head by writing "a book of advice for the vanishing individual," a "book of disempowerment." See "Adorno's Advice: *Minima Moralia* and the Critique of Liberalism," *PMLA* 126.2 (2011): 398–411; pp. 404, 407.

46. Schiller, *Aesthetic Education*, p. 215.

47. *The Force of Non-violence*, pp. 24, 27.

48. Ann V. Murphy, *Violence and the Philosophical Imaginary* (Albany: SUNY Press, 2012), p. 12. I have argued in *States of Terror* that our collective problem in anglophone culture may well have been the opposite: an imagining of violence as always outside or optional to core subjectivity.

49. *The Neutral*, trans. Rosalind E. Krauss and Denis Hollier (New York: Columbia University Press, 2005), pp. 11, 211. Barthes's lectures were given during 1977–78.

50. *How to Live Together: Novelistic Simulation of Some Everyday Spaces*, trans. Kate Briggs (New York: Columbia University Press, 2013), pp. 72ff. Agamben's "potentiality" represents a more abstract formulation, not socially imagined: "To be able is neither to posit nor to negate." See Giorgio Agamben, *Potentialities: Collected Essays in Philosophy*, trans. Daniel Heller-Roazen (Stanford, CA: Stanford University Press, 1999), p. 257.

51. Helmuth Plessner, *The Limits of Community: A Critique of Social Radicalism*, trans. Andrew Wallace (Amherst, MA: Humanity Books, 1999), pp. 162, 165. See also Helmut Lethen, *Cool Conduct: The Culture of Distance in Weimar Germany*, trans. Dan Reneau (Berkeley: University of California Press, 2002); Corina Stan, *The Art of Distances: Ethical Thinking in Twentieth-Century Literature* (Evanston, IL: Northwestern University Press, 2018); and Katja Haustein, "How to Be Alone with Others: Plessner, Adorno and Barthes on Tact," *Modern Language Review* 114.1 (2019): 1–20.

52. *Tact*, p. 6. On tact as a core component of civility culture, see Mark Kingswell, *A Civil Tongue: Justice, Dialogue, and the Politics of Pluralism* (University Park: Pennsylvania State University Press, 1995), pp. 44, 224–48.

53. Goldsmith, *Blake's Agitation*, p. 36.

54. *Giving Way: Thoughts on Unappreciated Dispositions* (Stanford, CA: Stanford University Press, 2019), pp. 29–30. Connor offers the "active power of holding back" (p. 217) as potential mitigation, a way of "not doing" that is not the same as "doing nothing" (p. 19).

55. *Open Secrets: The Literature of Uncounted Experience* (Stanford, CA: Stanford University Press, 2008), pp. xvii, 3, 60.

56. Consider also Wai-Chee Dimock's "Weak Theory: Henry James, Colm Toíbín, and W. B. Yeats," *Critical Inquiry* 39.4 (2013): 732–53, as settling for a

"low threshold in plausibility and admissibility" (p. 736). Work on Romanticism has produced a notably dense interest in neutrality. See, for example, Jacques Khalip's "ethics of engaged withdrawal" as a "critical renunciatory force" in his *Anonymous Life: Romanticism and Dispossession* (Stanford, CA: Stanford University Press, 2009), pp. 135, 139; and Anahid Nersessian's *Utopia Limited: Romanticism and Adjustment* (Cambridge, MA: Harvard University Press, 2015), which pursues "self-abnegation in the face of planetary fragility" by "reclaiming the value of *less*" (pp. 4, 22).

57. Keane, *Global Civil Society?* (Cambridge: Cambridge University Press, 2003), p. xi.

58. *Visions of World Community* (Cambridge: Cambridge University Press, 2009), pp. ix, 120.

59. See Anne Goldgar, *Impolite Learning: Conduct and Community in the Republic of Letters, 1680–1750* (New Haven, CT: Yale University Press, 1995), which reminds us that scholars were often deemed by others rude and uncivil (and indeed unintelligible) even as they sought to assume and perform recognizable attributes of civility.

60. *In Theory: Classes, Nations, Literatures* (New York: Verso, 1992), pp. 1, 3.

61. Much debate has occurred around two 'big picture' accounts of world literature: Franco Moretti's work, in *Distant Reading* (London: Verso, 2013) and *Atlas of the European Novel*, on large data sets assessing the circulation of the novel form around the world and Pascale Casanova's *The World Republic of Letters*, trans. M. B. DeBevoise (Cambridge, MA: Harvard University Press, 2004). For a good account of the issues, see Christopher Prendergast, ed., *Debating World Literature* (London: Verso, 2004). See also David Damrosch, *What Is World Literature?* (Princeton, NJ: Princeton University Press, 2003); Emily Apter, *Against World Literature: On the Politics of Untranslatability* (London: Verso, 2013). For arguments about the refiguring of a future discipline of comparative literature in the light of a 'world' literature, see Haun Saussy, ed., *Comparative Literature in an Age of Globalization* (Baltimore: Johns Hopkins University Press, 2006); Spivak, *Death of a Discipline*; and Emily Apter, *The Translation Zone: A New Comparative Literature* (Princeton, NJ: Princeton University Press, 2006). Three important studies reflecting the new disciplinary profile are Bishnupriya Ghosh, *When Borne Across: Literary Cosmopolitics in the New Indian Novel* (New Brunswick, NJ: Rutgers University Press, 2004); Gikandi, *Maps of Englishness*; and Rebecca L. Walkowitz, *Born Translated: The Contemporary Novel in an Age of World Literature* (New York: Columbia University Press, 2015). See also Ahmad, *In Theory*, pp. 243–85, on the category of 'Indian literature.' On the complexities of Indian writing in English, see Ghosh, *When Borne Across*.

62. Juliana Spahr, *Du Bois's Telegram: Literary Resistance and State Containment* (Cambridge, MA: Harvard University Press, 2018), argues that the content

of literature is much less important than the mechanisms of production and distribution controlled by state and corporate entities that effectively limit its reach. Literary reading, she suggests, increasingly belongs to "dwindling and aging publics" (p. 186).

63. *Culture and Imperialism*, p. xii.

64. Dimock, *Through Other Continents*, pp. 15, 22; Cheah, *What Is a World?*, p. 192.

65. Joseph R. Slaughter, *Human Rights, Inc.: The World Novel, Narrative Form, and International Law* (New York: Fordham University Press, 2007), p. 4. See also Hunt, *Inventing Human Rights*. Majumdar, *The World in a Grain of Sand*, argues that the local (novel) is the normative medium for the universal.

66. *The Historical Novel*, trans. Hannah Mitchell and Stanley Mitchell (Lincoln: University of Nebraska Press, 1983), pp. 312, 321.

67. On the matter of poetry, Jonathan Culler agrees: "Poetry lies at the centre of the literary experience because it is the form that most clearly asserts the specificity of literature, its difference from ordinary discourse by an empirical individual about the world." See *Structuralist Poetics: Structuralism, Linguistics, and the Study of Literature* (London: Routledge and Kegan Paul, 1975), p. 162.

68. *What Is Literature?*, pp. 9, 42.

69. Mikhail M. Bakhtin, *The Dialogic Imagination: Four Essays*, trans. Caryl Emerson and Michael Holquist (Austin: University of Texas Press, 1981), pp. 279ff. All concepts, Koselleck tells us, must deploy ambiguous words in order to function as concepts. Philology is the record of those ambiguities. Richards, *How to Read a Page*, p. 23, notes that the most important words are the most useful because they are the most ambiguous.

70. *Seven Types of Ambiguity* (Harmondsworth, UK: Penguin, 1965), p. 236. On the play between poetic and journalistic conventions, see Culler, *Structuralist Poetics*, pp. 161ff.

71. While popular music, film and television include elements of literariness, they are not uniformly weighted toward it.

72. *The Three-Body Problem*, trans. Ken Liu (New York: Tom Doherty Associates, 2006), p. 395. Accessible in one way, to be sure, although the preferred plot knowledge of mathematics and physics can seem daunting.

73. Liu, *The Dark Forest*, trans. Joel Martinsen (New York: Tom Doherty Associates, 2008), p. 39.

74. Liu, *Death's End*, trans. Ken Liu (New York: Tom Doherty Associates, 2010), p. 353.

75. *Maps of Englishness*, p. 214. For some of the vectors that have made a "mere reading" of Rushdie's novel now impossible, see Gayatri Chakravorty Spivak, "Reading *The Satanic Verses*," in *Outside in the Teaching Machine* (London: Routledge, 1993), pp. 217–41.

76. Ernst Jünger, *Storm of Steel*, trans. Michael Hofmann (New York: Penguin Group, 2004), p. 5; Vasily Grossman, *Life and Fate*, trans. Robert Chandler (New York: NYRB, n.d.), p. 19.

77. *Slow Violence*, pp. 2, 10.

78. *The Great Derangement: Climate Change and the Unthinkable* (Chicago: University of Chicago Press, 2016), pp. 9, 22, 66.

79. *Human Forms: The Novel in the Age of Evolution* (Princeton, NJ: Princeton University Press, 2019) makes the case for the importance of chaotic and polygenetic theories for the nineteenth-century novel: a form devised to explore formlessness.

80. Hegel, *Aesthetics: Lectures on Fine Art*, trans. T. M. Knox, 2 vols. (Oxford: Clarendon Press, 1975), 1:595.

81. *Friedrich Schlegel's "Lucinde" and the Fragments*, trans. Peter Firchow (Minneapolis: University of Minnesota Press, 1971), p. 190. Schlegel's other major *Tendenzen* were Fichte's philosophy and the French Revolution.

82. *The Aesthetic Dimension: Toward a Critique of Marxist Aesthetics* (Boston: Beacon Press, 1978), p. 8.

83. *Lessons on the Analytic of the Sublime*, trans. Elizabeth Rottenberg (Stanford, CA: Stanford University Press, 1994), p. 54.

84. *Lessons on the Analytic of the Sublime*, p. 239. See Lyotard's extended analysis on pp. 224–39.

85. I do mean aesthetics. David L. Clark's work has fully exposed Kant's preoccupation with human violence and militarism in eighteenth-century Europe. See, for example, "Unsocial Kant: The Philosopher and the Un-regarded War Dead," *Wordsworth Circle* 41.1 (2010): 60–68; and the related "Schelling's Wartime: Philosophy and Violence in the Age of Napoleon," *European Romantic Review* 19.2 (2008): 139–48. The Napoleonic campaigns were, after all, arguably the first time Europe experienced total war.

86. *Under Representation*, pp. 44–68.

87. Edmund Burke, *A Philosophical Inquiry into the Origin of Our Ideas of the Sublime and Beautiful*, ed. James T. Boulton (Notre Dame, IN: University of Notre Dame Press, 1986), pp. 143–44.

88. Pheng Cheah's work presents an important exception to my claim here, although his case for culture as formative comes to depend more upon Heidegger's ontology than on Kant's aesthetics.

89. The citation is from *The Theory of the Novel*, trans. Anna Bostock (Cambridge, MA: MIT Press, 1971), p. 12.

90. A positive case for national literature as countering global culture is Paik Nak-chung, "Nations and Literatures in the Age of Globalization," in Fredric Jameson and Masao Miyoshi, eds., *The Cultures of Globalization* (Durham, NC: Duke University Press, 1998), pp. 218–29. The case fits best with aspiring

or emergent nations. But see also Simon During, "Literature—Nationalism's Other? The Case for Revision," in Homi K. Bhabha, ed., *Nation and Narration* (London: Routledge, 1990), pp. 138–53; and, in the same volume, Timothy Brennan, "The National Longing for Form," pp. 44–70.

91. "The Future *in* and *of* the Novel," *Novel* 44.1 (2011): 8–10. Armstrong presciently called attention to the novel's relation to violence in 1989: see Nancy Armstrong and Leonard Tennenhouse, *The Violence of Representation: Literature and the History of Violence* (1989; repr., Abingdon, UK: Routledge, 2014). Armstrong develops her reflections on the breakdown of national community and of exemplary individuality in "Some Endangered Feeling," *Daedalus* 150.1 (2021): 40–61.

92. *A Passage to India* (San Diego, CA: Harcourt, Brace, 1984), p. 43.

93. For example: "Suspicion in the Oriental is a sort of malignant tumour, a mental malady" (p. 311).

94. *Under Representation*, p. 100. Spivak is largely responsible for literary studies taking on the term, which she takes over from the historians; see *Critique of Postcolonial Reason*, pp. 198–311.

95. Bhabha's notion of mimicry as that which simply repeats rather than represents produces a similar disjunction, a metonymy that impedes any access to essence or 'self.' See *The Location of Culture*, pp. 85–92. Compare also the "tropicopolitan" that Srinavas Aravamudan specifies as the "fictive construct of colonial tropology *and* actual resident of tropical space, object of representation *and* agent of resistance": *Tropicopolitans: Colonialism and Agency, 1688–1804* (Durham, NC: Duke University Press, 1999), p. 4. Forster's Aziz has mastered sly civility: "He was skillful in the slighter impertinences" (p. 336).

96. For a brief history, see Debjani Ganguly, ed., "The Subaltern after Subaltern Studies: Genealogies and Transformations," *South Asia: Journal of South Asian Studies* 38.1 (2015): 1–9.

97. "Subaltern Studies: Deconstructing Historiography," in Ranajit Guha and Gayatri Chakravorty Spivak, eds., *Selected Subaltern Studies* (New York: Oxford University Press, 1988), pp. 3–32; see pp. 4, 6, 16. See also Chakrabarty, *Provincializing Europe*.

98. *The Wretched of the Earth*, p. 227. See Betty Joseph, *Reading the East India Company*, pp. 92–122, for a conjunction of subalternity and the uncanny. Consider also the unstable imaging of the *babu* figure as described by Sartori, *Bengal in Global Concept History*, pp. 101–8.

99. *What Is a World?*, p. 183.

100. See *The Law Is a White Dog*, pp. 39–70.

101. *The Civilizing Process*, p. 350.

102. *Europe, or the Infinite Task*, pp. 322–23.

103. *Mere Civility*, pp. 14, 79.

104. *The Company We Keep: An Ethics of Fiction* (Berkeley: University of California Press, 1988), p. 485.

105. *An Aesthetic Education*, p. 27.

106. *The Reluctant Fundamentalist* (Orlando, FL: Harcourt, 2007), p. 1.

107. *Robinson Crusoe*, p. 198.

108. *Heart of Darkness*, p. 87.

109. Forster's *A Passage to India* also opens with a perhaps surprisingly Marlow-like impression of Chandrapore: "The very wood seems made of mud, the inhabitants of mud moving . . . like some low but indestructible form of life" (p. 4).

110. *Almayer's Folly* (Harmondsworth, UK: Penguin, 1976), p. 84.

111. J. M. Coetzee, *Age of Iron* (Harmondsworth, UK: Penguin, 1990), pp. 86, 130. Verceuil's name plays upon various Afrikaans words suggesting being tricked, being hidden, differing (David Attwell, personal communication): an icon of subalternity.

112. Recall also the utopian gesture that has Dickens exclude mention of any of the historical leaders of the French Revolution in *A Tale of Two Cities*. The events in the novel are all carried out by ordinary people.

113. *Love's Knowledge*, p. 265.

114. The Shelleyan view of metaphor is primarily affirmative: forming relations between disparate items is a good thing. But metaphor (always a covert metonym) can also work to divide and disfigure.

115. *Conviviality* is Paul Gilroy's word: see *After Empire: Melancholia or Convivial Culture?* (Abingdon, UK: Routledge, 2004). I suspect he intends something of the literalness of the French *vivre ensemble*, but in English there is an inevitable association with lively and cheerful manners. We lack the words for what he wants. A number of terms are available for helping think through the subaltern predicament. Mary Louise Pratt's *Imperial Eyes: Travel Writing and Transculturation* (London: Routledge, 1992) gave us the "contact zone" and, in a negative sense, the "myth of reciprocity." Stephen Clingman, in *The Grammar of Identity: Transnational Fiction and the Nature of the Boundary* (Oxford: Oxford University Press, 2009), comes up with *transfiction* as "a writing whose every contemplation is the nature of the transitive, of the boundary, of its protocols and obligations" (p. 185). Said's "contrapuntal reading" (*Culture and Imperialism*, p. 51) aims to hold together hegemonic and non-hegemonic histories but arguably cedes (in its musical metaphor) too much potential for an imagining of ultimate harmony. The subaltern event is perhaps better imagined as prescribing cacophonous reading without foreclosing on unison.

116. *Violence and Civility*, pp. xii, 65, 128.

117. *How to Read a Page*, p. 140.

118. *The English Auden*, pp. 246–47.

119. "The Study of Poetry," in *Essays in Criticism, Second Series*, p. 15.

120. Resources of hope is "a phrase used on a number of occasions by Raymond Williams," as we are told by Robin Gable in his edition of Williams's essays, *Resources of Hope: Culture, Democracy, Socialism* (London: Verso, 1989), p. viii.

121. From "The Resourcefulness of Words," in *Speculative Instruments* (London: Routledge and Kegan Paul, 1955), p. 72.

122. *Speculative Instruments*, p. 59; *The English Auden*, p. 245.

Index

Cultural Memory in the Present

Michael P. Steinberg, *The Afterlife of Moses: Exile, Democracy, Renewal*
Alain Badiou, *Badiou by Badiou*, translated by Bruno Bosteels
Eric B. Song, *Love against Substitution: Seventeenth-Century English Literature and the Meaning of Marriage*
Niklaus Largier, *Figures of Possibility: Aesthetic Experience, Mysticism, and the Play of the Senses*
Mihaela Mihai, *Political Memory and the Aesthetics of Care: The Art of Complicity and Resistance*
Ethan Kleinberg, *Emmanuel Levinas's Talmudic Turn: Philosophy and Jewish Thought*
Willemien Otten, *Thinking Nature and the Nature of Thinking: From Eriugena to Emerson*
Michael Rothberg, *The Implicated Subject: Beyond Victims and Perpetrators*
Hans Ruin, *Being with the Dead: Burial, Ancestral Politics, and the Roots of Historical Consciousness*
Eric Oberle, *Theodor Adorno and the Century of Negative Identity*
David Marriott, *Whither Fanon? Studies in the Blackness of Being*
Reinhart Koselleck, *Sediments of Time: On Possible Histories*, translated and edited by Sean Franzel and Stefan-Ludwig Hoffmann
Devin Singh, *Divine Currency: The Theological Power of Money in the West*
Stefanos Geroulanos, *Transparency in Postwar France: A Critical History of the Present*
Sari Nusseibeh, *The Story of Reason in Islam*
Olivia C. Harrison, *Transcolonial Maghreb: Imagining Palestine in the Era of Decolonialization*
Barbara Vinken, *Flaubert Postsecular: Modernity Crossed Out*
Aishwary Kumar, *Radical Equality: Ambedkar, Gandhi, and the Problem of Democracy*
Simona Forti, *New Demons: Rethinking Power and Evil Today*
Joseph Vogl, *The Specter of Capital*
Hans Joas, *Faith as an Option*
Michael Gubser, *The Far Reaches: Ethics, Phenomenology, and the Call for Social Renewal in Twentieth-Century Central Europe*
Françoise Davoine, *Mother Folly: A Tale*
Knox Peden, *Spinoza Contra Phenomenology: French Rationalism from Cavaillès to Deleuze*

Elizabeth A. Pritchard, *Locke's Political Theology: Public Religion and Sacred Rights*
Ankhi Mukherjee, *What Is a Classic? Postcolonial Rewriting and Invention of the Canon*
Jean-Pierre Dupuy, *The Mark of the Sacred*
Henri Atlan, *Fraud: The World of Ona'ah*
Niklas Luhmann, *Theory of Society, Volume 2*
Ilit Ferber, *Philosophy and Melancholy: Benjamin's Early Reflections on Theater and Language*
Alexandre Lefebvre, *Human Rights as a Way of Life: On Bergson's Political Philosophy*
Theodore W. Jennings, Jr., *Outlaw Justice: The Messianic Politics of Paul*
Alexander Etkind, *Warped Mourning: Stories of the Undead in the Land of the Unburied*
Denis Guénoun, *About Europe: Philosophical Hypotheses*
Maria Boletsi, *Barbarism and Its Discontents*
Sigrid Weigel, *Walter Benjamin: Images, the Creaturely, and the Holy*
Roberto Esposito, *Living Thought: The Origins and Actuality of Italian Philosophy*
Henri Atlan, *The Sparks of Randomness, Volume 2: The Atheism of Scripture*
Rüdiger Campe, *The Game of Probability: Literature and Calculation from Pascal to Kleist*
Niklas Luhmann, *A Systems Theory of Religion*
Jean-Luc Marion, *In the Self's Place: The Approach of Saint Augustine*
Rodolphe Gasché, *Georges Bataille: Phenomenology and Phantasmatology*
Niklas Luhmann, *Theory of Society, Volume 1*
Alessia Ricciardi, *After* La Dolce Vita*: A Cultural Prehistory of Berlusconi's Italy*
Daniel Innerarity, *The Future and Its Enemies: In Defense of Political Hope*
Patricia Pisters, *The Neuro-Image: A Deleuzian Film-Philosophy of Digital Screen Culture*
François-David Sebbah, *Testing the Limit: Derrida, Henry, Levinas, and the Phenomenological Tradition*
Erik Peterson, *Theological Tractates*, edited by Michael J. Hollerich
Feisal G. Mohamed, *Milton and the Post-Secular Present: Ethics, Politics, Terrorism*
Pierre Hadot, *The Present Alone Is Our Happiness, Second Edition: Conversations with Jeannie Carlier and Arnold I. Davidson*
Yasco Horsman, *Theaters of Justice: Judging, Staging, and Working Through in Arendt, Brecht, and Delbo*
Jacques Derrida, *Parages*, edited by John P. Leavey
Henri Atlan, *The Sparks of Randomness, Volume 1: Spermatic Knowledge*
Rebecca Comay, *Mourning Sickness: Hegel and the French Revolution*
Djelal Kadir, *Memos from the Besieged City: Lifelines for Cultural Sustainability*

Stanley Cavell, *Little Did I Know: Excerpts from Memory*
Jeffrey Mehlman, *Adventures in the French Trade: Fragments Toward a Life*
Jacob Rogozinski, *The Ego and the Flesh: An Introduction to Egoanalysis*
Marcel Hénaff, *The Price of Truth: Gift, Money, and Philosophy*
Paul Patton, *Deleuzian Concepts: Philosophy, Colonialization, Politics*
Michael Fagenblat, *A Covenant of Creatures: Levinas's Philosophy of Judaism*
Stefanos Geroulanos, *An Atheism That Is Not Humanist Emerges in French Thought*
Andrew Herscher, *Violence Taking Place: The Architecture of the Kosovo Conflict*
Hans-Jörg Rheinberger, *On Historicizing Epistemology: An Essay*
Jacob Taubes, *From Cult to Culture*, edited by Charlotte Fonrobert and Amir Engel
Peter Hitchcock, *The Long Space: Transnationalism and Postcolonial Form*
Lambert Wiesing, *Artificial Presence: Philosophical Studies in Image Theory*
Jacob Taubes, *Occidental Eschatology*
Freddie Rokem, *Philosophers and Thespians: Thinking Performance*
Roberto Esposito, *Communitas: The Origin and Destiny of Community*
Vilashini Cooppan, *Worlds Within: National Narratives and Global Connections in Postcolonial Writing*
Josef Früchtl, *The Impertinent Self: A Heroic History of Modernity*
Frank Ankersmit, Ewa Domanska, and Hans Kellner, eds., *Re-Figuring Hayden White*
Michael Rothberg, *Multidirectional Memory: Remembering the Holocaust in the Age of Decolonization*
Jean-François Lyotard, *Enthusiasm: The Kantian Critique of History*
Ernst van Alphen, Mieke Bal, and Carel Smith, eds., *The Rhetoric of Sincerity*
Stéphane Mosès, *The Angel of History: Rosenzweig, Benjamin, Scholem*
Pierre Hadot, *The Present Alone Is Our Happiness: Conversations with Jeannie Carlier and Arnold I. Davidson*
Alexandre Lefebvre, *The Image of the Law: Deleuze, Bergson, Spinoza*
Samira Haj, *Reconfiguring Islamic Tradition: Reform, Rationality, and Modernity*
Diane Perpich, *The Ethics of Emmanuel Levinas*
Marcel Detienne, *Comparing the Incomparable*
François Delaporte, *Anatomy of the Passions*
René Girard, *Mimesis and Theory: Essays on Literature and Criticism, 1959–2005*
Richard Baxstrom, *Houses in Motion: The Experience of Place and the Problem of Belief in Urban Malaysia*
Jennifer L. Culbert, *Dead Certainty: The Death Penalty and the Problem of Judgment*
Samantha Frost, *Lessons from a Materialist Thinker: Hobbesian Reflections on Ethics and Politics*
Regina Mara Schwartz, *Sacramental Poetics at the Dawn of Secularism: When God Left the World*

Gil Anidjar, *Semites: Race, Religion, Literature*
Ranjana Khanna, *Algeria Cuts: Women and Representation, 1830 to the Present*
Esther Peeren, *Intersubjectivities and Popular Culture: Bakhtin and Beyond*
Eyal Peretz, *Becoming Visionary: Brian De Palma's Cinematic Education of the Senses*
Diana Sorensen, *A Turbulent Decade Remembered: Scenes from the Latin American Sixties*
Hubert Damisch, *A Childhood Memory by Piero della Francesca*
José van Dijck, *Mediated Memories in the Digital Age*
Dana Hollander, *Exemplarity and Chosenness: Rosenzweig and Derrida on the Nation of Philosophy*
Asja Szafraniec, *Beckett, Derrida, and the Event of Literature*
Sara Guyer, *Romanticism After Auschwitz*
Alison Ross, *The Aesthetic Paths of Philosophy: Presentation in Kant, Heidegger, Lacoue-Labarthe, and Nancy*
Gerhard Richter, *Thought-Images: Frankfurt School Writers' Reflections from Damaged Life*
Bella Brodzki, *Can These Bones Live? Translation, Survival, and Cultural Memory*
Rodolphe Gasché, *The Honor of Thinking: Critique, Theory, Philosophy*
Brigitte Peucker, *The Material Image: Art and the Real in Film*
Natalie Melas, *All the Difference in the World: Postcoloniality and the Ends of Comparison*
Jonathan Culler, *The Literary in Theory*
Michael G. Levine, *The Belated Witness: Literature, Testimony, and the Question of Holocaust Survival*
Jennifer A. Jordan, *Structures of Memory: Understanding German Change in Berlin and Beyond*
Christoph Menke, *Reflections of Equality*
Marlène Zarader, *The Unthought Debt: Heidegger and the Hebraic Heritage*
Jan Assmann, *Religion and Cultural Memory: Ten Studies*
David Scott and Charles Hirschkind, *Powers of the Secular Modern: Talal Asad and His Interlocutors*
Gyanendra Pandey, *Routine Violence: Nations, Fragments, Histories*
James Siegel, *Naming the Witch*
J. M. Bernstein, *Against Voluptuous Bodies: Late Modernism and the Meaning of Painting*
Theodore W. Jennings Jr., *Reading Derrida / Thinking Paul: On Justice*
Richard Rorty and Eduardo Mendieta, *Take Care of Freedom and Truth Will Take Care of Itself: Interviews with Richard Rorty*
Jacques Derrida, *Paper Machine*
Renaud Barbaras, *Desire and Distance: Introduction to a Phenomenology of Perception*

Jill Bennett, *Empathic Vision: Affect, Trauma, and Contemporary Art*
Ban Wang, *Illuminations from the Past: Trauma, Memory, and History in Modern China*
James Phillips, *Heidegger's* Volk*: Between National Socialism and Poetry*
Frank Ankersmit, *Sublime Historical Experience*
István Rév, *Retroactive Justice: Prehistory of Post-Communism*
Paola Marrati, *Genesis and Trace: Derrida Reading Husserl and Heidegger*
Krzysztof Ziarek, *The Force of Art*
Marie-José Mondzain, *Image, Icon, Economy: The Byzantine Origins of the Contemporary Imaginary*
Cecilia Sjöholm, *The Antigone Complex: Ethics and the Invention of Feminine Desire*
Jacques Derrida and Elisabeth Roudinesco, *For What Tomorrow . . . : A Dialogue*
Elisabeth Weber, *Questioning Judaism: Interviews by Elisabeth Weber*
Jacques Derrida and Catherine Malabou, *Counterpath: Traveling with Jacques Derrida*
Martin Seel, *Aesthetics of Appearing*
Nanette Salomon, *Shifting Priorities: Gender and Genre in Seventeenth-Century Dutch Painting*
Jacob Taubes, *The Political Theology of Paul*
Jean-Luc Marion, *The Crossing of the Visible*
Eric Michaud, *The Cult of Art in Nazi Germany*
Anne Freadman, *The Machinery of Talk: Charles Peirce and the Sign Hypothesis*
Stanley Cavell, *Emerson's Transcendental Etudes*
Stuart McLean, *The Event and Its Terrors: Ireland, Famine, Modernity*
Beate Rössler, ed., *Privacies: Philosophical Evaluations*
Bernard Faure, *Double Exposure: Cutting Across Buddhist and Western Discourses*
Alessia Ricciardi, *The Ends of Mourning: Psychoanalysis, Literature, Film*
Alain Badiou, *Saint Paul: The Foundation of Universalism*
Gil Anidjar, *The Jew, the Arab: A History of the Enemy*
Jonathan Culler and Kevin Lamb, eds., *Just Being Difficult? Academic Writing in the Public Arena*
Jean-Luc Nancy, *A Finite Thinking*, edited by Simon Sparks
Theodor W. Adorno, *Can One Live after Auschwitz? A Philosophical Reader*, edited by Rolf Tiedemann
Patricia Pisters, *The Matrix of Visual Culture: Working with Deleuze in Film Theory*
Andreas Huyssen, *Present Pasts: Urban Palimpsests and the Politics of Memory*
Talal Asad, *Formations of the Secular: Christianity, Islam, Modernity*
Dorothea von Mücke, *The Rise of the Fantastic Tale*
Marc Redfield, *The Politics of Aesthetics: Nationalism, Gender, Romanticism*
Emmanuel Levinas, *On Escape*

Dan Zahavi, *Husserl's Phenomenology*
Rodolphe Gasché, *The Idea of Form: Rethinking Kant's Aesthetics*
Michael Naas, *Taking on the Tradition: Jacques Derrida and the Legacies of Deconstruction*
Herlinde Pauer-Studer, ed., *Constructions of Practical Reason: Interviews on Moral and Political Philosophy*
Jean-Luc Marion, *Being Given That: Toward a Phenomenology of Givenness*
Theodor W. Adorno and Max Horkheimer, *Dialectic of Enlightenment*
Ian Balfour, *The Rhetoric of Romantic Prophecy*
Martin Stokhof, *World and Life as One: Ethics and Ontology in Wittgenstein's Early Thought*
Gianni Vattimo, *Nietzsche: An Introduction*
Jacques Derrida, *Negotiations: Interventions and Interviews, 1971–1998*, edited by Elizabeth Rottenberg
Brett Levinson, *The Ends of Literature: The Latin American "Boom" in the Neoliberal Marketplace*
Timothy J. Reiss, *Against Autonomy: Cultural Instruments, Mutualities, and the Fictive Imagination*
Hent de Vries and Samuel Weber, eds., *Religion and Media*
Niklas Luhmann, *Theories of Distinction: Re-Describing the Descriptions of Modernity*, edited and introduced by William Rasch
Johannes Fabian, *Anthropology with an Attitude: Critical Essays*
Michel Henry, *I Am the Truth: Toward a Philosophy of Christianity*
Gil Anidjar, *"Our Place in Al-Andalus": Kabbalah, Philosophy, Literature in Arab-Jewish Letters*
Hélène Cixous and Jacques Derrida, *Veils*
F. R. Ankersmit, *Historical Representation*
F. R. Ankersmit, *Political Representation*
Elissa Marder, *Dead Time: Temporal Disorders in the Wake of Modernity (Baudelaire and Flaubert)*
Reinhart Koselleck, *The Practice of Conceptual History: Timing History, Spacing Concepts*
Niklas Luhmann, *The Reality of the Mass Media*
Hubert Damisch, *A Theory of /Cloud/: Toward a History of Painting*
Jean-Luc Nancy, *The Speculative Remark: (One of Hegel's bon mots)*
Jean-François Lyotard, *Soundproof Room: Malraux's Anti-Aesthetics*
Jan Patočka, *Plato and Europe*
Hubert Damisch, *Skyline: The Narcissistic City*
Isabel Hoving, *In Praise of New Travelers: Reading Caribbean Migrant Women Writers*
Richard Rand, ed., *Futures: Of Jacques Derrida*
William Rasch, *Niklas Luhmann's Modernity: The Paradoxes of Differentiation*
Jacques Derrida and Anne Dufourmantelle, *Of Hospitality*

Jean-François Lyotard, *The Confession of Augustine*
Kaja Silverman, *World Spectators*
Samuel Weber, *Institution and Interpretation: Expanded Edition*
Jeffrey S. Librett, *The Rhetoric of Cultural Dialogue: Jews and Germans in the Epoch of Emancipation*
Ulrich Baer, *Remnants of Song: Trauma and the Experience of Modernity in Charles Baudelaire and Paul Celan*
Samuel C. Wheeler III, *Deconstruction as Analytic Philosophy*
David S. Ferris, *Silent Urns: Romanticism, Hellenism, Modernity*
Rodolphe Gasché, *Of Minimal Things: Studies on the Notion of Relation*
Sarah Winter, *Freud and the Institution of Psychoanalytic Knowledge*
Samuel Weber, *The Legend of Freud: Expanded Edition*
Aris Fioretos, ed., *The Solid Letter: Readings of Friedrich Hölderlin*
J. Hillis Miller / Manuel Asensi, *Black Holes / J. Hillis Miller; or, Boustrophedonic Reading*
Miryam Sas, *Fault Lines: Cultural Memory and Japanese Surrealism*
Peter Schwenger, *Fantasm and Fiction: On Textual Envisioning*
Didier Maleuvre, *Museum Memories: History, Technology, Art*
Jacques Derrida, *Monolingualism of the Other; or, The Prosthesis of Origin*
Andrew Baruch Wachtel, *Making a Nation, Breaking a Nation: Literature and Cultural Politics in Yugoslavia*
Niklas Luhmann, *Love as Passion: The Codification of Intimacy*
Mieke Bal, ed., *The Practice of Cultural Analysis: Exposing Interdisciplinary Interpretation*
Jacques Derrida and Gianni Vattimo, eds., *Religion*

The authorized representative in the EU for product safety and compliance is:
Mare Nostrum Group
B.V Doelen 72
4831 GR Breda
The Netherlands

www.ingramcontent.com/pod-product-compliance
Lightning Source LLC
LaVergne TN
LVHW091112080826
845145LV00008B/1877

* 9 7 8 1 5 0 3 6 3 3 0 8 7 *